I AM
A
SURVIVOR

Janice E. Holliman

Author's Tranquility Press
Marietta, Georgia

Author's Tranquility Press
2706 Station Club Drive SW
Marietta, GA/30060
www.authorstranquilitypress.com

Publisher's Note: This is a work of fiction. Names, characters, places, and incidents are a product of the author's imagination. Locales and public names are sometimes used for atmospheric purposes. Any resemblance to actual people, living or dead, or to businesses, companies, events, institutions, or locales is completely coincidental.

Ordering Information:

Quantity sales. Special discounts are available on quantity purchases by corporations, associations, and others. For details, contact the "Special Sales Department" at the address above.

I Am A Survivor/Janice E. Holliman

Paperback: 978-1-956480-22-1
eBook: 978-1-956480-38-2

Contents

POEMS TITLES

Knowing Myself, Knowing My How, And My Why
Losing Weight Puts Me on A Natural High
The Joy of Knowing You Were Meant To Be
Having More Babies Were Not In My Future
Who Are You?
Thank You for Sharing
Surviving A Big Lost
What Is A Survivor?
I Will Never Get To Know This Little One
Pay Close Attention To Yourself
My Mental Brown Paper Bag And My Mental Drawer 'Method'
What Is My Purpose?
Treat Me with Respect
Controlling Myself, Controlling My Life
How Would I Feel If I Could Not Hear A Sound?
Oh, The Pain Will It Ever Stop?
What Does It Feel Like to Be Hit Over the Head with A Hammer?
Losing Weight Was Not on My Mind
I Will Never Let Anyone Stop Me for Being Strong
What Can Make Me Become Paralyzed?
Examining The Things I Have To Swallow
Things Do Change Us
You Are Not the Person I Married
What Is Joy?
Why Not in Private
The Smell of Foul Gas That Has A Mind of Its Own

Dedication

I have three dedications I would love to say thank you too, they are my husband, my son, and my mom.

To my dear and loving husband Willie, thank you for the forty plus years we have shared. We started out as friends, then buddies, and spouses to each other. We are like two hearts beating as one, but with our own identity, our own goals. We have always been here for each other, pulling and holding each other up even when we don't want it. Thank you for our son that we raised together, if there were some bad times, we knew we can pull through as long as we know there is still love between us. Just remember that as we get older or become sick, we do change sometimes for the good or for the bad if we let it, continue to work on the good. Love comes in all kinds, all sides, all colors, it conquers all things. With true love we will endure, with our faith we will endure, as long as we have or keep our joy we will endure, and if we keep peace, we will endure all things and much more.

Thank You! (Husband) Willie H. Holliman

To my dear son Ramono, thank you for the past thirty plus years we have shared. We have always been close, and we have always been able to talk. Ramono, you for being the son we raised and thank you for being the person you have become. We did our best. Sometimes I wish you were more like me, but you are your own person and that is great too. Just keep doing the things you are doing and keep looking forward and find good in all you do, that is good as long as you keep putting your best foot forward. And remember good things are waiting for you if it's things, or if it's people. Always find the good in them, if you do, you will find the good in yourself. We hope and wish the best for you and the new chapter in your life.

Thank You! (Son) Ramono Z. Holliman

To my loving mom Nancy, who has been there for me all my life, who has raised me, us the best way you knew how. Being a single parent raising my brother and myself alone. You did your best and you made sure we learned how to treat people, to be kind to people, you taught us to be and do our best. You have been there for me the best way you know how; you have tried teaching me things the way you feel was right. The way you learned from your parents of old(smile). But now you have learned it may not have been the right way, so you taught me differently. Thank you for all the things I have learned to do or not to do.

Thank You! (Mom) Nancy A. Byrd

An Introduction to this True Story

My story will show how I live my life as successfully as I can. It will also show how I survive the things I have faced in my life. Each chapter will tell you how things unfold in our life as a family and as an individual. Yes, the things you read are true. I change the names of everyone except my immediate family and the ones that have died.

You will read about some of my illnesses, my family illnesses, our trials, the tests we faced, facing, and will face. You will read about the names of my illnesses, my medications, and medications that I have become allergic to, some of my surgeries, hospital stays, and ER visits.

You will get an idea of what I deal with each, and every day. You will read how I chose to deal with each situation, you will also learn I am not perfect, I am human just like you. The one thing I know is I look to find ways to better myself in the best way I can. I am always saying "I am a work in progress," "I hold on not hang on because I must be aware of my surroundings, so the wind or anything else cannot come along and blow me or take me away."

My earnest desire is to deepen your appreciation of life, to give you insight as to the reason why I fight, why I keep surviving. How I keep beating the odds I face. Why I view things the way I do and why I take things from others the way I do. Please remember, I work hard at viewing good in others even when they do not show me goodness or when they are mean to me.

You will read about nine words that I will focus on as time goes on, and how I will focus on how to use each word and what I learn from each of them. You will read the dictionary's view and the Biblical viewpoint of each word each time I use them.

My aim is to help others understand how I survive things, why I say, "I AM A SURVIVOR!" Why I want to share my life with you, why I want to bring a smile to others, and why I love helping people the best way I can.

The objective is to let everyone know that I appreciate anything and everyone in my life because I am who I am because of them, no matter how big, how long, or what they did or didn't do for me or to me. I appreciate all the things I have gone through because it also made me who I am today.

Coming across as being Humble, I want people to know I am funny, approachable, funny crazy, able to listen, and very shy. But I talk to cover my shyness, I love putting others first. I am guided by and with whatever I learned from the one who created all things including us. I also know I cannot and do not do anything on my own or by myself.

Above All Other Things I want everyone to know, without my faith I would not be the person I am, and I would not be able to fight and say, "I AM A SURVIVOR!" Without my joy I would not be a joyful person. What about my Endurance without it I feel like I would not be here? I must keep my hope because without it, my hope of believing in the things I do I could not handle things the way I do. The reason I do what I do, and why I do it I must say most of all it takes love, without love there is no way I would become me.

I AM A SURVIVOR because I have an open mind and an open heart. So, I know, or I am willing to learn what makes me a Survivor, a person who love life, who love people, who love to share, because whatever I give, I get it back and more, I love to share my most precious gift which is my strength I give it freely to all I see and know each and every day. Therefore, this is the reason why I survive and why I can say "I AM A SURVIVOR!

I AM A SURVIVOR

BY LEARNING MYSELF, MY HOW, AND MY WHY

Being a Survivor is especially important and powerful. It helps me in so many ways, it has strengthened me, it has helped me to listen to others, it has helped me to listen to myself and my body and most of all It has saved my life so many times in so many ways.

Knowing each, and every breath I take, I thank my Grand Creator above for each, and every breath, for each and everything I have learned, and each and everything I do because I know my life really depends on it.

Getting to know one's-self is the most powerful weapon one can have, to protect one's-self from anyone and everything we may come across in our life. Knowing one's-self will help one save their life and maybe someone else's. I am who I am because of everything I have gone through and how I handle it and knowing that I cannot do anything of my own, or on my own. You may be asking what I am talking about, well, let us see. First, may I ask how well do you know yourself?

First, knowing yourself is truly knowing when there is the smallest change in your body, your mind, and your inner self. The way you do this is to pay close attention to yourself, your mind, your inner self and all your surroundings.

If you do not pay attention to yourself how in the world can you know yourself?

I can tell you this, it is not an easy thing to do because you must have the right mind set, the will power, the strength, the endurance, and most of all you must be strong, and let no one tell you what is and what is not wrong with you and your body. The reason why is because they are not God because the very first thing, they say to you or ask you when they come in is "How are you today or What brings you in today?" Remember that they do not ask for it to be ugly, it is because they really do not know you or what is wrong with you. I am not being ugly; it is just the truth.

The reason why you want to get to know yourself is because you are the only one that can help them save your life because you have all the information, they will need to know in order to tell you what's wrong and to help you feel better or get well. The questions they ask you is because they need a map to guide them on the right path or road to help you. So, remember to help yourself, is to know yourself and your body.

Knowing yourself will empower you in whatever you face in life, and it will also give you the strength to fight and live. So, buckle up and let us take this ride together. There is something that we will need, let us find out.

Knowing Myself, Knowing My How, And My Why

*By taking the time out, to really get to know myself, because I needed
to know what was happening to me.
I tried everything else and wondered what else it could be?*

*With me coming to know myself, I was incredibly determined to learn
everything I could because it meant I could save my life.
It means I will be able to have the answers that all my doctors need to
know without any trifle.*

*So, I begin to stop and look around, I would close my eyes, and
open my mind.
I would listen to the sounds, I could hear from both inside and outside
my body, and I learned to let them become entwine.*

*I first had to convince myself of my how, how can I help myself;
how can I know who I am, who I am meant to be.
I sat and wondered how life made me who I am today, wow I am
extremely interested in the things I found out about me.*

*As for my why I wondered why I am here and what do I have to offer.
I wondered why I was created then it hit me, stop and look at
everything that is around.
I am so glad I listened to everything I heard and to see everything
around me, I am incredibly happy with what I've found.*

That means I must always pay close attention; I must see what's
going on always
going on around me. That means I must be aware of everything and
everyone, keeping an open heart.
I truly realized this will be my best and the greatest place
for me to start.

Who Are You?

.

The Five Very Important Things I Need Is Faith, Hope, Joy, Endurance and Love

In the World of Illness. Before I Can Heal My Body and Have Inner Peace. The First Thing I Must Do Is Start the Healing, I Must Start with My Mind!

I Have Done It, So Can You, See I Am Still Alive Because Of It!

I Know Now What My Propose Is

Faith is when I have total and complete trust or confidence in someone or something. Faith is also having a strong belief in our Grand Creator loyally. It is when I have an allegiance to duty or a person with loyalty.

Hope is a feeling of expectation and desire for a certain thing to happen; it is a feeling of trust. It is a cherished desire with anticipation to want something to happen or to be true. It is what I feel in my heart. Yes, believing in something and someone beside myself I know I cannot live without it, and I will never want to.

Joy is what brings a smile on my face when I see I have brought a smile to someone's face. Joy is what makes me happy when I have done or said something kind for another person and not just myself. Joy also brings me peace of mind when I always bring peace to someone's life.

Endurance means to have the ability to keep doing something that may be difficult, unpleasant, or painful for a long time. It is to describe what I need to help me with my physical and mental strength to help keep me going, like I am running a marathon or like giving birth, as for mental strength it helps me deal with stressful times, it gives me the Endurance to bounce back from heartbreak even from death of loved ones. This also works very well when I am sick because illness affects me in so many ways and I cannot do anything without endurance if I want to survive.

Endurance is the fact or power of ensuring an unpleasant or difficult process or situation without giving way. It is the ability or strength to continue or last, especially despite fatigue, stress, or other adverse conditions or stamina.

Love is the most important thing I will always need and should have. Love never fails, it never has to say, "I am sorry," it never shows pride, it is not arrogant. Love is not selfish, and Love does not stumble! Love puts others first, yes before I can think of myself, I think of others, and it helps me treat others the same way I want them to treat me.

Love tells me what I may not want to hear. Love helps me accept when others tell me the truth even if it hurts. Love comes in when every one of us just says "thank you" for caring enough to enlighten me on the matter even though I may not like it. Love should be easy, wait it is, but we are imperfect. Sometimes it is the hardest thing to have, to give, to show, to feel, or even do.

It is so easy to say, "I Love You" but it is much harder to show "I Love You." Because saying "I Love You" is like drinking water because we may say it because we must, or we feel we should so we can get through life. Like we need to drink water to keep living, to keep surviving.

Love is an incredibly beautiful thing. All we need to do is show people that we love them, that we care for them, that we like them, that we will even die for them. Love is what really makes the world go around. There is so much I can say about love in the most positive way.

Why My Faith, Why My Hope, Why My Joy, Why My Endurance and Why My Love?

The reason why I begin to really investigate and tap into my Faith, my Hope, my Endurance, and my Love. My "FAITH" because it would, and it has kept me alive. My "HOPE" is because as long as I know I have something to hope for, it keeps me going. My "JOY" because it is a joy to be alive. I know, I "WILL" survive. That's when I realized I need "ENDURANCE." No, I can't do or have any of these if I don't have "LOVE." Because it is what makes the world go around and it's what keeps pushing me forward therefore, I can honestly say I Love myself and I love life, I hope everyone Love themselves too.

Which is my focus to keep pushing myself beyond my last step. To keep learning all I need to learn about myself and the things going on In my life or the things around me and my life.

Me learning myself, my how, and my why, as for learning myself I must see beyond what I can see with my naked eye. What was told to me by my family members which means it was passed down through generations. How many of us are told about our family history, and later we find out it may be more to it, or it may not be true. It can be more, or less of what was told so we really don't know what is true until we find out for ourselves.

You May Ask What About Me?
You may wonder and ask how can I save myself? I asked myself that same question and I came to this conclusion, and I am so happy that I did. Now I can't help myself, my family, friends, and anyone else who would need my help or who will let me help them. I do this because I know what it is like to be lost in a place where no one understands you or believes you. I have seen so many people have lost their lives. If they had the knowledge about themselves or had an idea of how to learn about themselves, they may have lived longer.

Again, I must tell you, knowledge is power, and power is knowledge. The very first thing you need to know is you 'can't' do anything on our own or think that we know everything because 'believe me' we know nothing about ourselves because we 'can't' guide our own footstep. This is something that we all must learn, in doing so we must first have an open mind and heart and be willing to learn. Then do as much reading, research, and meditation about the matter as we can. If you are like me before you do any of this, you need to pray in order to really learn what you need to learn, and to understand what you will learn about yourself.

Doing these things, it will help you have faith, hope, joy, endurance, and love. When you have all these things it will give you the tools to be a Survivor as it did me. It will give you the strength to be a Survivor like it did me too. When you master these things or train yourself by using them the right way you can and will be able to say too, "I Am A Survivor."

This book is about me and my look at the world of illnesses which a lot of us are facing every day. I am writing this book to let people know that as long as we have Faith, Hope, Joy, Endurance, and Love, we can endure anything we face, what doesn't kill us will make us stronger.

You will see how I view life and how I handle my illnesses, how you can live with yours, by you ruling it and not letting it rule you. I will include my intake on life while I take on all my illnesses and trials. The first thing I will need is faith, which comes from my heart. I need to take a good look in my life, meaning I must look deep within myself. As you read this book you will read about my life during my good and bad days. There will be laughter, joys, tears, and wows. I am dedicating this book to all my family and friends. I will also share some of their illnesses and trials. Some of the joys that come from my heart, I share with others.

This book is about me going through so many illnesses to the point that a few of my doctors told me I should write a book and tell people about me and how I deal with all the things I have through the years. I told the main doctor that I should write a book. I told him he can write it; all I want is only 10% we both laugh.

See, the reason why they want me to write this is because all the things I have faced and still are facing. The reason why is because they felt like people would like to know they can endure anything if they put their mind to it and have the will to live. Let me just say this "I am not like everyone else, and my body is so different it's crazy." You may have said or thought the same thing about yourself. I want to say, 'it's okay.'

As you read you will see what I mean when I say, "I don't see things the same way other people do, I don't think like others, I don't act, I don't expect anything like others, like how I should be, or how I should feel." You will understand that I have a lot of Faith, Hope, Joy, Endurance, and Love which is not by myself or man, they all come from above. Just because we are living in a dark world, I don't have to live in a dark world, I don't have to live my life dark. I have learned I can have faith, hope, joy, which helps me have endurance as well, which has shown me there is also love all around me. If I just look for them and show them, yes, they are here, yes, they all are real. As you read this book it will become clear, and you will understand me and my life. Hope you will enjoy it!

Chapter 1

THE BEGINNING ON OUR WEDDING DAY

I will begin with the day of our wedding it was in March of the year 1978. The morning of my wedding it snowed, that was a big deal because thatwas the first time it snowed in the south that I can remember.

There were 25 people in our wedding party and our colors were burgundy, pink, power blue, and white. The groom 'Willie' matched the bride maids who wore burgundy, and the bride 'me' matched the groomsmen including the two best men and a ring bearer who wore white. I had a maiden of honor, and maid of honor which both wore pink, and my two flower girls wore powder blue, cooled by breezes, which a few hours previous were out of sight of land. Look at the crowds of water-gazers there.

It was a nice wedding. I must say we did not have a honeymoon till this day. That Monday after the wedding I was so happy to be able to cook and have my husband eat my food. When he came home, he was shocked because it was a dish that he never had or heard of, we called it Goulash on a bed of White Rice. I really can say it was very good... a good meal, we ate it with Corn Muffins, with a glass of Iced Tea.

After we ate, I cleaned the kitchen and after washing the dishes, I started wiping down the countertop and the dining table.

I looked back, and I saw my husband coming behind me wiping down where I had already cleaned. I looked at him and I put my hands up in the air.

"You want it! You got it!"

March 6, 1978 was the beginning of Willie spoiling me. I cook and he did most of the cleaning for most of the past forty-one years. He was my dishwasher and sometimes he would also cook. I never took out the trash and before we got a washer and dryer, he would go to the laundromat for the first seven years.

We were noticeably young, over forty-two years of marriage

I am very happy; I would not start my wedding until I got my flowers.

This is one of our Wedding Pictures where we are eating cake!

I have so much fun laughing at him and with him. He did and still says some of the funny's things. Like the time we went to visit his family he ran into the corner of a box then he looked at me and said,

Willie: "I am going to die, because I just swallowed a piece of plastic."

"Everything you are putting me through you are going to get it back in spades through your children."

We began laughing so hard his family asked us what was so funny when we told them they began laughing too, I remember the time I asked him to go and get me some Shrimps from the 'Shrimp Boat,' he got himself a plate of Fried Fish, he brought it home and said,

Willie: "I'm not going to eat this because of what I saw."

He then threw it away; I just shook my head thinking man you are so crazy.

"Don't tell me because I don't want to throw-up."

Before we got married, I got on birth control pills because we wanted to wait a while before starting our family. I noticed they were not only making me gain weight they were making me sick, so I started taking only half of a pill, but that didn't work either, they still were not good for me. After three months I stopped, because they really began to make me sicker.

I gained like eighty pounds and that was the beginning of my health downward spiral. Within the first three months of my marriage my body began to change. I began having so many changes like pain, 'man oh man' the pain was very severe. I was so sick around that time of the month each month then about four months later I went to the doctor who examined me and ran tests, told me.

Dr. Jefferson: "You have two tumors, one the size of an orange and the other the size of a grapefruit."

Tumors are abnormal and function with less mass of tissue that is not inflammatory and arises from pre-existent tissue.

I wanted a second opinion. Meanwhile I went home and while I was there, I could barely walk. So, I went to the doctor. It was a female doctor, she examined me, and she told me the same thing, but she also told me.

Dr. White: "You have two choices to make, one is to have the surgery, or you can take (vitamin E,) which will dissolve or shrink the tumors, but I want you to know they can or will come back."

"I have nothing to lose so I chose to take the (vitamin E.)"

About a week later I began to feel better, so I continued taking them and they did dissolve or shrink. The reason why I know is because I went back to the doctor, and he said they were gone. I was so glad. About two years later I dealt with another female problem, this time it was to the point that I needed to have a D & C. this was the very first time I had ever been in the hospital or put to sleep. I was in the hospital for three days during our third year of marriage. As time passed, I never will forget this about a year later one of my friends told me.

Kendrick: "I was told that you were picking fun at them."

"I didn't do any such thing, that's not in me because I know how it feels when people pick on me. I know how it feels when people lie on me."

That troubled me so bad that I had to go to the ER. They ran a lot of tests because they thought I was having a heart attack, but they found out that it was stress. I was relieved, I said.

"Oh, that's good to know I am not having a heart attack."

ER Doctor: "If you don't stop stressing out over things you will have a heart attack and die."

This is the very day I decided I will not ever let anyone, or anything stress me out like that again. So, I sat down and thought about how I should handle the issue because I don't like hurting anyone's feelings, if I am wrong, I will own up to it and make things right. So, I decided to go to that person and have a talk with them about the matter. We got things straight and we are better friends. I didn't know it then, but I use my mind to help heal my body and inner self, I did so by thinking about what I needed to do to help myself. I reminded myself that I could not rely on myself or do it alone. This has been over 35 years ago and that was the beginning of me "starting with the mind" without knowing how, or anything about my true self, without knowing what it takes to endure whatever trial I may face.

I have tried losing weight many times through the past three years, but it's like being on a roller coaster ride, because of the birth control pills. I tried different diets. I just couldn't lose the weight and keep it off, because those pills really did a number on me.

A year later I decided I wanted to lose weight again, so I worked extremely hard to do so. We were living in an apartment on the second floor, when I came home from work, I would drop my bag, pick up my jump rope and head to the parking lot and I would jump rope for thirty minutes. Then I would go back inside and work out another thirty minutes. I dieted Mondays - Fridays but I would eat whatever I wanted in moderation on Saturdays and Sundays for seven months I lost weight. I didn't know how much until I went to my doctor for my checkup. I got on the scale, and it said I lost 80 pounds.

"Oh, yeah I did it, I did it oh, yeah!"

I was so happy when I came out of the doctor's office, I was walking down the street, downtown no. I was dancing and singing downtown, people were looking at me. I felt like I was making a movie like a scene in the movie 'Singing in the Rain.'

I didn't care who and how they were looking at me, because I was on a natural high of winning the battle of losing all that weight. Not only was I singing and dancing, but I also decided to treat myself. Yes, I treated myself with food on a Wednesday in the middle of the week! I decided to have Chinese Food at our favorite restaurant. In our fourth year of marriage, we decided we were going to Hawaii the next year for our honeymoon and anniversary. So, we set down and made our plans like how many days, what we were going to do and the cost.

Losing Weight Puts Me on A Natural High

*Losing weight is not an easy thing to do, but I know I need to
get some of this weight off me, I really need to shed
some of these pounds.*
*What do I need to do? How am I going to feel better about myself? I
know it's not an easy thing to do, I wonder if I can hear myself say, I
have lost weight, I have shed pounds, I wonder how this will sound.*

*Wow! Losing weight puts me on a natural high, because it makes
me feel great about myself, it will help me learn something about
myself, it will help me be the person I want to be and intend to be,
it will help me see what I need to see.*

*Being on a natural high from losing weight 'Wow,'
with me singing
and smiling because I have reached my goal of
losing weight I really, feel great.*
*With me knowing I have reached my goal, of losing all this weight.
I am on a natural high because I feel good about myself,
now I truly can say what it truly means for me to lose this weight.
What it means truly to me to be on a natural high, to be able to say it
truly feels good to me for losing weight I really feel great.*

*As for me being on a natural high, it really makes me want to sing,
it makes me have the biggest smile on my face, because I feel
healthy, and now it makes me feel like it came so naturally.
This is one of the most wonderful things I could have done.
Because now I can honestly say I am on a natural high.
Yes, it really is something I truly can identify.*

This is the very first dress he bought me

Pictures after Losing Eighty Pounds   What a joy!

Chapter 2

FOUR YEARS LATER

One day after work while waiting for the bus I began feeling sick. As soon as I got on the bus, I was feeling sicker. Before I knew it, I had to throw-up. I put my hand over my mouth because I didn't want to throw-up on anyone. By me pulling the cord to get off didn't get the bus driver to stop, I had to wait for the next stop, but I couldn't wait so I had to say.

"I am about to throw-up!" He stopped to let me off as soon as my right foot touched the ground it came up, and up, and up. As I was jumping over it, I thought I was finished, but I was not. As I waited for the next bus, I was still feeling so sick.

"Oh man," when I got home all I could do was go to bed. My head hit the pillow. I slept until my husband came home. I told him I was not feeling well so he told me to go back to sleep and he would cook after he got out of the shower, so I went back to sleep. I didn't even wake up to eat besides, I was not hungry; and I was too sick to eat.

I was sick for a week. I began thinking what could be wrong, so I decided to make an appointment to see my (OB/GYN) doctor for the next day. I went to work feeling extremely sick. I was sick as a dog. As soon as I got off from work, I went straight to my doctor's office. They called me back, she examined me, she ran tests. One was using "the urine cup" yeah, "the urine cup" she came and said,

Dr. Mick: "Mrs. Holliman I did a pregnancy on you, and it came out half positive of being pregnant."

"Pregnant and only half pregnant, what do you mean?"

Dr. Mick: "I want you to take a blood test and come back in two weeks for the results."

It was vacation time, so we went on vacation. I hated that vacation because I was so sick the whole time, I hated every time Willie touched me. All I did was 'sleep and throw-up' two weeks later I went back to my doctor.

Dr. Mick: "You are pregnant, you are about three months."

What came to mind was all the miscarriages I had during the past four years then it hit me. Is this really happening after we made plans to go to Hawaii the next year, but I was still incredibly happy. I went to work until it got to the point, I couldn't do it anymore, so I quit because I stayed sick. Six months I stayed sick. I couldn't even hold water and I was running to the bathroom all day. I couldn't hold up my head and with every move I made it caused me to barf.

"Tell me, why do we call it 'morning sickness' if I am barfing all day? It should be called 'awake sickness' because as long as I am awake, I am barfing."

I couldn't take the prenatal vitamins which my doctor gave me because they made me sick, so I took something called Bee Pollen pills in its place. I will never forget what my mom told me.

Nancy: "You will not have that baby naturally because you fell in a tree when you were about twelve."

I fell on a big tree limb like a rock, and I was a pair of scissors, "ouch." On my fifth month office visit.

"Doctor, I am not going to take Lamar's classes because I am not going to have this baby naturally."

Dr. Mick: "You don't know until the time comes."

I didn't take Lamar's classes. I remembered to this day you couldn't tell if I was pregnant specially if I was sitting down. One day I went to the hospital thinking I was about to have my baby. I was in my six month. I just knew I was in labor. The craziest thing happened knowing I was not showing until I got up on the table in the ER thinking that this is it but no it was a false labor. It was so funny as I was laying on the table my stomach popped out like Tom in the Tom and Jerry cartoon show when he shut out a cannon. The next thing I knew was my stomach popped out like I was a cartoon character three times as big, now, you really could see me both sitting and standing, I was huge.

ER Doctor: "I hear two hearts beating."

"No, you don't!"

They begin laughing. I have always wanted a set of twins, girls first or one of each. Anyway, I am incredibly happy with what I got; my neighbor told me I was going to have a Sittindive. Sittindive at birth was a 22-pound baby boy so you can see how big I was at six months, that really frightened me just thinking of something that big passing through me.

During that time while my husband was in the shower, I was in the middle of the bed. I had to get up to pay my 'water bill,' {urinate.} Being that big I couldn't get up, so I had to rock and roll I was glad my husband moved the bed closer to the wall with enough room for me to get by, anyway I finally got to the edge and slide down to the floor on my knees and then I use the bed and the wall to pull myself up and I went and paid my 'water bill,' {urinate.}

I had a friend that was like my mom. She would take me to all my doctor's visits. My last two months I was huge, and I really was wobbling like a duck. I had to use the wall to get up each time I went to see the doctor. They would call us back to take our weight, our blood pressure and our temperature and then send everyone back to the waiting room. I was so big they would tell me to go in one of the rooms because I had to slide to the floor and then use the chair to push myself up because I was so huge. I was miserable and angry because a lady was the same amount pregnant as I was, but you could not tell it, so I told myself I really dislike that woman.

Dr. Mick: "If you haven't gone into labor by next week, I will take your baby."

When I went back to the doctor, she told me she wanted to wait another week. I was so mad because I was a week overdue, and I was extremely big the next week. Dr. Mick said the same thing, man I really was upset I walked out of that office that day I called her everything except the name her mother gave her.

"That slew footed, knock kneed, pair toed woman makes me sick. She promised me she was going to take this baby weeks ago."

My friend Wade, had to park across the street because the parking lot was full, to get to the car cross the street there was a brick wall about two feet high instead of me going around it I jumped it and walked into the middle of the street while cars was coming, I stop and said,

"Hit me if you want too!"

Boy, was I mad, I was not my normal sweet self, I was there before she could tell me.

Wade: "Janice be careful!"

But I was in the middle of the street, she took me home, and, on the way, I asked her to take me to the neighborhood store. As soon as the car stopped, I jumped out to go into the neighborhood store so I could buy some milk. When I got out of the car a man came out of the store and he looked at me. Those hormones really made me crazy I know because one day I was standing in line in the grocery store, a pregnant woman was in line, and she looked at me and cursed me out because I was looking at her. I was about to tell her I remembered being pregnant with my son. It's so funny when I think about it because she said the same thing to me.

"What are you looking at?"

Anyway, I went in and got my milk; she took me home. I had to walk up ninth-teen steps to get to my door. I had the key in the lock before my friend could turn around to say to me.

Wade: "Be careful going up the steps. That's a mad woman there."

She started laughing because it normally took me a while because I was so big. That day it was as if I had wings and I flew to my door. My doctor's appointment was on Mondays. After two weeks she said if I haven't had the baby that next Monday, she really was going to take my baby, I told my husband and friend.

"Okay, before I have this baby, I want some Greens, Rice, Cornbread, Ham and an Apple Pie because after I have this baby, I am going back on my diet to lose all my baby fat."

Yes, I was really looking forward to that great tasting meal of Greens, Rice, Ham, Cornbread, and an Apple Pie. I really was looking forward to getting my eat on. My friend was to bring the Apple Pie that Sunday because I was going to get my eat on. When we went to bed that Saturday Night it was pouring down raining like cats and dogs. I slept all night when I woke-up the next morning, which was Sunday about 7:00a.m., I went to pay my 'water bill' by the time I got to the restroom and started paying my 'water bill' my water broke.

"Call the doctor to tell her my water broke."

Willie called our friend, and she brought the Apple Pie. We called my doctor again, but they still couldn't find her. I told them let's go to the hospital if she's not there when we get there, I will find someone else to deliver my baby. She was not there still when we got to the ER.

ER Nurse: "We can't find her."

After a while Dr. Mick showed up.

Dr. Mick: "There goes my big baby! I have been going between two hospitals the whole weekend."

Remember the lady that I said was the same amount of pregnant as I was? Anyway, she was the last mother whose baby she delivered that morning before me at another hospital. My labor pains were about three minutes apart when they put me into a room anyway. She put me in a room to prep me for labor. I was laying there by myself. I could hear a lady in the next room, with the nurses and the doctors. She was screaming so loud.

One Nurse: "Push! Push!"

Lady: "I'm pushing ....it."

Another Nurse: "You weren't saying that when you were getting it." I started laughing to myself and before I knew it a pain hit me so hard. I said,

"Oh, that's what she's feeling, boy that hurt."

Dr. Mick came in to examine me to see how far I had dilated as she examined me.

"Please knock me out!"

Dr. Mick: "No! Because it will make the baby be slow."

She had another doctor come in and examined me also. The male doctor said,

Doctor Liam: "She only dilated one centimeter and she is not going any further, so you are going to have to take the baby."

Dr. Mick: "Prep her for surgery."

Another doctor named Dr. Epic came in and gave me an upper epidural shot. Suddenly, my right leg began to jerk and jump, then my right arm began to jerk and jump. My left leg began and left arm also before I knew it my head and then my whole body began jerking and jumping. Dr. Mick ran into the room and saw me jerking. She started asking me questions.

Dr. Mick: "Who are you, do you know where you are? What year is this and who am I?"

"Yes, you are my doctor, I am in the hospital, it's 1983."

I was able to answer her questions once my body and limbs calmed down.

Dr. Mick: "We have to put you to sleep and take the baby."

"You should have done it when I asked in the first place."

She went out to tell my husband and friends what was going on.

The next thing I knew I had my baby, and I had a bikini cut and a 9 lbs., 11 ounces and 21 ins., long baby boy, yes, he was big. I didn't get to see my baby for two days because he had Yellow Jaundice and they had to put him under the lamp. I couldn't even feed him. My husband came and told me what was going on the next day.

Willie: "He came out hungry, but he can't eat for a day because of Jaundice, but when they did let me feed him, I couldn't get the bottle in his mouth fast enough."

The doctor who gave me the epidural shot came to my room the next day to talk with me, he couldn't understand what happened with the shot, he was wondering why I reacted to it the way I did. He said,

Doctor Epic: "I want to give you another shot to see what happens."

By that time as he finished saying what he said Dr. Mick walked in and overheard him.

Dr. Mick: "Can you please step out of the room for a minute?"

Dr. Epic: "I just want to see what happened with her when I gave her an epidural shot."

Dr. Mick: "You are not going to touch her and don't come back."

She came back and said,

Dr. Mick: "I am so sorry that he came in to ask you that. Your blood pressure is so high that you can't see your baby until tomorrow besides, he has Jaundice, and he needs to be under a lamp, in the meantime you just lay here to get your pressure down."

"Okay!"

On the third morning she came to see how I was doing.

Dr. Mick: "You have to go on blood pressure medications, and you would not be able to breastfeed your baby."

That didn't upset me because I didn't have any milk anyway, I was just glad to be alive to see and raise my baby. I was not shocked about being on the blood pressure medications because it runs in my family on both sides. A lot on my mom's side, many of them have, and had strokes and died.

Dr. Mick: "Oh you can see your baby today."

When she said that, I was so glad because for nine months and three weeks we were together. I can remember how I would talk to him, play music to him, rub him, sing to him, and pray with him. When they brought him in and I held him for the first time, that was a feeling no one can take away from me. I remembered when I put my hand on his back, he would push back like he was saying.

Baby Ramono: "I don't need you to support my back!"

I removed my hand then put it back a few times and he pushed back each time.

"Wow!"

Two days later I was laying in my bed and 'oh boy' pains began to hit me so hard I just cried. Remembering I didn't have but one labor pain when I was laughing at the lady in the other room when she was having her baby. But these pains were much greater, or you can say very much harder than that one labor pain, I called for someone to examine me.

"What in the world is happening to me, am I dying?"

Nurse Linda: "You are having after birth pains."

"No! No! No! I am dying over here. It can't be that because this is worse than labor pains."

"This is not funny!"

"We see this all the time. It's just after birth pains, and they are much harder than labor pains."

It went on for hours when it did stop, I was so glad. On the fourth day I walked to the nursery to see my baby. I was standing there looking at him and a family came in from another race.

The Grandmother: "This is him; our grandson and he is the biggest baby in here."

"Nooo... That's my baby!"

They didn't believe me because of his color. What was so funny was their baby boy was born the same day as mine and I once worked with his mother a few years before. We were close while we worked together. Neither of us did not know the other was having a baby which was also a baby boy. But funnier than that I can see why they thought my child was their grandson. See they were white, and he was exceptionally light even after they put him under the lamp that was why I had to tell them no he is mine.

Without me realizing it this is where my faith, hope, joy, endurance, and love comes into play. I prayed we both come out okay and that I would be around to raise him. Because he is not mine, he was a gift that our Grand Creator, who gave him to me so I can take care of him. So, I prayed for help to raise my child the way I can, and I did, here we are 37 years later, he is our heart.'

I was eight in my month.

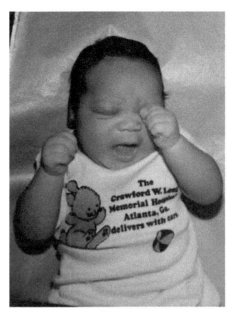

Ramono's day view before he came home from the hospital.

Ramono and his dad

Ramono and his mom/ (mom)

Ramono in his baby bed.

We are matching, he was three years old .

I stayed in the hospital for eight days. By the six day I was so ready to come home.

Nurse Mary: "You can't go home because your blood pressure is still up but if you want to go home you have to lay here like you are dead."

So, I did, when my friends came to visit, they tip in my room, and they talked extremely softly. They kept looking at me as if I were dying.

"Please don't do that, I am not dying or dead."

Ann & Sallie: "We were told to be very quiet to keep your blood pressure down."

"You two are acting like I'm on my deathbed, and you are afraid to come close to look at me so just stop."

Ann & Sallie: "Okay!"

For days I laid there like I was dead, but it did not help me. The only thing that happened, it made me more agitated, on day seven I told them.

"The only way my blood pressure is going to go down is if go home."

Nurse Linda: "Try and do your best to get it down."

I begin telling myself if I want to go home and raise my baby, I must do everything I can, so I did. Without me realizing it I began digging deep into a place where I really didn't know I had in me, but I realized I have a little boy that was counting on me, so I had to live.

The Joy of Knowing You Were Meant to Be

*It's a joy knowing people, but to get to know someone from the
beginning of their existence is the biggest joy of all. The day I felt
sick I just knew you were there.
It's so funny thinking back on it, it's like
you were saying hey mom, I'm here.*

*I was so sick like I never felt before I couldn't even ride the
bus home from work that life changing day.
I had to keep getting off the bus and I kept bringing up
everything I ate that day and more.
I just knew something was happening to me because
it was like I never felt before.*

*When I went to the doctor to see if anything was wrong,
deep down inside I just felt something different, special,
and strong.
I felt a special presence inside of me and I just knew, there was
nothing wrong.*

*As sick as I felt it was nothing compared to the joy I felt.
The joy of feeling something growing inside of me was the greatest
joy of my life.
Truly, just knowing and believing you were there.
Brought me the biggest smile without anyone telling me, you were
real I already knew I really do declare.*

I felt a special kind of bond that only a mother, yes, a mother can have
with her unborn child. Yes, you were my unborn child and
me having proof you were real, and I was going to get to know, and I
was going to see.
Yes, from the start it was a joy getting to know you
and I really felt you were really meant to be.

The joy of getting to know you little one and the joy
knowing you was really meant to be.
Knowing that, brought the greatest joy to me because I know you
were meant to be that was the greatest day for me.

Chapter 3

OUR LIFE WAS CHANGED WITH BIGGER JOY

After seven days in the hospital, we came home after I kept saying I wanted to go home. Yeah! That day my in-laws came up to see our son. They were at our apartment when we came home, what a joy it was to be home! When we got home the TV was on and Tarzan was playing, he looked at it like he knew just what he was watching, I couldn't believe it, so I called everyone to come and see. I need to see if it was just me or was, he really watching TV. Everyone saw it too. It was a great day.

I remember he never wanted anyone to put their hands to his back when we did, he would push back hard like he is saying,

"Remove your hand, I can support my own back."

He did that every time we would put our hand to his back, he would just fight us each time. He did that from the day he was born he was a big baby.

Willie's two sisters were pregnant with their second pregnancy that same year, one was about four months, the other one was six months, they both had girls. That was the year for babies because I also had three of my friends who had babies also, Willie named our baby and his sisters' too.

Our son was growing so fast we couldn't keep up with his progress, I couldn't keep up with his growth because he was growing so fast. He was turning over when he was about two months old. At three and a half months he was setting up by himself then two weeks later he was walking around his baby bed. I couldn't believe it, but he truly did. The saying 'crawl before you walk,' well he never did because he walked on his hands and feet.

When he was about six months old, we were with a group of friends. He answered a question, we all heard someone say the answer in a funny baby voice. Everyone turned around and looked at him so the person asked the question again, he said it again we couldn't believe it because the answer he said was right the year 1914. He made all of us so proud to hear him say that and none of us were crazy, we all just looked at each other and began laughing.

That was not the only time he gave an answer to hard questions, we were very proud parents. I prayed telling our Grand Creator he was not mine; he was a gift from him which he had given to us to raise and teach, and I thank him for entrusting us to do so, he was a good baby, he was a good child, and he still is, I am not just saying this because he is my child it's the truth.

He was a happy child. The only thing I regret is that I only had one. It wasn't from the like of trying because we did, but it just didn't happen. He grew up so fast, people would say he was getting out the way for another baby, which didn't happen, we tried until he was eight years old.

We Didn't Have Any More Children Why?

I began to get very, sick with more severe pains, so I went to see my doctor and he told me that I needed to have a "D & C' for the second time.

(OB/GYN) Dr. Harm: "You need to have this surgery, but I won't do it until you lose 40 pounds."

I can really tell you it really hurts, believe me.

"You mean to tell me that I will have to hurt until I lose 40 pounds?"

(OB/GYN) Dr. Harm: "Yes, You Do!"

After he said that, I was so angry and before I left that office, I had made up my mind that I needed to find another doctor because he really hurt my feelings. I began looking and I found a new doctor when I went in to see her all kinds of thoughts ran through my mind like what if she tells me the same thing, about losing 40 pounds? She came in to examine me.

Dr. Brown: "I can do the surgery."

"I don't have to lose 40 pounds before you do the surgery do I?"

Dr. Brown: "No, size doesn't have anything to do with what you are feeling."

I was so happy, thinking now I can get rid of this severe pain, this showed me there is help out there I can't or must not give-up. I had to have hope because there was a need to find someone to help me. I prayed, I thought, and I did research on my problem. I read any and everything I came across to help me understand everything that I was feeling. I learned how my body works, I even learned to listen to my body and really listen to what I was feeling, even what can make me have the problems I had. I still do the same to this day, not only was this the day I decided I was going to do everything I needed to do to help myself. This was the day I decided to be who I am, the day I decided I am going to survive whatever I face, plus that's the day I decided not to ever let anyone make me feel the way Dr. Harm did.

I learned what I can and can't eat, what I can and can't drink, what I can and can't be, if I can and can't smile, and what I can and can't do. So, when something comes up, that didn't, do, or don't make me feel quite right, I would and still and do, is, I will go and find out what is going on with me what I am feeling and how it makes me feel meaning I will go to the doctor, but before I go, I will educate myself. I began thinking how through the years in the past when the tumors kept coming back, I would take vitamin E, but this time it didn't help. I had to take care of them by having them removed. I begin to think how the first doctor just did not want to do the surgery and he didn't care about me or my pain, he didn't want to do surgery on an overweight person. I never went back to him, that taught me that I should not let anyone tell me what I need to do before they can help me. And most of all, I had to have faith and hope, I can endure whatever comes my way. I realize endurance is what I will need to keep living. I realized I love myself and life and I am not going to give-up without a fight. I became a fighter that very day. All of this reminded me of something that a doctor told me years ago.

Dr. Lime: "Let me tell you something, don't ever let a doctor ever tell you what is and what 'ain't' wrong with you. You see me in this wheelchair? One day I was working under my car, it was on a jack and the jack failed. I broke my back and now, I am in this wheelchair for life. I now know both sides as a doctor, and as a patient and I have learned 'No One' knows me better than myself. I am truly telling you please, get to know yourself, know your body, and don't let any doctor ever tell you otherwise."

I live by Dr. Lime's words ever since.

Faith is a complete trust or confidence in someone or something. It is a strong belief in God or in the doctrines of a religion, based on spiritual apprehension rather than proof. Faith is trust · belief · confidence · conviction · Credence, reliance and [more]. Faith is without doubt, and I realize if I want to live, I will need it more and this is how I must view my life and myself.

Hope is a feeling of expectation and desire for a certain thing to happen. Hope is an optimistic state of mind that is based on an expectation of positive outcomes with respect to events and circumstances in one's life or the world at large. So, I needed to "face my outcome with expectation, with confidence 'and' I also must have a cherished desire with anticipation." I did just so, but before I did, I wondered how I was going to do this. This is where faith and hope come in. Then a light came on ahh... "It Starts with The Mind" I asked myself how bad do I want to live and what will it take for me to fight to live?

I kept saying "It Starts with The Mind" over and over until a calm peace came over me. This is when I realize I must heal my mind before I can heal my body or have that inner peace.

Meaning that if I am not at peace in my mind, how in the world can I calm my body down? So, I will have the strength to heal and get well. Through the years I have learned and mastered these qualities.

Having More Babies Were Not in My Future

I love children and I always wish I were a twin but that didn't happen
so, I wish I had twins that didn't happen either,
no, that didn't happen neither.

I wish I had a set of each, even though I knew it would
not be a walk on the beach, or in the park.
I just love kids; I love taking care of the greatest gift that our Grand
Creator can give me to have a life grew inside and
to give birth is a great way to leave my mark.

Not feeling alone, always having someone, a special person to talk
with and share my feelings and my thoughts.
To eat and enjoy the food I eat. I won't get to know what their
likes and dislikes are, that's really saying a lot, whether
its days or nights.

Yes, as long as we teach them right from wrong, love and kindness,
joy and peace, mildness and self-control,
goodness and faith, along with patience we can never go wrong.
With these tools my child, I knew you would
grow up and be extraordinarily strong.

I wish I had more children for a long time. I didn't, but it's okay, at
least I did get to bring one in the world,
and I cherish every moment of it,
no matter how bad I felt, or how sick I felt.

Thank you little one for letting me share my life with you, thank you
so much little one for letting me be your mother,
too bad you didn't have a sister or a brother.

Thank you so much little one for letting me teach you from the
moment I learned you were due.
I began teaching you what I learned from the person that created both
me and you.

Ramono, is getting some sun.

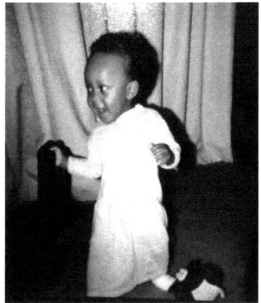

Ramono, is walking at my dad's house.

These two are his school pictures

Chapter 4

WHEN IT CAME TIME FOR MY SURGERY

realized I had to prepare myself for surgery, so I did all my due diligence, meaning that I investigated everything I could so I could understand everything that I was going through, what I was feeling and why. No, I was not doing an overkill on the matter because as I see it, knowledge is power, and I needed to empower myself. So that's where knowledge comes in, I decided to use the pros and cons method which really worked. In doing my due diligence I've learned more than I can say, and I am so glad I did. My potential evaluated conclusion was just to empower myself to get through the surgery. But as time and things in life happens, I would use it more and more.

The day I had my surgery I was not afraid because I knew what was going to happen not to say that things couldn't go wrong, I was grateful it didn't because that was the third D & C I have had since I got married. This time I felt like I needed to learn why I keep having this problem. I learned they just come back in some people. I knew I was one of those people that is not like everyone else. I felt special, not better but different. I call myself abnormal and through the years I was right.

Through the years I had many more 'D & Cs' come to think of it, for me wanting to and needing to learn more was a must. I didn't feel by myself knowing at that time I was learning how to help others. All I knew was I was in a lot of pain, and I needed it and wanted it to end. I remembered when I would go and pick my husband up from work, I would park the car and let the seat back or lay down in the back seat depending on what kind of car it was. I would keep going on until I could not sit anymore. When I was at my meetings it got to the point where I couldn't sit because it hurt too much, I would find myself staying home, it got so bad to the point I could only stay in bed.

Tumors Are Real and Painful

Tumors being real and to the point of needing 'D & Cs' which was very painful and my very first surgery of many. As the years went by and things kept happening. I stayed in the doctor's office; I have had so many doctors I could not count since I got married.

My female problems started since I first got married, from me taking birth control pills. I stopped because my problems worsened, and I was not regular after that with my monthly visit.

Having female problems and didn't know why or what was going on, each time I had tumors they were worse than the last one 'oh the pain the horror, oh the pain.' Anyone who ever had them have an idea what I am talking about. And I feel for them because with some of us we will or can have many before we stop altogether sometimes it will take more than just 'D'&'C's. Not only did I have female problems I also had other health problems.

Looking at my health report you can see just what I have and going through it can be extremely hard, but it can also make you stronger. I know because that's how and why I am the person I am today.

Thinking back on this I did not know where my life would take me but now, I am so glad I am the person I am. I don't like being sick but it's okay because it has made me the person I am today.

I thank my heavenly father for my life, I think him for helping me get to this point in my life. I see life in a special way, I know it has made me strong, it helped me to help and understand others as well.

I know I have a family, who needs me, but I cannot help anyone as long as I keep having these pains. I have thought long and hard about my family and what if I don't come through. Can I survive this? What if I don't make it? What will happen to my family if I don't come through?

I have talked to so many people through the years about their health. I truly know people need to have someone there for them. I know it's hard to know or think you are alone. This is why I never want anyone to feel that way, because life is hard enough and when you feel you are alone that is worse than any fear you may have. I have made it my goal to never let myself ever feel that way again or make anyone else feel that way.

Chapter 5

WHO ARE YOU?

As long as we remember that marriage is a three-cord fold not a two-cord fold. We will and we can weather any storm each, and every time things come up and as long as we work at them together, trust me we will continue to come out strong. I know because we have faced so many things no human can fight alone. We need to remember it takes two and both at a 110% each not 50-50%, nope, that won't do.

I can tell you this, things can put an extremely hard strain on any good marriage especially when a person themselves becomes ill or if it's your loved ones. An illness just doesn't affect the person that is sick, it affects the person(s) that is closest to you because it can and will take a toll on the strongest marriage and family. I want to show you just what I mean on how any family no matter how strong or how close we are it can cause an effect.

In the year of 1992, my husband Willie was at work. He was working with a beer company at that time he got to work at 5:00a.m., each day. One morning about 7:00a.m. I received a phone call to tell me. His co-worker Adam called and told me,

Adam: "Janice, Willie passed out here at work."

I rush to his side when I got to his job the paramedic was there working on him then they rushed him to the hospital the paramedic said,

Paramedic: "He had a TIA."

"What is a TIA?"

Paramedic: "It is a (mini-stroke) and as I now know that if a person keeps having them it can or will lead to a major stroke."

He was out of work for five months and he told his doctor what he wanted, Willie said he wanted to go back to work.

Dr. Cane: "I am totally against it because you are not ready to go back to work."

Willie became very agitated; he couldn't take being out of work that long.

Willie: "I really need to get back to work because I have to take care of my family and I can't just keep sitting around the house."

He went back anyway and a few months later he snapped his back which made him retire. Because of his TIA, and his back that year onward he changed which turned the whole family up-side down which caused nothing to be the same. What happened was that his personality changed. He was a different person and it got so bad. We got to the point that we were walking on eggshells. It was like being married to a totally different person, a stranger that was so mean. We walked on eggshells for a whole year, it was like I had to learn the person I had married over 15 years because that person was no more.

We did what we thought was right many times we set and talked about it, but it didn't help for long. Because neither one of us didn't understand what was happening. I knew he had changed, but he didn't and couldn't see it no matter how often we talked about it. It never was about love, it was about being there, for each other for better or worse. That's what love is all about when we said our I do's we meant just that because we both know our Grand Creator's views on marriage so there was no way we were going to take our vows lightly. Because our Grand Creator said,

"Whatever I have yolk together 'let no man,' pull apart."

And we were not looking at the death do us part. After a year something told me to step outside of the marriage, outside of the family and look in to see if I can help my family. And I did and the things I saw were shocking, meaning I didn't look at things saying it's all about me and I did not take anything personal. Because it was not about me but about my family and I was not going to give up until I found out what was going on and what we can do to make the changes so we can move forward.

I guess you are saying what I mean by stepping out of the marriage and family. Well, it simply means I put myself in a place mentally, where I could see and work on understanding what each person was saying and feeling and what we each meant when we spoke. What we say and how we understood what the other person was saying. When I did and I began to understand what was going on it was like a light came on in my head. We all sat down, and I began explaining what I did and what I saw and understood first I told my husband.

"You are not the same person."

Willie: "What do you mean I change?"

"After you had that TIA, that mini-stroke it changed you."

Willie: "What changes have I made?"

"You are quick tempered, you are so angry all the time, the lease noise sets you off. We are walking on eggshells, so we don't upset you, your own son, you are always fussing at him for being a child. I see things in you that you told me about your childhood that were abusive. You are making it a circle and you need to break it. You said you will never be like your stepdad the way he treated you all back then but here you are."

Willie: "No I am not."

"Ask your son what he sees you doing."

Willie: "Ramono you are not in any trouble, but can you please tell me how am I treating you?"

Ramono: "Daddy you hurt my feelings all the time, you are always screaming at me, and I don't know why you hate me so much."

Willie: "I am so sorry that you feel that way. I will do my best to stop but please know that I don't hate you, I love you. I didn't know I was doing these things to you, please forgive me."

Ramono: "Okay!"

Willie: "Can you come and give me a hug?"
Ramono: "Yes!"

"We are on the right track?"

Willie: "I guess you are right. I felt something was wrong, but I couldn't put my finger on it. I knew something was not right. That stroke messed me up and I wanted to go back to work."

Willie has always believed in taking care of his family's Spiritual and Physical needs. We both understood and totally agreed.

"Well, we can't see things when we are put in strange situations we have never faced before."

Willie: "I changed in other ways too. I will tell you later I am tired."

After 15 years of marriage and being a family, we had to totally reinvent ourselves. That's just what we began to do. It took some time to get it right, but we did, and we became the funny and happy family we were once again. We did it by first praying and not trying to take on things on our own, we went to the only person that knew who we were and who we became. It was our Grand Creator. I am not saying we are perfect because we live in an imperfect world, but we could do our utmost to stick with our Grand Creator's view of things and not our own.

By doing so we can say which is absolutely true we can feel when each other is sick or coming down sick. We both laugh about it when we tell the other. We Both say,

Willie & Janice: "You are not feeling well because you don't look or act right."

He always tells me I look wild when I am not feeling well and trying to keep it to myself, he would be right. I could and still can tell when he is sick, but a lot of times I don't say anything. I wait until he feels ready to tell me.

It's funny when I think about it, when a couple says their "I DO's" that really means for sickness and in health, for better or for worse, for richer or for poorer till death do us part. Those words are immensely powerful and at times those vows will be tested because of the time we live in and how bad the world has gotten. We should let nothing, yes, I mean nothing to pull us apart. It will be hard at times because we all are different, thanks to our Grand Creator for that because otherwise it would be a boring world and we would get sick of each other fast.

Some people do not take marriage and family life like our Grand Creator wants us to, because that is the way it was meant to be. Life is hard enough and if we have to do it alone, it will be much harder, we can, and we do make things worse. We are not created to be alone; it is nice to have someone to talk to or just laugh with. Remembering we are stronger with help from others or just having them around.

Just think for a moment what brings us joy, is it laughter, watching TV, fishing, cooking, camping, dancing, singing or helping others? These are just a few because there's so much more. The point is how many of these do we like to share with others, is it by having them there with us, or just taking it in and sharing it, or is it just telling them about it later? Do you see yourself having a smile on your face just thinking about it, or is it just when you talk about it? Let's take cooking if you love to cook, which I really do because my husband is always joking with me about it.

Willie: "She is in her zone because she is humming to herself. You can't tell her nothing."

Yes, I do because I love sharing what I do, and I do it with love, and from my heart. I love sharing things with others because it makes me happy and it brings a smile to my face and when that happens, I get a warm feeling in my heart. I love people and I want them to know I will fight for what brings me joy. Joy is very important, that's what marriage and family can do for us. It helps me have faith and hope not just in myself but also with others, my loved ones as well as strangers, this helps me have endurance. All of this is nothing but true love.

This is us before our son

Who Are You?

What would you say if I asked you who are you? Are you the person
I know?
Are you the person I fell in love with? Are you the person I married?

Who are you?
I am asking who are you?
Do you know who you are? Because this person sitting here is not
you, and this person will not do.

Who are you?
The person I married are not the same person that is sitting in front of
me, this is not the person I know.
Are you the person that makes me laugh? Are you the person
that makes me smile?
Are you the person that would carry me for a mile?

Who are you?
Are you the same person that I said, "I Do?"
Are you the same person that said "I Do" too?
You are not the person I know, no not you, who is sitting
in front of me.

Who are you?
You are not the same person that is sitting in front me.
So, I am wondering who you are and is this
the place we are meant to be?
This I must say, what would you say if I say who you really are?
No! No! I need to ask who are you sitting before me today?
Are you the person that talks to me at any given time and day?
Are you the same person that is here for me at any given time
and in any given way?

Who are you?
Really, are you the same person I know that is sitting in front of me
today?
Are you still the same person with whom I started a new life?
Are you the same person that made me your wife?

Who are you?
Please tell me who you are, because I do not know who I see
or this person that is looking back at me.
Can you please, tell me who you are?
You are not the same person you use to be.
You are not who you use to be not this person I see.

Who are you?
You are not the person I used to know.
So, who are you?
Do you know who you are?
Do you know, how you have changed so far?
Who are you?

We are at our 12th Anniversary

We are at our 25th Anniversary

I catered both Anniversaries.

This picture is when Ramono was about 10 years old.

This picture is doing our 40th years of marriage, we are at one of Ramono's friend's wedding.

This picture is of us when Ramono was about 12 years old.

This one is when we were at a convention.

Chapter 6

SURVIVING THE LOST OF OUR HOME

We lost our home which we were renting because the landlords let it go into foreclosure, one day the landlords took out loans on both and they lost both houses. The landlord came to let us know that they had let the houses go into foreclosure and we could stay there for free until they told us to leave. We both said what are we going to do? Well, we won't have to pay for rent.

Willie & Janice: "That's true because with neither one of us working we can use the money at this time while we wait on the judge's decision, so this came at the right time."

When Willie said he was thinking the same thing.

"I guess we need to start packing because we don't know when they will tell us to move."

Willie: "So we need to start getting some boxes tomorrow."

This was during the time when Willie was sick, and he had to retire because of his health. About three years later while we were waiting for his disability to start, and we had gone through all our savings. My mom has been living with us for about 12 years because of her health. We hired an attorney; I remember one day we were in his office, and he said something that was so strange.

Attorney: "I want to let you know that sometimes when a client wins their case Social Security decides to pull their case and reverse the finding."

"Just watch, we will be the one they choose."

I said it as a joke but by George that's what happened, we won his case, and we got a letter saying that they look at his case and they decided to turn the decision around. We had to fight their decision, we had to have another hearing with the judge they picked, who came from Fla., about two years later because they wanted someone that would rule in their favor.

As we were waiting, we got the letter letting us know that we had to move out by November which was about a year later. That only gave us about six weeks to move. We didn't want to, but we decided that we were going to move back to my hometown where my family lives 3 1/2 hours away. We would be driving back and forth to see our doctors, but some friends stepped in.

Gary: "We have been talking and why don't you all come and stay with us?"

Betty: "Yes, why not? But we want you guys to know we have rats; big ones."

Willie: "Do you want to move in with them?"

"No!"

Willie: "I don't either, but it would save us on gas and time."

"I don't want to drive-up and down that road three times a month to come to our doctors."

Willie: "You are right plus it will be hard on our car." "What about the rats I don't want to deal with that?"

Willie: "We have to check all our options; we only have two."

About two weeks before we had to move, we told them that we would take them up on their offer. We went out and bought a lot of big rat traps. And I put them down that first night. As soon as I put them down the traps start popping.

Gary: "I will get them up."

Betty: "Gary, you tell me you got us living in this place."

Their Oldest Son Carlos: "Daddy that make six that was caught by these traps why didn't we get some?"

"Are you awake and do you hear them? They are still popping and it's three o'clock in the morning."

Willie: "Yes I know I hear them; I am tired of hearing them pop. What did we get ourselves into?"

"A big mess!"

For three nights we kept hearing those traps pop. As time went on, we found out more things were happening. We have been living there for a while. It was a duplex, and they had both sides. They gave us the side where the oldest son slept. There was the living room, the bedroom, the kitchen, and bathroom. My mom slept on the living room sofa, Ramono slept on the living room floor. Yes, but we did not like him sleeping on the floor, their family slept on the other side.

We got Ramono off the Living Room floor and moved him in the bedroom where we slept on the sofa. I felt better with him off the floor because we didn't want him to get bit. Telling this story gives me the shakes, even just thinking about it.

"Momma at night I hear the rats on top of the cabinet where the chips are, they keep running across the bags."

Nancy: "Girl, that was not rats because if it was, they would have bit into those bags and eaten the chips."

"Oh yah, you are right I also hear them in the closet, I hear them crawling both day and night."

They had snakes also, yes, I said snakes.

"Momma, each time I go in that bathroom I would put my feet on the tub for fear of rats or snakes."

Nancy: "I do the same thing."

"Please no one is going to cut on my neck especially when there's only 30% in my favor, they must be crazy!"

I went home and I really did some hard praying with the main things I wanted to say. I asked to please let me get better, so I can get out of bed so we can move. I couldn't do anything but lay in bed listening to what was going on around me. When we bought groceries each month, we would put bags of chips on top of a cabinet in the space where the bathroom was, I remembered what I told my mom one day. Thinking about those snakes, I remembered looking at the light in the ceiling, it was just hanging with a hold around it.

"Momma, look at that snake tongue that keeps hanging out of the light hold?"

Ramono did Home School after he finished the third grade, he has a remarkably high IQ, so he jumped from the third to the eighth grade. He went into the kitchen and got a hotdog and put it on a stick.

Nancy: "Boy, stop feeding that snake, take that stick down with that hot dog."

"Yes, stop before that snake falls down on me, I will have a heart attack."

When Willie came back home, I said,

"We got to get out of here now, quickly, before I have a heart attack because I hate snakes and I have had enough. I don't care if I have to sleep in the car."

Ramono: "I want to go too; I hate it here I want to sleep in our car also."

I learned never say never about where we are not going to live. So, the next day I pulled myself up out of my bed and we went to housing so they could help us find a place to live. Three days later they called us and told us they had a place for us to live. It was out of two places; we were out of there in about two weeks.

Our friend, Wade would come to see us one day when we moved, she came to see us.

Wade: "You are going to get up out of that bed now that you all are getting out of all this mess."

"I hope you are right!"

With my prayers and my hard work, I did get out of my bed and moved on with my life that was in the 90's. About two months later Gary brought our deep freezer over and he told us a story.

Gary: "I know you all are so glad to have your own place again."

Willie: "Yes, we want to thank you guys for letting us stay with you guys."

Gary: "We were glad to do it but let me tell you all what happened three weeks ago. One day I cooked some neck bones and I put them on the table. I turned around to get the hot sauce to put on them and when I turned back around there was a raccoon on the table and he was eating my neck bones."

"You are lying!"

We all were laughing.

Gary: "No it's true, that was the second time, one it came in the house and got on the table eating."

"Why are you all still there?"

Gary: "We are working on getting out of there also like you guys."
Willie: "That's Great!"

"What does your family say about the raccoon?"

Gary: "They want out now."

"I am so glad we are out of there."

In the back of the house where the bathroom was, it was a long walk that connected both sides. The wall was separated from the floor by about 12 ins. You can see outside and that was another reason why we had to hurry and get out.

"I was in there earlier today and I heard baby rats while I was in there but just now it was very quiet."

Nancy: "I heard them too, so that means a snake came and ate them all."

Willie: "I heard them too that's what that was, we got to hurry and get out of here."

One night while I was asleep, and I turned on my right side and I heard something snapped in my neck, I could not move my arms or hands. I was stuck in bed for months, I couldn't feed myself, I couldn't bathe myself, or brush my teeth. That mean that I laid there for months, I remembered I went to see a neck surgeon to see what he could do.

Dr. John: "I can do the surgery, but it will only be 30% in your favor."

"How much it will cost?"

Dr. John: "It would cost about $50,000.00."

"Thanks, but no thanks!"

Gary: "I know you'll are so glad to have your own place again."

Willie: "Yes, we want to thank you guys for letting us stay with you guys."

Thank You for Sharing

I must and need to say this, beside I want to, not because I should or
because Gary died. I want to say, Thank You
for offering and sharing what you had, with us, Thank You,
for sharing your place.
We know it was not easy to have four more people in your home that took
over your space.

You all gave up so much, even though we contributed to the house and
shared what we had and making sure we had everyday
things done for you guys. Thank You, so much for sharing.
That proved your love for us, it showed your kindness, plus it showed you
have a heart for sharing and caring.

Thank You, for showing us true love, thank you for sharing your home, that
truly shows love.
It was in your hearts then, and now because we know it came from above.

Thank You, for sharing, thank you for caring.
We want you all to know we really appreciate your caring, and
your love for sharing.

Thank You, so much, you will never know just how much we appreciate
everything you all did for us.
Do believe me when I say this from the bottom of my heart, true friends are
no ways truly apart.
I mean this from the bottom of my heart!

When people like goes out your way to show how much you care.
This truly proves you are willing to share.
Thank You, for caring!
Most of all!
Thank You, for sharing!

Willie's Second Hearing

Sometime later they set Willie's second hearing with a Fla. judge doing the hearing the judge told us.

Fla. Judge: "You are still very young what are you going to do about working or taking care of your family?"

Willie: "We don't know we have to set down and talk about it. I can say this I am not able to work so we have to see what we have to do."

Fla. Judge: "They sent me down to rule in their favor, but I truly can't do this because I see you really can't ever work again, I am going to rule in your favor."

To make a long story short it was years later, we were in the six-year fighting. After winning his case for the second time it set on the judge's deck for two more years.

I would call about every four to six months. one day for the second time my dad told me.

Clifford: "Call your state Governor and tell him what is going on, let him know how long it has been, that you'll had two hearings and tell him what the judge had to say."

I call his office and I said just what my dad told me to say and within two weeks we had his check and our son Ramono's two weeks later.

Surviving A Big Lost

Devastation happens when something has been
taken from us, and we can never recover it but it's okay.
When we lose our way of life, or place
where we live all in one day.

Time will come when we all will lose what we have,
what we know, what we own, what is given to us,
what we buy.
We can survive no matter if it's a small or a
big lost, because nothing we have truly
do not belong to us no matter how hard we try.

All we can do is, do our best and keep surviving, from a big
lost and the best way we can do this is never worship what we own.
And do not let things own us.
We cannot make it our life, because that's not good for us, really, we
need to keep in mind, it do not matter if we are a child or if we are
grown, because it's truly not ours to own.

When the time comes when we must choose, if we are a person yes, a
person who will keep surviving after a big lost.
As long, as we keep during our best, and leave
everything we own, in its proper place it will not be
a big cost.
Devastation will not be hard on us if we keep surviving a big lost.
Because we will not let it become our big cost.

Endurance is the fact or power of enduring an unpleasant or difficult process or situation without giving way. It gives you the ability to do something difficult for a long time. You will have the ability to deal with pain of suffering that continues for a long time. You will have the ability to withstand hardship or adversity, it will especially help to have the ability to sustain a prolonged stressful effort or activity and more...

So, for me to help myself, endurance must play a big part in my life so I can heal my mind, body 'and' have inner peace. These are the three greatest tools to have in life and they will work if I use them for good and in the right way. Let's take our mind, it is very powerful it guides us to feel, to think, and make the right choices.

As for our body it is a powerful machine that works in so many ways that man will never totally understand, but what I do know is if I am willing to learn as much as I can about my own body, my own self, and what is in my mind that is the most powerful tool in the world. See when my body is not working right, my mind will fall out of place also. Which causes the effect on my inner self, which is what make me feel, make me say, and make me act the way I do.

When one is a loving kind person, a person that love to live, that love helping others which bring the biggest joy in our life are always there for us. Then suddenly, an illness happens, and you are not your loving kind self. This is speaking of a person that shows kindness to others and think of themselves as the lowest thing on the earth. Without thinking that they are not important and must also remember I too have something to offer, I too have something to give, I also have something to share. When I tell myself these things it will help me, no give me the faith, the hope, the joy, and the endurance to handle whatever comes my way that is truly love and it will move me to survive. Surviving is endurance, and endurance is surviving.

Chapter 7

LET'S GET TO KNOW WHY I SAY I AM A SURVIVOR

As you know I have survived many things; I don't want to call them small or little because every illness has its hardship on the person that is suffering from it. And no one should judge anyone whatever a person is suffering from or have. Believe me that person is in great pain otherwise, we wouldn't call it an illness.

Illness means a disease or period of sickness affecting the body or mind. It also a condition of being unhealthy in our body or mind. It is a specific condition that prevents our body or our mind from working well.

The synonyms of illness are affection, ailment, having a bug, complaint, complication, having a condition, having a disease, having a disorder, being distemper, having a distemperature, having a fever, being ill, being infirmity, having a malady, having a sickness, and being trouble are just some of the things a person may have or may face.

Now, that we have an ideal what this illness covers or do to our body or mind, it is never nice to tell a person, when someone says,

"You don't look like you are sick!"

When someone tells me this, I have, and I will tell them.

"Thank you I am so glad to hear that because I don't want to look like I am tore-up from the floor-up."

What about this one? When someone says,

Anyone: "You just wanted to get some rest!"

Yes, I did need rest and thank you for noticing that I look better, that makes me so happy with hearing you tell me this it makes me feel better."

Here is another one if you carry a cane or a walker, when someone says,

Anyone: "You don't need that cane you are just pretending, you do!"

"It's so good to see that you are free to walk without a cane, because for me, I have to use something to keep me from falling, it's good to see you don't need any help I wish I had that chose to stand on my own without help, keep up with the good work."

Those are just a few things people can and will say to me. Let's say they are not thinking or don't realize what they just said. I am going to repeat what a good doctor once said to me about how he ended-up in a wheelchair, he told me,

Dr. Lime: "One day he was fixing his car while it was up on a jack and I was under it, suddenly, the jack felt, and my car felt on me and broke my back, what I am telling you is don't ever let anyone tell you what is and what ain't wrong with your body because they don't know you or your body like you do."

I can still hear him say 'being a doctor he could see both sides.' For me to never let any doctor tell me otherwise.

"Thank you for this knowledge."

I began doing just so, I start letting doctors know that this is my body and I have lived with it all these years. I know they went to school many years to learn what they have learned, and I thank them for treating me, but I also let them know that they are not God because if they were, they would not come in and say what they say.

It's good to have doctors but we must remember they are imperfect humans just like the rest of us. They can only help us by asking us questions to guide them toward finding an answer to our illness. We need to remember they may not get it on the first or second visit. Sometimes they may not get it right until it is to late or they may never find the answer to help us because we may decide to go to another doctor for a second opinion.

On the other hand, we should not tell anyone that is suffering an illness it just in their mind. Or tell them they need to do what the doctor tell them to do even if that person keeps saying what they can or can't do or take. Please stop and think how you may feel if someone keep telling you what you know about your own body. Remember everyone is different, even if we have the same illness the same pain level, we all handle things different. Plus, dig this by saying what you say can do more harm to that person than good. Sometimes we may say something that we may think is helping but most of the time we may harm them more by what we say and how we treat them.

Remember it is not your body that is dealing with whatever illness is may be, so stop and think how and what you want them to tell you because words and action cuts like a sharp double edge sword. And please remember this if that person who is sick pay attention to their body, they know themselves better than you know yourself or your body. Think about this when a person is sick, they do not have the strength fighting with you they need all they got to deal with what's wrong with them.

Now back to why I am a survivor, here are just some of my illnesses, I will start in the end of the 90's. Here are their names here goes:

1. Crohn's Disease
2. Colitis
3. Vertigo
4. Muscle Spasms
5. Angina
6. TIAs
7. Immune Deficiency
8. Sleep Apnea
9. Asthma
10. Leak or Toxic Gut Syndrome
11. Osteoarthritis
12. TMJ
13. Rheumatoid Arthritis
14. Fibromyalgia
15. Everyday Swelling
16. Allergies
17. Burning & Itching
18. Chronic Anxiety
19. Stroke
20. IV Nerve Damage
21. Memory Loss due to Mold
22. COPD
23. Corbel Tonal (3 Surgeries)
24. Scar Tissues Removal (Many)
25. Gallbladder & Gallstones
26. Neck Infusion
27. Stomach Bypass
32. A Diabetic
33. High Cholesterol
34. Flatline (3 times on same day)
35. Bad Teeth (Due to Medications)
36. Pericardial Effusion
37. Bronchiectasis
38. Dehydration
39. Atherosclerosis
40. Cyst on Kidney
41. Cataracts (Removal)
42. Fuchs Corneal Dystrophy
43. IV Needle Nerve Damage
44. Damage Right Shoulder
45. 14 Blood Clots
46. Cervical Spondylosis w/Myelopathy and Radiculopathy
47. Enlarge Heart
48. Bariatric Surgery
49. Broke Back (In 2 Places)
50. Broke Neck
51. Damage Right Shoulder
52. My Own Car Ran Over Me Damage
53. Severe Sleep Attack (Where I almost die
54. Body Would Not Wake-Up (3 different times)
55. Mold Sickness (Due to Mold)
56. 2 Car Accidents (20 days apart)
57. Right Shoulder & Arm
58. Broke Toes (Many Times)

28. DVT-Blood Clots (14 at one time)

29. High Blood Pressure

30. Cystpscopy w/Hydration

31. Bladder Biopsy & Bladder Instillation

63. Sinuses

64. Over Compulsive Disorder (OCD)

65. Short Attention Span (SAS)

66. Severe Constipation

67. Severe Diarrhea

68. Cataract Removal (On Both Eyes)

69. Neck Snap

70. Shoulder Snap

71. Skin Break Out

72. Severe Gout

73. Knee Numbness

74. Hair Loss

75. Severe Joint Pain

76. Bladder Biopsy & Bladder Instillation

77. Large Intestine & Part of Small

59. Ablation

60. Hermia

61. Diverticulitis

62. Helicopter Bacteria

78. Eye Disease

79. Mold Skin Break Out

80. Coronary Artery Calcification (CAC)

81. Inflammatory Bowel Disease

82 Panniculectomy Surgeries (3 times)

83. Underactive Thyroid

84. Left Shoulder Injury

85. (SAS) Short Attention Span

86. Broke Toes (Many Times)

87. Endometriosis

88. Left Shoulder Snap

89. Nerve Damage Surgery on Right Hand

90. ************ (Will Let You Know Later)

91. ************ (Will Let You Know Later)

This is all true and I can prove all of them.

I live with them every day. Can you see why I say I am a Survivor. Can you say the same about yourself? I believe you can because you may have faith, hope, joy, endurance, and love just like I do.

Before I tell you about some of my illness let me tell you that I am allergic to a lot of different medicines. These are the ones I kept up with and or remembered. The allergic reactions which I notice all started after I found out about my Crohn's Disease.

I used to take seventy-two medicines a day including five Diabetic shots, and two Blood Thinner shots a day in the pass years not including vitamins. Then my body just began rejecting some of my medicines which some I too for years. Now I cannot take many different medicines, I will give you a list of these.

I still take seventeen different medicines a day some two or three times a day and I am down to one Blood Thinner shot a day. So, this means I drop well over half of my medicines. Oh yeah, I also take many vitamins also about fifteen different ones. Oh, I forgot I had to go and get somethings from a natural herb store because I can't take the medication the doctor gave me. This is still, a lot of different things going into my body.

Here are the names of just some of my medications which I became allergic. "Are you ready?" Here you go!

1. Hydrocodone (Acetaminophen)
2. Actos (Pioglitazone)
3. Ciprofloxacin HCL
4. Nafcillin
5. Pentasa (Mesalamine)
6. Contrast (IV Dye)
7. Demerol (Meperidine)
8. EntocortEc (Budesonide)
9. Ibuprofen
10. Medroxyprogesterone
11. Retinol
12. Oxycodone
13. Elmiron
14. Fluticasone
15. Micardis (Telmisartan)
16. Adhesive
17. Steroids
18. Ketamine
19. Avandia (Rosiglitazone)
20. Azelastine 137 MCG NASAL
21. Pervaicd (Lansoprazole)
22. Carafate (Sucralfate)
23. Azithromycin Tablets
24. Fentanyl
25. Coumadin
26. Lidocaine
27. Lexiscan(Regadenoson)
28. Glipizide Er.
29. Sulfur
30. Humira
31. Escitalopram
32. Codeine
33. Valium (Diazepam)
34. Lexapro (Escitalopram Oxalate)
35. Vancomycin (Analogues)
36. Tetracyclines Dyes
37. Metformin HCL
38. Albuterol
39. Purinethol
40. Anoro Ellipta
41. Steroidal Neuromuscular Blocker's
42. Doxycycline HYC 100 MG Cap
43. Mercaptopurine Analogues (Thiopurines)
44. Metformin Er
45. Dexilant (Dexlansoprazole)
46. Loratadine 10 mg
47. Indomethacin
48. Hydromorphone 2 MG Tab
49. Paxil (Paroxetine HCL)
50. Pentazocine-NALOXONE Tablet
51. Penicillin (All of kind)
52. Proventil HFA (Albuterol Sulfate Inhalation Aerosol)

This is all for now, no telling what may happen at any time. My pharmacist says: My Allergies also Includes Prednisone, Asacol, Troldine, Angiotensin Rec. Sio. Salicylates Non-ASP & Proton Pumps.

ANYTHING WITH STEROID COMPONENTS LIKE: Metformin, Prednisone, Prevacid (Lansoprazole), Steroidal Neuromuscular Blockers. So, I must be very careful with whatever I take. It's funny I have taken some of these medicines all my life but after I had my surgery in 2001 for my Crohn's Disease my immune system began to drop.

Are you saying to yourself Wow? What? How can she take all those medicines and become allergic to all the ones she has taking and become allergic to all these medicines? Believe me you are not along every time I give my Medical History Report to the nurses and doctors in the office or in the ER and hospital for surgery.

Doctors & Nurses: "I never in my life seen so many allergies and I am so glad to see you have this report it covers everything."

"Thank you!"

I did it because I cannot keep everything in my mind, and it just is too much go on with me. So, I decided to make this report.

My Report looks like this, this is just an ideal if you want to make one.

MY MEDICAL HISTORY REPORT: (Sample)

Pharmacy's name: Phone #: _____   Address:

_____
My Faith:

My Ethnicity: (ALL MY RACES) MEDICINES I AM TAKING

Medications: How Many Times A Day: What They Are

for:

MY OVER-THE-COUNTER MEDICATIONS:

The Items: How Many a Day: What They Are

for:

ALL MY ILLINESSES

WHAT TO GIVE ME FOR ALL OF MY ALLERGY REACTION (IN BOLD AND ALL CAP AND COLOR

CODE THIS STATEMENT)

ALL OF MY ALLERGIES, REACTIONS & SYMPTOMS State: (PLEASE READ)

Medications: My Reaction & Symptoms to All:

MY SURGERY HISTORY, HOSPITAL STAYS & ER VISITS

Dates: Hospital Stays & ER Visits: Why I was There & What Was Done:

MY FAMILY HISTORY ON BOTH SIDES

Illnesses: Who Had or Have It: Alive or Decease:

ALL MY PHYSICANS

Doctor Names: Address:_____   Phone #:_____   Fax #:

_____

A COPY OF MY LIVING WILL

I always keep this with me, I have all my doctors make a copy to put it into their records. I even do it in the ER and when I go in for surgeries. This is one of the most important things I carry with me because I will never know if or when I may need it, matter of a fact I have three copies, I keep one in my car. I never know if I can be in a car accident, or I maybe can't talk which has happen already.

I hope it don't happen to anyone else, but if it does don't feel bad, things can happen at any time to anyone. This can be extremely hard for anyone do they can become overwhelmed. It will be extremely hard, for me to believe or understand myself if it was not me. Now you can see why I keep saying I am a Survivor, but really am I?

What Is A Survivor?

*A Survivor is a person who survives, whatever their body and or mind goes through. No matter what comes about, that Survivor will
find the strength from deep inside,
especially if that person wants to remain alive.
Even after an event happens even when no one expect that
person to survive.
A Survivor is a person, who copes well with difficulties in their life
and who will do all, they can stay alive.
Being a Survivor means that person will fight to keep living, and
that is the person who will survive.*

*What Is a Survivor?
A Survivor is another word for an Endura, a person who is the Remainer of
what they may just gone through.
A Survivor is the person who outlive others, the person who outlast
others, for real that person will not just make-do.
A Survivor is a person who survive whatever the case maybe, as if
they land on their feet.
A Survivor is a person who is not discreet, or lunch met, no, this
person is concrete.*

*What Is a Survivor?
A Survivor is a tough person, a Survivor is an arriver who shows even when
things become difficult and when it seems like when all is lost,
no matter what the cost.
That is a person you really may not ever, want to cross!
A Survivor is a person who have great character, this is a person
who really loves to volunteer.
A Survivor is a person who do not wavier, this is a person that is
their nature, and they are a keeper.
A person who takes pleasure in life because that person is not
an impostor.
No, that person always makes it, truly clear!*

What Is a Survivor?
A Survivor is the person who will find their inner strength, who will find
inner peace, when that person is facing and who faces the darkest minutes of
their personal life.
That person is who keep pushing, who keep pulling, who keeps knocking
until that person's inner self finds peace
to keep enduring life's strife.

What Is a Survivor?
A Survivor is the person who has wisdom, and that Survivor will
let wisdom come in play.
A Survivor is the person who has wisdom, and that Survivor will let wisdom
come in play, when the Survivor began to think what they
need to do to stay alive.
Yes, a Survivor will always think about what is needed for them
to survive.

What Is a Survivor?
A Survivor is a person who is a successor, a person who is just a plan tough
cookie, a person who is just a tough nut to crack, a person
who is a survival, a person who is an extender, a person who is alive.
Yes, a Survivor is a person who will, do what it takes to survive.
Yes, a Survivor is a person who will survive.
These are just a few things that makes a person a Survivor.
Am I really that person you, see?
Am I a Survivor, can you please, tell me is that person really me?

⮞ *Chapter 8* ⮜

AM I A SURVIVOR OF CROHN'S DISEASE?

Now knowing what a survivor is; let's see if this person is me. Crohn's disease is a relapsing inflammatory bowel disease (IBD) it mainly affects the gastrointestinal (GI) tract. It can result in abdominal pain, fever, bowel obstruction, diarrhea, and even the passage of blood in stool. The exact cause of Crohn's disease is unknown. Potential drivers of Crohn's disease are compared to a combination of several factors, including our immune system, our genetics, and our environment.

The symptoms of having Crohn's disease include abdominal pain and cramping, blood in my stool, having bowel obstruction, having diarrhea, being nausea, and vomiting. The severity of my Crohn's Disease symptoms is:
(1.) Mild to Moderate, (2.) Moderate to Severe, and (3.) Extremely Severe.

I must keep track of all my symptoms not only it helps me, but it helps my doctors keep track and understand if it is being controlled or if it is getting worst. My Crohn's disease symptoms are not always easy, so therefore knowing my body is very important and it is the key to my survival.

When I have severe abdominal pains with tenderness, this is when my intestines become very inflamed. It's when I have chronic inflammation of my digestive tract, and there is no known cure for it but there are treatments available which can be lifelong.

I found out about my Crohn's disease in the late 90's through the years I would find myself going to the bathroom a lot. If I were to go anywhere that morning before I go, I would have to use it three or four times before I could leave the house.

I went to my (OB/GYN) doctor one day the same one that did my 'D & Cs' through the years.

Dr. Brown: "Janice how many times you go to the bathroom to do number two, a day?"

"It's anywhere between 8-15 times a day."

Dr. Brown: "That's not normal you need to go and see an (GI) doctor."

Which I did, he examined me, ran tests on me, and had me to come back to his office about two weeks later. He examined me then he asked me to come in his office.

Dr. Downy: "You have Cancer."

"Cancer, What! What! What are you talking about?"

I was thinking Cancer, Cancer, Cancer. I kept repeating it over and over in my head,

Dr Downy: "It is called Helicopter Bacteria we don't know where it came from or how it got started. What I can tell you is it comes from something we eat."

He was right because till this day I must be very careful with what I put in my mouth. I can't drink water from the faucet because it will make me very sick, and I will be barfing and pooping at the same time this includes ice also.

Having Crohn's disease is not fun at all because I never knows with each other breath. I may have constipation, or it could be diarrhea. Which can go on for days at times sometimes it about two-three days then it switches over to the other it's for two-three days.

This is what I do when that happens, which ever one happens first, I watch what I eat. I only eat what I need to eat to stop it then when the other one comes up; I will only eat what I need to eat to stop that also.

With my Crohn's disease flaring-up as much as it does, I should be very skinny. Not true for me I gain weight how do that happens well my body has always had a mind of its own I just go on its ride whichever way my body say go I go. Because I have learned that I cannot control this illness I can only know what is happening when it is happening and understand what's happening and do what I can to help myself and most of all stay calm with my mind and my body.

I have learned for me to survive each flare-up I must be prepared. I must have the right frame of mind; I cannot let anyone, or anything get me upset to the point that I can make things worse. So, I must keep telling myself be calm, be calm, be calm.

Sometimes so many things can be going on until I forget what's happening and I snap. When that happens, I say what I have to say to release some stress. Because surviving is being stress free that is my key to helping myself. Life can and it will get me at times, but I am only human, but I do not use that as a reason to be mean or ugly with people.

I will let anyone know that I am a peaceable person, but I am not one that will let anyone push or run over me I will let anyone know nicely. See, I have learned that I must be true to myself and others because that is the only way I can survive. I have had to get some people off my back I do my best, to do it respectfully and if that don't work, I have had to use the words 'you don't know me, so you better ask somebody' I really hate saying that, so through the years I had to learn not to say it, it's been over fifth teen years since I have use those words in that way.

I work hard at bettering myself, to help myself survive my illnesses, so if it means for me to carry myself a certain way so be it, I've learned I need to do what I have to do to help myself both mind and body. But I also must remember I have to be tactful because I don't like hurting people feelings. But I also know no matter what I do everybody are not going to be please with me. I know I cannot please some of the people some of the times and I cannot please none of the people all the times. I realize as long as I know I am doing my best it is their problems not mine.

People do not have the faintest idea what I am going through or how I feel or what it takes for me to get through every minute of the day. I do not wish anything I have to deal with, on anyone. I wonder if they can they handle it; I realize I handle whatever I am facing because I always says, 'what can I learn from this not Oh why me?' For me I come to realize when I am weak that is when I am strong. And each time I come out on the other side I am stronger and a better person because I feel as if I have something to share with others to help them and that is my joy of dealing with everything, I come face to face.

Therefore, I can tell anyone who are willing to listen about me and my story as my (GI) doctor told me one day. As you know I have Crohn Disease is a chronic inflammatory bowel that affects the lining of the digestive tract. Crohn's disease can sometimes cause life-threatening complications. I pulled up this site so that anyone that do not want to look it up I did it for you. Believe it or not this disease is rare, guest how many people are diagnosis in US cases per year.

<u>10 Symptoms of Diverticulitis - RM Healthy</u>

Crohn Disease

Description

Crohn disease is a complex, long-lasting (chronic) disorder that primarily affects the digestive system. This condition involves an abnormal immune response that causes excess inflammation. It most often affects the intestinal walls, particularly in the lower part of the small intestine (the ileum) and portions of the large intestine (the colon). However, inflammation can occur in any part of the digestive system, from the mouth to the anus. The inflamed tissues become thick and swollen, and the inner surfaces of the digestive system may develop open sores (ulcers).

Crohn disease most commonly appears in a person's late teens or twenties, although the disease can begin at any age. Signs and symptoms tend to flare up multiple times throughout life. The most common features of this condition are persistent diarrhea, abdominal pain and cramping, loss of appetite, weight loss, and fever. Some people with Crohn disease have blood in the stool from inflamed tissues in the intestine; over time, chronic bleeding can lead to a low number of red blood cells (anemia). In some cases, Crohn disease can also cause inflammation affecting the joints, eyes, or skin.

Intestinal blockage is a common complication of Crohn disease. Blockages are caused by swelling or a buildup of scar tissue in the intestinal walls. Some affected individuals also develop fistulae, which are abnormal connections between the intestine and other tissues. Fistulae occur when ulcers break through the intestinal wall and passages form between loops of the intestine or between the intestine and nearby structures (such as the bladder, vagina, or skin).

Crohn disease is one common form of inflammatory bowel disease (IBD). Another type of IBD, ulcerative colitis, also causes chronic inflammation of the intestinal lining. Unlike Crohn disease, which can affect any part of the digestive system, ulcerative colitis typically causes inflammation only in the colon.

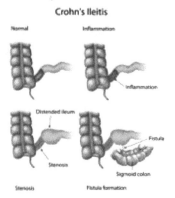

Crohn's Ileitis

The symptoms are Crohn's disease can cause abdominal pain, diarrhea, weight loss, anemia, and fatigue. Some people may have symptoms that never go away. I just learn nearly half of people with Crohn's disease battle mental illness. We all deal with some form of mental issue glad to say for me as I know it for now that is not my problem for now. This condition cannot be cured, but treatment can help for some not me.

I also have Diverticulitis which is a common ailment that roughly develops in over 200,000 patients per year. It's somewhat of a mystery illness, as even the most qualified of specialists find it challenging to come up with a cause, but they do know that it has been common on those that have a low fiber diet. Fiber is necessary to help avoid the condition from forming entirely as without adequate amounts of fiber going through your body on a regular basis, the colon has to work overtime just to be clearing the stools from the body.

As an infection that targets your digestive system, diverticulitis occurs
when the diverticula (small protruding pouches that form on the lower part of your colon), become inflamed. While this condition is not life-threatening, it can cause a tremendous amount of pain to those who suffer from it. The forming pockets of diverticula mostly appear in individuals over the age of 40, and the risk of diverticulitis increases for those who smoke, suffer from obesity,
lack proper dietary fiber, and who don't partake in a regular exercise routine.

Wondering what signs are associated with this illness? Here are the 10
symptoms of diverticulitis.

10 Symptoms of Diverticulitis

10 Symptoms of Diverticulitis - RM Healthy

1.**Digestive Issues**-Unfortunately, there is no 'in-between' phase when it comes to diverticulitis. Those who suffer from the illness either experience high levels of constipation, or extreme diarrhea. Often, there is no happy medium to be found.

2.**Gas**-A result of the bowel issues caused by diverticulitis, patients can also experience massive bloating and gas issues. Individuals will generally feel extreme pain and cramps when suffering through this symptom. It can occur, on and off, or the course of a few weeks.

3.**Stomach Pain**-Those who have diverticulitis typically report a persistent lower pain on the left side of their stomach. Stomach pain can be tricky to diagnose properly considering there are so many variances of digestive disorders.

4.**Tenderness**-The inflammation of the diverticula can not only cause pain in your abdomen, but it can also be quite tender to touch, or when slight pressure is added to your stomach.

5.**Fever**-Patients with this condition can experience the typical signs of infection, which include a temperature that reaches or surpasses 100.4 Fahrenheit.

6.**Vomiting**-Unfortunately, another symptom of diverticulitis is nausea and vomiting. As this mirrors the flu, (especially if individuals are experiencing diarrhea as well), many shake these signs off as a minor infection.

7.**Loss of Appetite**-Abdominal pain and uncomfortableness will cause diverticulitis suffers to lose their appetite when it comes to solid foods and liquids.

8.**Urination**-A condition known as fistula can often occur when patients are suffering from diverticulitis. Fistula results when the infected diverticulum erupts, and the inflammation and bacteria from your diverticula moves to
organs near your bowels, which include your bladder. The end result can mean frequent and painful urination.

9.**Blood in Rectum**-If stool gets backed up within your bowel, it can harden and affect nearby blood vessels. This ultimately will cause patients to notice traces of blood when going to the bathroom, or rectum bleeding.

10.**Peritonitis**-If diverticulitis remains unnoticed, the infection can spread across an individual's abdominal cavity, and a condition called 'peritonitis' can develop. Life-threatening, symptoms of peritonitis include fever, abdominal pain, and bloating. Unfortunately, if diverticulitis progresses into peritonitis, a patient will require surgery, and hospital care. I have this also. Helicobacter pylori (H. pylori) Diagnosis, Treatment & Tests.

Helicobacter pylori (H. pylori or, as it is sometimes termed, stomach bacteria) is a spiral-shaped gram-negative bacterium that can cause chronic inflammation of the inner lining of the stomach (gastritis) and in the duodenum (first part of the small bowel) in humans. This bacterium also is considered a common cause of ulcers worldwide as many as 90% of people with ulcers are infected with H. pylori. However, many people have these organisms residing in (colonizing or mucosa-associated) their stomach and upper digestive tract and have few or no symptoms. LPS (lipopolysaccharide) is part of the H. pylori outer membrane and can be toxic when the bacteria die and lyse.

Chapter 9

MY CROHN'S SURGERY

One day I was at the laundromat with a friend while she was washing her family clothes, we just loss her in death last month to cancer. I received a phone call from Dr. Downy, which I have not heard from in many months, he called me himself.

Dr. Downy: "I am calling you to let you know about your Crohn's Disease you need to have surgery."

I just froze because first it had been months since I have seen him, he's now calling me out of the blue to tell me this.

"Why Now? What Changed? And Who do I go to see about it?"

He gave all the information I needed to go and see a (GI) surgeon. I made an appointment with the surgeon I went in to see him, he ran a lot of tests himself. During that time, I began to hurt more and more. For you to understand my pain you would have to feel what people like me go through when our intestines become inflame, I will tell you what we feel to some extent.

Back then when I use to pass this very foul gas before I knew anything about having Crohn's Disease my son would say.

Ramono: "Momma, I really think you need to go and see a doctor."

"I think so too."

The reason why because I would have this foul-smelling gas coming from inside me. Back then it was not as foul as it is now, even now it can be so foul, I will have to remove myself where I am when it comes out of me on its own really, so I have to get out of the bad smell.

As time passes without noticing or feeling anything noticeable, this is because my body has become so use to the pain or inflammation. I go to the restroom a lot like today I have gone five times and today is not over. I get use to going to the restroom, so I don't pay it any attention. It's when my bowel becomes loose, and I barely can make it to the restroom if I do. Which makes me realize, my intestines are so inflamed that's when I realize it, it has become in a severe state. Sometimes they may even bleed and the only way I will know is if there is blood in my stool or if I have stool tests done and blood is found.

I do have a good day every now and then, but when I do hurt it hurts so bad, I cannot set anymore so I get to the point all I can do is stay home and stay in bed. But again, I do have good moments in a day or night. The only time I will leave home is to go to see my doctor.

During that first-time many months passes, and I beg the doctor to put me in the hospital and do the surgery, but he made me wait for more test, I got to the point.

"You don't care about me because you were making me suffer with all my pain."

Dr. Williams: "I do, care about you it's just that I have to make sure of everything before I go cutting on you."

Then I finally got my surgery date from the doctor.

Dr. Williams: "Just because you are having this surgery don't mean that you will be cured. It will come back; the surgery will only help you with the inflammation you are dealing with at this time."

"I don't care, if I can get six months free of pain, I will be happy."

Three weeks later, my mom came up to be with me for my surgery. My dad also, they were never married even though he wanted her to, but my mom said no before she had my brother. See, my dad was just like a popular song once said: 'Papa was a rolling stone wherever he laid his hat was his home.' How true that song was it was as if it was written just for him. The morning of my surgery I rode with my dad to the hospital and on the way, there was a billboard showing a strawberry, it looked so good I start craving it.

"I wish I had some strawberries and shrimps right now."

We began laughing, my mom rode with my husband and son. Some of our friends came to set with my family. We all arrive at the hospital by 7:00 a.m.. We all went to the floor we were told to go. The nurse came and got me, I told everyone I would see them later. And I went with the nurse she took me to my room, a nurse came and asked me a lot of questions, a nurse came in to run tests on me and she drew my blood, and she took my urine. Another nurse came in and we start talking.

Nurse Pebbles: "I am so tired because I have a 22-year-old and a 2-year-old." I laughed so hard.

"Boy you really did start over."

Just as I was saying that the nurse who took my blood and urine came back in the room.

Nurse Emma: "I just got through talking with the doctor."

As she was talking, I was looking at the two pregnant tests she had in her hands, I was thinking I wish she would take those tests wherever she is going to them.

Nurse Pebbles: "And he told me to tell you that he will not be able to do your surgery today."

"Why Not?"

Nurse Emma: "Because you are pregnant."

My eyes went up toward the left corner ceiling. I said,

"How that happen?"

She just laughs.

Nurse Emma: "He said before you leave for you to call your (OB/GYN) doctor and them you need to come in ASAP."

Now, I know how that happen, I just couldn't believe it because I was told when my son was eight years old during a time of my ('D & C') surgery.

Dr. Brown: "Janice you will never get pregnant again unless you have a certain surgery."

But I never did when my (OB/GYN) doctor told me that I really {I don't want to say this, but I did feel this way at that time, I dislike that woman at that time because of what she told me, and she was eight months pregnant. I didn't hate her because I hate no one I just was very angry.} Ramono, was 18 at the time and it came to my mind I was starting over also. I had to tell everyone that morning that I was not going to have my surgery and the reason why and when I did everyone was shocked.

Nancy: "I thought she was too sick to do anything like that."

Ramono: "Me too beside I thought they over there watching TV."

"You can only watch just so must TV."

Before I left the hospital, I called my doctor's office before I left the hospital.

"This is Janice Holliman I was told to call you'll and let you'll know that I was about to have surgery this morning, but I can't have it because I am pregnant, and I am to tell you all before I leave the hospital."

Dr. Brown's office: "Oh my goodness can you come in today?"

"Yes, I can."

I was thinking about that all the way to my doctor's office. On my way to the office, I begin to think about a conversation I had with one of the nurses during one of my pap smear exams.

Nurse Barbara: "You are at the end of menopause."

"How can that be, when I told you'll years ago that I was going through the change in my 30's, each time I would tell you, I was told, I was not because I was too young so, again how can that be?"

Nurse Barbara: "Because you are dry."

"I knew I was right!"

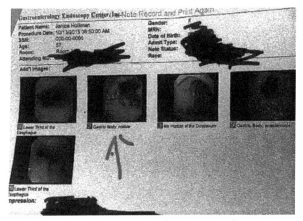

Pictures of my intestines from one of my testes

As I said earlier the exact cause of Helicopter Bacteria is unknown, but I do know heredity and a malfunctioning immune system play a major role. Along with abdominal pain, diarrhea, malnutrition there is fatigue. There are anti-inflammatory drugs and immune system suppressors can help in long term remission.

I used and tried many treatments, but through the years my body began to reject a lot of my medicines. I remembered taking Pentasa for about six years, give or take then I realized things began to happen I start feeling sick, each time I took my medicine I couldn't breathe. My chest began to hurt, it felt like I had and have a heavy weight on my chest, I began to itch, and I began to break out in rashes each time I took a pill.

When I realized it was the medicine, I stop taking it, but I didn't tell my doctor for three years.

Dr. Downy: "How's the Pentasa doing?"

"I stop taking it about three years ago."

Dr. Downy: "Why didn't you tell me you stopped taking Pentasa?"

He was mad.

"I am sorry, but I really thought I told you, but I guess not."

I was sorry about it, I guess I didn't want him to give me anything else because I was tired of taking medicine that was hurting me. Now I don't and can't take anything he even realized everything he gave me made me sick or hurt me, so he stops giving me anything.

I remembered with one of the medicines, it was the Humira which they did an infusion in the doctor office. They hooked me up and within about two minutes I began itching, I couldn't breathe, the office was connected to the hospital. Becky came back in the room about three minutes later and she saw what was going on, so she rushed, and I unhooked me from the infusion, and she walked me down to the ER. On my way walking down to the ER, I was walking in a way that I could rub myself with parts of my body that a person couldn't normally do walking straight. It was funny when Becky that was taking me down turned and saw me doing what I was doing.

Becky: "You are good and graceful because if that was me, I would have people looking at me like I am crazy."

Willie was with us, and we all just laughed. When we got to the ER, they took me right back. And they hooked me up with an IV I was not paying any attention to what they were giving me like I normally do because I was too busy taking care of my itching. It was a good thing Willie was there.

Willie: "What are you giving her?"

ER Nurse: "We are giving her steroids."

Willie: "Oh no you can't give her steroids because if you do, she will be in a worst shape than she is in right now."

ER Nurse: "Thank you for telling me I do see she is allergic to steroids; I am so sorry we didn't pay attention to her allergies we could have killed her."

This showed me I must be on top of my game and be aware of what is going on even when I put myself in the hands of others. That was my first and last time of letting anything like that happen again. I was prepared from that very day I began keeping an eye on what they do to me I ask about everything.

And if you don't suffer with intestinal problems like I, do you would not understand what it is like living with Helicopter Bacteria and most of all Crohn's Disease or the other stomach problems I am living with.

Having these diseases don't make me a survivor, do it? No, it doesn't! What makes me a survivor is how I view it and handle it. First, this shows me just how bad our fore parents didn't care about us. What they were looking at was the fact they could be gods or god like then they wouldn't have to rely on our Grand Creator, they were very selfish.

Adam was weak to follow Eve when he was told by our Grand Creator, when he gave the command to Adam: "From every tree of the garden you may eat to satisfaction. But as for the tree of the knowledge of good and bad, you must not eat from it, for in the day you eat from it you will certainly die."

Then he made him a helper because it was not going for him to be along. And he was to tell her everything our Grand Creator told him. But as we see it that didn't work or matter because look where we are today. How many of us have lost loved ones in death because of the sin our fore parents put upon us with their greed and their selfishness?

Then he had the audacity to blame our Grand Creator for what they did, no by what he did by saying,

"That woman whom you gave me, she gave me the fruit from the tree, so I ate."

Now why didn't Adam tell Eve, "No" he was not going to touch the fruit or eat it because it was going against the commandment? He didn't just follow 'that woman,' instead of saying 'that woman was broken' and he couldn't fix her and that he needed another helper because she was not a good helper.

Nooo... he just had to show who and what he loved more, and it wasn't the Creator. Maybe, he didn't want to be along again, or he loved her more, whichever, he was wrong.

Therefore, I am dealing with my illnesses like many of others and facing death because of the state they put us in, and we have to deal with their sin because they passed it to each and every one of us.

Remembering what a Survivor is it is a person who endure is this me?

Let us see how I did with Goodness this time around.
Dictionary's View: Is the quality of being morally good or virtuous. It is the quality or state of being good. It is having generosity, kindness, and it's the best or most valuable part of anything, essence.

Biblical View: Simply put, yes goodness is the quality of state of being good. It involves moral excellence and virtue, without badness or rottenness. Goodness is evident by its beneficial effect on others. It is an active, positive quality manifested in helpful deeds. God is good and his works are good.

As for me I know I must pray for goodness, and I want it to be genuine. So, I must love what is good and hate what is bad, that means I will reject the badness I will face this week. I know it will not be easy, but I will keep in my mind and forefront, how I am working on goodness, and I will do my best to show goodness to all. I want to be equipped with goodness, I want it to fill m my heart, I want to add it to my treasure so I can put it when I need it yes this will be a good week let's see.

∽ *Chapter 10* ∽

MY (OB/GYN) DOCTOR OFFICE'S VISIT

When I arrived, my pregnancy was buzzing all over the office I overheard them talking about me as I was coming in, they were very shocked because I was turning 42 years old in a few months, that year so that meant that I was having a baby on the change. And I would have started over again being a mother it would have been like I was a new mother.

Because everything I knew raising my son would have been different because I was different, my life and my health was different. When I got there, they called me back and the first thing she said when she came in was.

And I would have started over again being a mother it would have been like I was a new mother. Because everything I knew raising my son would have been different because I was different, my life and my health was different. When I got there, they called me back and the first thing she said when she came in was.

Dr. Brown: "What happen?"

"You tell me, because you told me, I would never become pregnant unless I had that surgery which I never did."

Dr. Brown: "I know, I remembered."

"How could this happen when I was told I would never have another baby."

Dr. Brown: "This is why I told them Nobody, touch her, only me!"

"When You told me that I could not get pregnant, you were about eight months yourself I really dislike you. The fact that I was told I couldn't get pregnant again made me so angry."

Dr. Brown: "I know! I am so sorry I know how mad you were!"

"So, tell me what happen? How did this happen?"

Dr. Brown: "I don't know, things just happen sometimes."

She then went on to tell me the different kind of pregnancies and she wanted me to have an ultrasound which was set up and done. Then I went back to see Dr. Brown and she told me about the test, the kind of pregnancy it was. She told me she was worried about the pregnancy; she was worried that my body may abort it. I heard what she said but my mind was on the fact that I was pregnant after all those years, something that I was told would never happen. I was pregnant again beating all odds, me at the age of forty-two having a baby. Wow! What! How!

"Okay! We will have to wait and see."

After I left the office, it really hit me what she said. But I felt fine were not having any problems I was three months. I told a group of my friends I was pregnant; they knew how I wanted more children. They asked what did I meant about being pregnant and how far was I?

I told them I was three months at my age, and I talked about how they knew how I wanted more children.

As time went on, I began thinking about all the medications I were taking, I began wondering if all my medicine could have an effect on my baby. I do not agree with abortions by the removal or expulsion of an embryo or fetus before it can live or survive outside the uterus is killing a life, the reason why is because life began at the moment of conception. I know that life only happen because that is what our Grand Creator wanted and the reason why he created mankind in the beginning. When this happens, it is called a deliberate step when taken to end a pregnancy, it is called an induced abortion.

Now as for an abortion that occurs without intervention by the hands of any human is known as a miscarriage or spontaneous abortion. Which is out of the hand of the mother, what happens when something goes wrong, and the baby cannot survive in any form it just is a bad pregnancy or the baby is not healthy.

I began worrying that my baby may not have a healthy life or survive the whole pregnancy and I did not want it to suffer in any form. But I really wanted my baby and I know that I had to stay on all my medications also for me to survived. Plus, I stayed in pain, and I was taking pain pills to stop the pain.

I prayed extremely hard that my baby will be alright, but I had to come to the realization what Dr. Brown said may come true. So, I told myself and made myself believe if I lose my baby, it was not meant to happen at that time. That stayed on my mind all the time it got to the point I worried about it the whole time.

I was in my fourth month, then one morning about 8:30a.m. I woke-up I with was in so much pain. It hurt so bad I start crying because of the pain. But most of all because I knew what was happening, I was balling up with pain and then I started bleeding then it happened. I took and picked it up and put it in a zip lock bag. Then I began cry of what had just happened because I lost what I wanted for many years more children. Something that we all wanted it to hurt my husband and my son as well as myself. I was laying there crying, and my phone ring and it was Dr. Brown.

Dr. Brown: "I calling to see how you was doing? I just had a feeling I needed to call and check-up on you. How are you doing? Is everything alright?"

"No, it just happened! Besides losing the baby and the severe pain and crying from the lost I will make it."

Dr. Brown: "I am so sorry you lost the baby I had you on my mind, so I said I needed to call you to check and make sure you were alright. I want you to come in and bring me what you miscarried. I want you to come in tomorrow."

"Thank You for caring enough to call. Okay what time?"

She connected me to the front desk so they could tell me what time I should be there.

Oh, I forgot to say it was a girl which, we wanted. That made it hurt even more, it still hurt till this day. Just think about it if I were four months in August, which meant five months later it would have been around January or February of 2001. And from that year until now she would have been 18 years old this year. But I will never get to know her to teach her. The same things we taught our son or more since we have learned from raising our son.

I was three months pregnant in this picture, but I didn't know it.
The way I found out knocked me and others off our feet!

I Will Never Get to Know This Little One

This little one is the person I will never get to see or get to know.
She is the person I wish I can see but it was not meant to
be, because of the world we are living in.
The bad things that were put upon us all, because of all the
sickness in the world and because of our fore parents' sin.

I am so, so sorry I have to say, I will never get to know
this little one, I will never see her grow, she will never
hear me say, I love you little one.
Because of my illnesses, I am deeply sorry I will never get to
know this little one, no I will never, be
able to say, please forgive me, for what I have done.

If I could tell her and let her know how we really wanted to meet
her, we really wanted to tell her how beautiful she would have
been. If we could let her know just how wonderful, she was made
which would be wonderful.
But we can't because she is not here. She will never hear our voices I
must say it wasn't me, it was my illnesses that was responsible.

Even though I will never get to know this little one, I wish she
could know how loved she was and still is loved because our
Grand Creator made her even though she is not alive.
I will never get to know this little one, it still hurts my heart to
know she Is not Here, I which I can say, I really fought for us
both. It's sad for me to say that she was not strong enough, no not
enough to survive.

I will never get to know this little one, I will never get to teach
her, the love we have and had for her, the love
we could have shown her.

Sometimes I wonder what I could miss someone whom I never meet, or I wish the pain would leave and it is all said and done. Our Grand Creator did let me know that she was there, even though I will never get to know this little one.

I will never get to teach her, to show her any of the wonderful things in life I am deeply sorry, I wish I could, I would want her to know, I do love her as far as the sun. I know she will never get to hear these words because she never got to take a breath. I still feel, I really need to see these words and say, I will never get to know the one that is not Here with us today.

I must say this today, I have learned as time goes by, I must say, and things become clearer each and every day.

Yes, I have learned there may be a chance to see my little one, and things are not all said and done. All I need to do is be patience, to wait and see what's can be, in storage for her and me.

It would be nice to see her, to hear her cry, to hear her laugh, and to see her smile, it will be the greatest thing for me, to see this little one, It's good to know things are not all said and done.

This week my word was Faith.

Dictionary's View: Faith is having complete trust or confidence in someone, something, or concept. Its allegiance to duty or a person: loyalty.

Biblical View: Faith is the assured expectation of what is hoped for, the evident demonstration of realities that are not seen.

Moreover, without faith it is impossible to please God well, for whoever approaches God must, believe that he is and that he becomes the rewarder of those earnestly seeking him.

This week I looked at my faith knowing and showing myself that I do have faith in myself. Knowing that I can do the things that I set out to do, even if I fall short, it's okay to fall as long, as I pick myself up and keep moving forward.

I also focused on the fact that my faith in my Grand Creator is real even though I cannot see him. I know he is real and that he is here for me because I see the things, he does for me each, and every day. And I also know he is here for others as well as long, as they let him be there for them, by putting him first in their lives as well as myself.

This too hurts and I will not forget this trail of what happened, but I will take and learn what I can so I can become stronger and so I can help others by telling them about me and what I have to deal with. I will work hard to survive also because this is what Survivor.

⌒ *Chapter 11* ⌒

THANKS TO MY CROHN'S SURGERY

After I lost the baby, I wanted to hurry and have my surgery, I just wanted to end the pain. I wanted to feel better, I wanted to move on, to get on with my life. It took a while for me to have my surgery, Dr. William told me I needed to get my blood level back up because of the miscarriage.

I did everything I needed to do to build up my blood level. I got the green light for my surgery; it was a bittersweet thing to hear. The day came for my surgery it went well, I healed well.

It was hard to know that I had my right side of my large intestines and part of my small intestine removed. I remembered some of my friends who came to see me in the hospital.

Betty: "If I was not there, I would not have believed you had that surgery because you look very well you don't look like nothing ever was wrong with you."

"Thank you for those kind words and it makes me feel good to know I don't look like I am tore-up from the floor-up."

We both laugh!

Chris: "Wasn't nothing wrong with you, you just wanted to get some rest."

"Thank you this mean so much to me because it is so good to hear that I don't look like I am tore-up from the floor-up."

I don't mind anyone telling me I don't look sick because I am one person that don't like looking sick. I take great pride in how I feel and looking nice, because taking care of my looks is part of my way of help healing myself. See, being a skin care consultant, I must always, look my best because it makes me feel good, and it helps me feel good about myself, plus it's my business.

Another way I help heal myself first and foremost is having a calm and peaceful mind and being happy. I remember while I was out sick, I would spend many hours looking out the window thinking and seeing the wonderful things our Grand Creator created. All the beautiful colors of flowers, the beautiful sky, the beautiful trees, and grass.

I remembered and kept it in my mind how I always thank our heavenly Grand Creator for all the wonderful things he has given me starting with my life and for letting me survive. I was so happy I had my surgery I felt so much better, I did keep it in mind that was not a cure for because there is on fire. And I also remember saying that's okay if I get six months free of pain, I will be a very happy woman.

The day came when I went to see my gastroenterologist for my six months check-up and my colonoscopy test, I got my test results.

Dr. Downy: "Okay I have the results I am sorry to say that it is back, and it is bleeding."

"It's okay! I got my six months free of pain."

Dr. Downy: "No we don't want it to bleed but with all your problems with medicines all we can do is just keep an eye on it. I am going to give you a diet to go by."

I have had so many diet plans for him it's okay. The thing is I can't eat some of the things that is on the diet plan. So, I must eat what my stomach allows me to eat because I deal with constipation and diarrhea.

Through the years I have had to deal with one then the other. It can be a pain living one's life like this not knowing which one it will be that day or for the next two or three days. So, whichever it is, I have chosen which way I must eat so I won't get sick or make it worse.

Through the years I have colonoscopy about every 6-8 months. To see how my Crohn's Disease is doing or my Scar Tissues, doing and anything else that may be acting up.

I have learned I always need to take another look at the results one day or two after the drugs ware off. Because they can make a mistake and give me someone else results. I have received a male's test result before.

This is the reason why; it is especially important for me to start paying close attention to my health because things can go wrong. So, learning my body and who I am is the most important thing in life because it has saved my life many times.

Surviving is such a joy knowing what I have just went through and I am still alive. I feel like this makes me a Survivor!

Pay Close Attention to Yourself

Attention is the act or state of applying the mind to something. As
taking notice of someone or something as regarding them of or it as
in testing or important.
Stop, and look at me what do you see, do you see me?
Pay close attention to what I may be.

Know and learn what life has to offer by paying close
attention to yourself you will feel free.
Stop and look at me, I see what I can be, what about you,
what can you see?
Do you want to feel like me, feeling free?

The closer you pay attention to yourself the more you will learn
about yourself.
By doing so, you will feel better about yourself,
when that happen, you will feel and there is nothing
else left.

Stop, pay close attention to yourself because
if you don't you should not be surprised if anyone say they won't.
Pay close attention about and to yourself,
don't let what you find out about yourself get you down.
Take what you learn and do the best you can and turn your life around.

Stop and see what you can learn about
yourself and be the best you can be,
because it will help you feel free.

*Pay close attention to your mind, to your body, to your inner self, in
doing so you will have good physical wealth.
When you do then you will know this is the start of good health.*

*Stop pay close attention to yourself, please pay close attention
and see, if you do you will find, you can be fine, just like me,
no matter what the outcome may be.*

*So, please stop pay close attention to yourself, pay close attention
to yourself, yes, pay close attention to yourself,
and don't depend on no one else.*

⌒ *Chapter 12* ⌒

THE BROWN PAPER BAG AND THE MENTAL DRAWER

Let's say there is a problem, and you don't know what to do, all you do is worry, worry, worry. That's not good for your health and you don't get anywhere worrying about the problem because you worry to the point you cannot think. So many people let themselves worry about everything in their life. I am not saying there is anything wrong with worrying which is good for us because it will keep us humble, and it will keep us from thinking that we are better than anyone else.

I also must say if we spend all our time worrying, we will never get anywhere. I use a method that I heard while they were telling a story about one family it goes like this:

Think Do Not Worry

There was a happy family of three, one day the father died as time passed the mother meet someone, she fell in loved and married. The son was having a problem and all he did was worry, he worried so much it got so bad to the point it drove him crazy. The stepfather asked the son what was wrong, he told him what was going on with him at school. The stepfather had been watching the son for a while he told the son that he had notice he and his mother worry about everything. And that he could give him the answer, but he was not going to tell him what he should do, but what he told him to do was for him to go upstairs and think of two ways to solve his problem.

He told him not to come down until he can come up with something that can help him with his problem. The son did, hours later he came running downstairs and told his stepfather the two things he came up with, the stepfather asked him how he felt after he solve his problem. The son told him he felt great, the stepfather told him that since he had a plan (A) and a plan (B) the next thing for him to do was to put it away until it was time to handle the problem.

I loved hearing that story and that method, so I begin using this method for myself many years ago. To hear about his wife and her son having a big problem about letting things get the best of them. After he told him what he meant about getting two great ideals. The stepfather told him to stop crying about the matter because he could not think while he was doing all that crying, and that he needed to use his brain and not his tears. He came running downstairs with his ideals or a way out the son told his stepfather listened and then asked the son did he feel better, the son said yes sir. Then stepfather asked the son what he was going to do with all that time he had since he had solved his problem, the son said he was going outside and play.

That was a happy ending which I really love so I decided to try it and I still uses it till this day. That is how and why I came up with the saying, "The Brown Paper Bag."

As for the brown paper bag I say it like this, I will come up with two or three ideals put them in a mental paper bag and put them in a mental drawer and leave it there until it's time to handle the problem and then and only then do I take them out. Which means I take it a step further by adding a plan (C) and by also adding the mental drawer, I really do live by it.

See if the first one doesn't work out; I will use the second one and if the second one doesn't work; I will pull out the third one. Now if the third one doesn't work well, I tell myself I did my best and no matter what I come up with, it just won't work so there is nothing else I can do. That means I should just move on and not let my problems take over my life, don't let it rule me, I rule it, I am in control of my life and not my life in control of me. Yes, you are in control of your live when it comes down to handling our problems with help.

I am telling you, remember not to let anything or anyone ever take your joy away if it comes to the point you can't think about anything but your problem. That's not the way to live your life, it was meant for you to enjoy life and not let your life run you but for you to run it. I know I am not alone, and I don't do anything on my own, I know this because I truly do this strongly!

My Mental Brown Paper Bag
and My Mental Drawer
'Method'

I have solved many problems in my life thinking
and using the brown paper bag method
I will think of two or three ways to solve my problems,
I call it plain A, B, or C this means it will take preplanning.
I love the brown paper bag method, it is so helpful, so
peaceful, so calming, and most of all it makes me feel good,
and it is undemanding.

After pre-planning I then will put plan A, B, or C in a mental brown
bag, which I then will put it in a mental drawer. I will leave it there,
and I do not think about it until the time come to use them after I have
said a good size prayer.

When the time come then, and only then, I will open the drawer.
I will use plan A, if it doesn't work, I will use plan B, and if I have to,
I have a plan C, I will use it also, but if it doesn't work,
what's next should it be?
I realize and say it's okay what's the worst can
happen to me!!!

YES! I have realized something new in life, it will not kill
me if they don't work, I tell myself well... I have learned
something new, I have learned what not to do. Yes, I have learned as
long, as I do my best.

I realize and say it's okay what's the worst can happen to me!!!
YES! I have realized something new in life, it will not
kill me if they don't work, I tell myself well... I have learned
something new, I have learned what not to do.
Yes, I have learned as long, as I do my best.

I will realize, no I have realized, I have passed a great big test.
Guest what, it still doesn't matter what I do, it still may not work!
Yes, what I've learned no matter what happens, I have learned it's
okay and it's time to give it a rest.
Yes, I know what I must do what is best.

Yes! I have learned somethings just do not work no matter what I do,
maybe it out of my hands so I must give it a rest
because I then realized I have done my best.

I also realize, life is filled with a lot of zig zag.
This is why I do the brown paper bag.

⟶ Chapter 13 ⟵

WHAT IS MY PURPOSE?

The very first thing you must know about me is I am a very shy person. People find that is extremely hard to believe but it's true I am shy, but I talk to hide my shyness. I used to wonder what my purpose in life is and through the years I have found out. One of them is the gift of gab because I love to talk, I love telling others what I have learned in life. Wait a minute how can I be shy and love to talk at the same time? I told you I do not think like other people do. I love helping people because I am a people person and I hate seeing people sad or down and out, I love to keep busy. I love seeing and making people happy, I love bringing smiles to people faces, I love bringing joy to people and I have found many ways to do just so, if that means that I have to step out of my comfort zone that is helping others because it helps me.

During the times I'm up, I'm really on the move. I love cooking so I would have dinner parties. That makes me feel so good even though it is hard work I love every minute of it. I just don't have people over and put food on the table no, I had to serve it by courses sometimes it's a five-course meal and sometimes it's a seven-course meal. And I always make dishes I never cooked or taste before but when I do, it always turned out great. I will try new dishes and if I invite the same people over, they will say. "What are we having, never mind we know it will be something different and great."

My family and friends always tell me not to do too much, but I know with my illness it can knock me down in a blink of an eye. Despite my illness I am going to enjoy every second I can. Being up and doing things I love like helping people by telling them about our Grand Creator. I am a person that loves bringing joy to others, I really love cooking, but more is going on with me than just cooking, I love a lot of things and I work extremely hard at whatever I do. I do my best, and I work extremely hard at not worrying about the rest.

I love it if I can just get a creak of a smile from a person that's my joy, this is my how and my why. I found out how I can bring joy to others even when I am extremely ill. This reminds me when my friends would call me to give me encouragement, I would find a way to make them laugh and they would let me know that I encouraged them, and I would thank them for letting me do so. I would tell them it makes me feel good, and it bring joy to me and my heart. Besides, they are letting me store my treasures in heaven and they have helped me do what I love doing that is making others happy in whatever way I can and that is just one way I bring joy.

My purpose is making people feel better about themselves no matter what is going on in their life. My purpose is to put a smile on everyone's face no matter how small it is or how big it can be just as long, as I do what I love to do. This is to bring faith, hope, and show them how to have endure when they have a problem no matter how big or how small just as long, as I stay true to myself. I hope others can see it in me, and I always want to give someone some of my strength everyday even when I may need all of it for myself. I can't keep them all to myself I have to share whatever I have with others because this is part of my purpose. Just like God give me my strength I must share with others.

My purpose in life is to live and to bring joy to as many people as I can. My purpose is to make others life a little easier when dealing with me. I know you may be thinking this woman is crazy. But please believe me I am not, because I know there is too much darkness in the world today, so why would I, or why should I add to their problems.

I am not a push over because I will let you know just how far you can go with me. This is why, I am who I am, and this is why I chose to look at the good in others and if I find myself doing wrong toward anyone I will go and say.

"I am sorry about anything I may have said or did because that's not my purpose to hurt anyone's feelings."

Besides, it is enough of darkness in this world today so why would I want to add to anyone's problems. Just like the greatest man who ever lived on earth he had a purpose he also set the greatest example for us to follow. This brings me to knowing my what, my why, and my how when it come to my purpose. I am a purpose, not just a planner, I will set down and work things out in my head and put it down on paper but if something get in its way, I will work around it until I reach my goal.

Another reason why I see myself as a planner because I see myself as an orange carrot is because it is orange all the way through. This means as a planner when I run into a problem, I will find a way around the problem and find myself back on course or track even if it takes me longer to get where I am going or doing.

Right now, my goal is to live as long, as I can, to do all I need to do to stay alive, that means I must keep my mind in a good place. I must work hard at keeping focus on the more important things in life. While I am still able to talk, to see, to hear to get up, and think. Because my purpose is to fight with everything I have; to live, but I wonder do "this" make me a Survivor?

The reason why I know my purpose is because I love people just as our Grand Creator is a purpose. And he has shown us the finest way of life because we are made in his image. So, the best and easiest way to know my purpose is to know our Grand Creator, to know his ways, to know his likes and his dislikes. To follow his rules, to agree with him totally every day and in every way.

I do not to pick what I like and leave what I don't like he don't do that to me the reason why is because he gave us his most pressures gift.

Something else he gave us is the fruitage of the spirit. Which is Love, and its aspect is: hope, faith, peace, joy, kindness, self-control, patience, and mildness. I have picked and used each one for years for a week. I will tell you which one I pick each week and how I only focus on that one word. You will see we cannot do one without the other. We will see and learn they all work together because they are all linked.

Using this method have helped me in the best way of my life it has showed me how I look for the best in people. How I will do my best to work the word I picked for the week. I will fall short at times, but it is okay because I am not perfect, and I will keep working them repeatedly. The words will have different meanings each week because I find new ways each word will help me each week, first let find out what each word mean from the dictionary and the Biblical view of each. I do this because I now know I am truly a Survivor!

What Is My Purpose?

My purpose is the reason for which I want whatever
I need to do, be done. It is my intention or my
objective to finish some of the things I would like to
finish, my purpose is to keep faith, alive.
It is to see my hope not only alive but also with
a lot of vibe.

My purpose of my joy, is for me to help as many people as I can, I
want to bring as many smiles as possible to anyone's face,
without anyone ever feeling uneasy or feel out of place.

What really is my purpose when it comes to my endurance,
for me it is to put up with life with as
much ease as I can or decide to just let it be,
I think I can do it without hindrance.

What is my purpose? I got it, I got it! It is the
way I show love, to whomever and whatever I
do for others,
It is also my purpose when and what I do for my sisters and
to my brothers.

My purpose is not simple because my life is not
simple, I have a multi-purpose life because I
have so many things going on at one time.
Yes, more than one thing at a time and I truly do not mine.

Because my purpose is to be kind to all I meet,
because I know my purpose is to show
love and by giving everyone a great big kind greet!

I pulled the word Love this week.

Dictionary's View: Love: Is a profoundly tender, passionate affection for another person or thing. It's a warm personal feeling of attachment or deep affection. It is tenderness, fondness, predilection, warmth, passion, adoration. Love, Affection, Devotion all mean a deep and ensuring emotional regard, usually for another person. Love may apply to various kinds of regard: the charity of the Creator, reverent adoration toward God or toward a person, the relation of parent and child, the regard of friends for each other, romantic feelings for another person, etc. Affection is a fondness for others that is ensuring and tender, but calm. Devotion is an intense love and steadfast, ensuring loyalty to a person; it may also imply consecration to a cause. So, liking, inclination, regard, friendliness.

Biblical View: Love: God is Love "God gave us not a of cowardice, but that of power and of love and of soundness of mind" See God gives us courage which is strengthened by love.

I will look at love in a courageous way because love can impel me to show outstanding courage in what I may face this week. So, I that mean I will beware in advance by keeping myself awareness of ridicule, abuse speech, anger from myself or others. I must remember love is from God and we should continue to love one another. Because everyone who loves gains the true knowledge of him and because if we do not love or show love, we do not really know God because he is love.

I did okay I am a work in progress which I know I will always have something to work on because I am not perfect. But I do know this I am a Survivor that will do everything I need to do to do the right thing even if I fall short, I know I will miss the mark every day.

What do Survivor mean to me, well it means for me to learn all I can to help save myself and others because I know I cannot survive alone we all needs help from time to time. But sometimes there may not be anyone there to

help you, so I know for me I always looks to our Grand Creator because I truly know I am not alone. This is what makes a true Survivor knowing just how far to go and never think I can do it by myself, surviving is truly a Survivor!

⌒ *Chapter   14* ⌒

THE BEST HOT DOG I EVER ATE

Before I tell you about the best hot dog I ever ate. Three days before I ate the hot dog, I just got out of the hospital which I was in for nine days, because I was having severe stomach pain. When I checked in, I asked them to put leg pumps on me I always get them through the years.

Nurse Mary: "We will, the other week there was a lady that was on this doctor show, and she said that if you put soap under your leg it will break up blood clots."

"You can do that, but I still want the leg pumps."

Nurse Mary: "Yes we will put them on you."

She did get the soap and put it under me. Believe me or not but this is true. It did cause something to happen because I felt it when it broke away, but I did not put too much stock in it.

During that stay, my blood pressure drop extremely low this happens a lot. My heart rate also drop they did all they could to get it back it was not easy. After I got out, I had a doctor's appointment on the third of the month.

We went to see Dr. Downy that morning, after leaving the doctor's office.

"I am hungry, and we both need to eat."

So, we stop at the Varsity and ate hot dogs, onion rings, Willie had a Coke, and I had an Orange Freeze. Boy that was good, or was because I was hungry?

"Wow that was so good I didn't realize I was so hungry."

Willie: "Now we can go to the bank and handle our business."

We got to the bank, and we took money out of that bank and went to put it in the second bank to pay our monthly bills. When we got to the second bank, I begin to not feel well, I am glad I were setting on the passenger's side of the car. I was the one that was going in the bank, but I couldn't get out of the car because I was not thinking straight. We set there and counted out the money to make sure we put enough in for the monthly bills.

"What did I say this was for? What is this for?"

Willie: "Janice let me go in and handle it."

He went in the bank and as I was setting with my eyes close because I felt so bad, I couldn't keep my eyes open. Suddenly, I felt like I had to throw-up, but I wouldn't throw-up in my car, so I held my mouth close, and I threw-up in my mouth. Then I open the door and opened my mouth so it would fall out then I open my eyes to close the car door as I was doing so, I looked down and I saw my money laying in my throw-up it was folded. Then I remembered I had some in both hands and my lap, but I didn't know how much it was. I said to myself.

"I don't care if it is only one dollar, I want my money."

The next thing I remembered; I was laying in my own throw-up with my head facing under the car. I saw my folded money under the car than the wind blew, and the bills came apart.

"It's twenty-two dollars, 'Oh' 'No', I know I want my money."

Then the wind blew again this time one dollar went toward the back-passenger's tire and twenty-one blew on the other side of the car and no other car was there.

"I can't let anyone get my money I will let him get that one dollar and I will go around and get the twenty-one dollars."

I got up, and the next thing I remembered I was on the ground at the back door. There was a man there the whole time, he never left my side. I truly wish I can meet that person I want to tell him from the bottom of my heart. I really need to say, "'Thank You so much, Thank You! Thank You! Thank You!' I realize I were not alone even though I could not say a word, I heard his voice the whole time. He will never know how much I appreciate what he did for me, it will always mean so much to me. I wish I could meet him to tell him thank you for what he did for a person he did not know and for him to call 911. To let them know what was going on with me even though he could not believe the things I done, again 'Thank You' so, much."

Man: "Miss! Are you okay? Miss! Are you okay?" He kept talking to me, the hold time.

Tammy: "Mr. Willie, something is happening to Miss Janice, you need to go and see."

Willie: "I need to get out there and see about her."

Bank Teller: "I will watch your money for you go ahead and see what's happening with her."

When he came outside and asked.

"What's going on with her?"

When he got outside, I told him this even though I could not talk.

"There's a dollar at the back tire."

Willie: "Okay! I got to get back in there."

Tammy: "Go ahead and I will watch her for you."

He got the dollar and then he went back into the bank to finish his transaction. My neighbor did stay and watch me, but I don't remember anything about her after that. I got up and the next thing I remembered I were at the back tire.

Man: "Miss! Are you okay? Miss! Miss! I am going to call 911. Hello, you'll need to get out here this lady is doing some strange things. The things she is doing you would not believe it."

I heard him tell them this, but I could not respond because I had tunnel vision. I got up and the next thing I knew I woke-up at the back tire on the driver side then I passed out again. I woke-up at the spot of my money I got it then I found myself back on the ground.

"I am going to crawl to the back tire, and I am going to pull myself up and walk back around my car."

The next thing I remembered I were at the back-passenger side of the car. I passed out again because I woke-up at my passenger back door, when I next woke-up I was setting in the passenger's door, then I was setting back in my car when I woke-up I heard voices one was a female behind my head.

Female Paramedic: "We got to hurry and get her out."

Male Paramedic: "Okay let's swing her legs so we get her out."

They pulled my legs around to the door then they pulled me out I stud-up then I saw myself going down. The male paramedic picked me up, threw me on the gurney, and put me in the ambulance to start working on me. By that time, my husband came out of the bank, and I heard him talking.

Willie: "I need to get back there to see what they are doing to her."

Male Paramedic: "You have to wait a minute. Mr. Holliman where do you want to take her?"

Willie: "I want her to go to the hospital she just came out in Cobb County."

Male Paramedic: "We can only take her to one of two hospitals and that's not one of them."

"Noooo... Grady's!"

Male Paramedic: "Mrs. Holliman you can't talk but you are letting us know that you do not want to go to Grady's."

They took me to the other hospital the same one where I had my son. Then I passed out, I felt a pain, but it was very, very faint then I heard noise and voices way, way off. I was out again then I felt the pain again that it was harder, and the voices were closer. Then I went out again then the pain hit me much harder for the third time, I heard the noise and the voices that time it was very, close. The pain hurt so bad it made me snap.

"If you, do it again, I will knock you out."

I can still feel that pain every time I thank about it or talk about it till this day; I did not know I flatlined at the time. I flatlined three times that day, Wow!

ER Doctor: "Let's do one more test."

When the test came back, she said,

ER Doctor: "You have a blood clot."

I was in there for fifteen days. They put me on Lovenox blood thinner. Seven days later on a Sunday about 12:00p.m., Willie and I was talking.

Willie: "We was just talking, and she went to sleep, and I couldn't wake her up."

Nurse Tan: "Miss Holliman, can you wake up?"

Willie: "Janice can you please wake-up?"

"I want to, but I can't."

I could hear a lot of them talking I heard them call in a doctor. He examined me and kept calling me, but I couldn't say anything.

The Doctor: "She is very tired just let her sleep, but someone stay with her the whole time."

It's after 12:00a.m., that night, I know because my eyes went right to the clock on the wall. Then I saw out of the corner of my eyes in the doorway there was a nurse standing there I moved.

Nurse Sandy: "Mrs. Holliman you are awake, good we all were afraid because you slept all day long, you been out over 12 hours."

Days later one of the nurses came in to examine my IV and I saw something fall from her face. I didn't know what it was, so I didn't say anything. The blood lab tech came in took my blood like they have every night but this time they came back within an hour to redo it again then the Lab. doctor came in an hour later.

Dr. Martin: "Mrs. Holliman we had to come back to make sure of what we found, do you have, or had you had a fever or night sweat?"

"Yes, at night I notice it."

Dr. Martin: "We found out you have a Staph Infection."

"What?"

Dr. Martin: "Are you allergic to penicillin?"

"No!"

Dr. Martin: "We have to let the CDC know about this because it is a health issue. Mean time we will get you started on the Penicillin this happen when someone is in the hospital at times."

The next day the CDC came, and they explain everything to me. They let know me know how serious it were and they were sorry it happened.

(CDC) Doctors: "We will have to put a stencil in your shoulder so that the medicine can work, and we are the only one that can have it removed."

While I was in the hospital, they had me doing therapy because I was weak in one of my leg, I worked with a therapist, doing therapy it went on for a few days then she came to me to tell me this.

Therapist Connie: "Mrs. Holliman the doctor me that they are going to send you to rehab."

"No, I am not!"

Therapist Connie: "Yes You Are!"

"No, I am Not!"

Therapist Connie: "Just wait and see!"

She went to tell the doctor what I said, he came in.

Dr. Martin: "Mrs. Holliman how are you doing?"

"I was doing okay, until the therapist told me you were going to send me to rehab. I 'ain't' going!"

I didn't say, I am not going!

Dr. Martin: "Are you sure?"

"Yes!"

Dr. Martin: "Are you a 100% sure?"

"No, I am a 110% sure."

Dr. Martin: "If we let you go home are you willing to do therapy there?"

"Yes"

Dr. Martin: "Okay we let you do it at home."

"Thank You!"

They had me take a test to make sure the Staph Infection did not get on the stencil or my heart I am glad it didn't. As the days went by, I hated that hospital food with a passion and the only way I could endure the horrible food, I had to put lemon juice on it and look at pictures of my food I had cooked on my laptop.

I was to go home on day 14, I woke-up that morning about 6:00a.m., I couldn't breathe. Willie was asleep on the floor, but he did not hear anything. I called the nurse; she called the doctor.

Dr. German: "I understand you are having trouble breathing. Why are you breathing like this? This is happening because you suppose to go home today. Why is this happen, this morning? What's going on? What made you wake-up with this happening? How did you wait until today to have this happen to you?"

"Wait a minute, let me tell you something; I am setting here can't breathe, and you keep asking me the same question you just changing it around. I had a life before I came in here and I want to get back to it. I want to be out of here more than you want me out of here. So, all your questions will be the same, no; matter how you change it around."

She ordered an (EKG), the (EKG) Tech came in and hooked me up then suddenly, she pulls them off all at one time, I had to ask.

"What's wrong, is it me?" EKG Tech: "No it's the machine!"

I said to myself, "Yeah, I know it was me you are not telling the truth."

The (EKG) Tech came back with another machine and took the test again then the doctor came back and said,
Dr. German: "Your EKG, I need to get your last test when did you have you last one?"

"In June."

Much later! She came in with a different attitude.

Dr. German: "It looks like there is a different in the two tests. We are going to keep you over night and see what going on."

The next day came it was about 4:00p.m., by that time I was so ready to get out of there because I was so sick of that place. I had some friends visiting me when the doctor came.

Dr. German: "I need to talk with you."

"You can say what you need to say in front of them."

Dr. German: "We are going to let you go home today but I want to tell you, your heart has become enlarge, you may want to get another opinion."

"Okay, I just want to get out of here."

Treat Me with Respect

I wish people would treat me with respect because I am human and so are, they, I need to show them the same respect. Respect is our behavior we show to please others, it a courteous expression of feelings of friendship, and family in order for us to connect.

The reason why we need to show respect to others it's because we want them to take us seriously, it's because we do our best to respect others and we want them to respect us. When we all respect each other, it is the best thing that can happen between people and that will be a great start for everyone, will or can this be a big plus?

Why do we treat people the way we treat them, why we say and do the things we do? Is it because we are empowered with control or is it of what we have gone through?

People should show respect to each other because this will make life easier to deal with in these hard times. We see little or no respect in the world today, this is incredibly sad to see things keep going this way and this is why, today we see many crimes.

Why do people not respect each other why is this, what is the real reason, why is it this way? What's the reason why people do not show or treat others with respect, is it because we as people don't live the way they pray?

Respect is a way to show love, respect is the way and what we say, to one another, it is the way we need to show toward each other today is every way.

Treat Me with Respect

*I wish people would treat me with respect because I
am human and so are, they, I need to show them
the same respect.
Respect is our behavior we show to please others,
it a courteous expression of feelings of friendship,
and family in order for us to connect.*

*The reason why we need to show respect to
others it's because we want them to take us
seriously, it's because we do,
our best to respect others, and we want them to respect us too.*

*When we all respect each other, it is the best thing
that can happily happen between people and that
will be a great start now for every one of us, I know
it will or can be a big plus.
Why do we treat people the way we treat them,
why we say and do the things we do?
Is it because we are empowered with
control or is it of what we have gone through?*

*People should show respect to each other
because this will make life easier to deal with
in these hard times.
We see little or no respect in the world
today, this is incredibly sad, to see things
keep going this way and this is why today
we see so many crimes.*

JANICE HOLLIMAN

Why do people not respect each other why
is this, what is the real reason, why is it
this way?
What's the reason why people do not show
or treat others with respect, is it because
we as people don't live the way we pray?

Respect is a way to show love,
respect is the way and what
we say, to one another, it is
the way we need
to show toward each other today in every way.

So please treat me with respect, respect me and I will respect you!
I will show you the respect in what you say and do,
so if you want people to respect you,
you know what You must do, you must show respect too!

⌒ *Chapter   15* ⌒

THE NEXT DAY AFTER I LEFT THE HOSPITAL

I was, so glad to leave the hospital, I hated when I must fight with anyone, but I had to stand my ground. I had to let the doctors know I am human, and I wish they would treat me with respect like they want me to respect them. All I wanted was to leave that place as fast as I could, and I didn't really care what they found I just wanted out.

I left the hospital that Saturday around 5:00p.m., as soon as the doctor said I could go home I was out of there not caring what she said about my heart. I was so glad to be home because I had been in that hospital for fifteen days and nine days in another hospital just three days before that, when I got home, I went straight to bed.

Remember I was in that hospital due to a blood clot and I also flatlined three times the day they brought me in the ER. While I was there, they couldn't wake me up no matter how hard they tried to or no matter how hard I tried to also it just wouldn't happen until my body said it was time. Oh yah, they wanted to send me to rehab, I almost forgot I end up with staph infection, and before I left, I found out my heart became enlarged.

It was the next day on a Sunday, one of my friends called me and we had a long talk then I began not feeling well. I began noticing I could not breathe, and I was dizzy and sick on the stomach.

Remember I was hooked up with two medications one for the staph infection, the other one for my blood thinner. It was the same feeling I had five days before I left the hospital even though I told them about it they did nothing. As the day going by it got worst so I call my husband.

"I don't feel well it's very hard for me to breathe I need to go to the ER."

Willie: "Ok let's get you on some clothes and I will take you." Before I left home, I disconnected myself from both medications that was hooked to my stencil by the CDC because my breathing got worst as time passed. We got to the ER remember I was dizzy, and things became fuzzy to me.

ER Doctor: "Why are you here?"

"I can't breathe, and I have this stencil in which I were hooked up to two medications with me not being able to breathe I disconnected them both."

ER. Doctor: "What are they?"

"They were Penicillin and Coumadin and I read my papers and it said it had steroids in it and I am allergic to steroids so that's why I disconnected myself from the medications."

They examined me and they read my papers which I brought them. The nurse came in and talked to me.

The ER Nurse: "The doctor will be in shortly."

The doctor came in the room.

ER Doctor: "There are no steroids in your medicines."

"It does, can you change my medications?"

After him telling me there was no steroids in my medicines and he also said it was nothing he could do for me.

He left the room, and I am terribly upset, and the nurse was still in the room, so I started talking to her telling her how I end up there that day.

"I don't want to be in here anyway I just want to go home." She went and told the doctor what I said he told her.

ER Doctor: "I don't know what to do for her."

After she told him I didn't want to be there, and I wanted to go home. He told her since he could not do anything for me, he would let me go home when he came back in the room he said.

ER Doctor: "Mrs. Holliman it's nothing I can do for you, and I understand you wants to go home."

"Yes, if you can't help me, what else is it for me to do?"

ER Doctor: "Okay I will let you go but before you go, I need to tell you that your heart is enlarge and you may want to get a second opinion."

"You are my second opinion less than twenty-four hours."

The food person kicked on my door without coming in said breathing got worst I asked Willie could he please stop the car and look in my bag and get me my aspirins so I could take one because my chest hurt?

He gave it to me, and I took it, and we went home, and I went to bed, and I reread the side effect sheet and I realized I was the word sterile instead steroids. That made no different because my health didn't get any better and by 10:00p.m., it was really, bad.

"I believe I need to go back to the hospital."

On the way the hospital, I looked at Willie to let him know what to do.

"Hey, pull over there at the fire station so they can work on me while they take me to the hospital."

We pulled over and the paramedics came out and asked,

"What's going on?"

Willie told them I couldn't breathe.

Paramedic #1: "Let's check her oxygen level, and her blood pressure."

Paramedic #2: "Her blood pressure is very low, it's 95/65, and her oxygen level is 65%."

Paramedic #1: "We better get going now before we lose her."

They jumped in and away we went. My husband drove to the hospital. While we were going to the hospital I started to pray.

Paramedic #1: "We got to step on it because she is heading toward a low-pressure stroke."

Paramedic #2: "Okay!"

Paramedic #1: "Mrs. Holliman I need you to breathe."

"I am, along with praying."

Paramedic #1: "Okay just as long as you remember to breathe."

The paramedic called in to the hospital to let them know what was going on with me. When I arrived at the ER, they examined me and asked my husband a lot of questions. When they found out that I had just got out of the hospital with the staph infection things went crazy. It took a long time for them to put me in a room.

ER Nurse: "We are going to put you in the new wing of the hospital, but we have to find a bed for you."

Hours later they put me in this room that was new, but it was so funny it set off and away from the other rooms it was setting off to itself. They worked on me the rest of the night. That Monday I ordered lunch and I waited for hours and still no lunch then they brought it but not in the room.

"I ordered lunch and I had to wait for hours and when they did bring it, they left it out in the hallway."

Nurse Sandy: "I am so sorry about that they were afraid of your staph infection."

"I am the one who need to be worried that nothing happens to me not them."

Nurse Sandy: "You are right, I will order your food over."

The food person kicked on my door without coming in said,

The Food Person: "Your food is here I am going to put it out Here."

"No give it to the nurse so she can bring it in."

Nurse Sandy brought my tray to me. I thanked her and said,

"It's a shame for me to be treated like this."

I have to say the food was better than the other hospital. About 3:00p.m., the doctor came to visit me and introduce himself. You know what he said so I told him why, he then what medications was I given.

"Because I was in another hospital for a blood clot and I was in there for fifth teen days and while I was in there, I got a staph infection."

Dr. Jake: "What is it that you want me to do?"

"Change my medications please."

Dr. Jake: "I can't change your medications."

"Why not?"

Dr. Jake: "Because your insurance will not let me change it."

"Why Not?"

Dr. Jake: "Because they will not pay for it."

"So, You, are saying even if my medications are killing me, they will not let you change it?"

He told me yes and I told him I could not go back on those medicines no matter what. He said he didn't feel he needed to change my medications I did get upset with him because I knew better so I said.

"Why you don't know me? You just met me, and I know my body better than you do because I have lived with it for fifty-two years and you just known me for the last five minutes."

Dr. Jake: "I know my job because I am the doctor Here."

"Yes, you are the doctor, but you are not God Almighty because if you are when you came in you would not have asked me how I am doing and why am I in here."

Dr. Jake: "No I am not God."

"But coming at me as if you know everything about me and you don't. See let me tell you this long time ago I was told by a good doctor his exact words were 'Do not ever let a doctor ever tell you what is and what's not wrong with your body because they do not know. I am telling you this because you see me in this wheelchair I am in it here because one day I was under my car fixing it; the jack failed which I was under it and it broke my back, I will never walk again so I am telling you this because I am on both sides and now I know both sides from a patient's view and as a doctor's view and I learned why and how a patient has to fight with the doctor to get him to hear, listen, and understand. So, I tell you never, never let them tell you that they know more about you than you do.' I promise him from that day I will do just that, and I have, and it always have saved my life, so for you to tell me that you can't change my medicines is not true because if you tell them that I cannot take what I was on they will change it."

Dr. Jake: "If I change your medicines and put you back on what you were on in the hospital the cost will be about $10,000.00."

I told him I felt my life was worth it so could he please call them, he told me,

Dr. Jake: "No he would not!"

Then I told him,

"I will not let you or anyone else kill me I am going to fight for my life as long as I can with all I can."

Dr. Jake: "Mrs. Holliman can we agree to disagree?"

"Yes, we can agree to disagree; but I still need you to change my medicines."

He then said he would change it, I thanked him for doing so.

That night as I was sleeping, I kept itching then I realized something was biting me, so I called the nurse. I told her something kept biting me and I asked where did they get that mattress from? She told me it was down in the basement.

"You all just threw me anything just because I have a staph infection? Get me out of this bed now I want a new mattress, you see all these bumps on me."

Nurse Amy: "Okay let me help you out of the bed and I will order a new bed for you."

I was so mad, and I just wanted to go home and get out of that place, the next day the doctor came and examined me I showed him the bumps, but he just let it go I was too tired to say anything else.

Dr. Jake: "I placed a change on your medicines, and you can go home today."

I thanked him the nurse came back in the room with some supplies and laid them next to the bed. I asked her,

"What is that for?"

Nurse Chantel: "The doctor told me to remove your stencil."

"Oh no you are not going to touch this plus you have not even cleaned your hand; you are not wearing a paper gown and you are not wearing a mass. Plus, you cannot touch this I was told by the CDC they are the only ones that has the right to remove this."

Nurse Chantel: "I am going to take it out because the doctor told me to."

"I don't care what he told you to do, the CDC is over him and he can't touch this or have you to touch it."

Nurse Chantel: "I am going to tell the doctor and he will have me to remove it."

"I don't care what he says but just know this you nor him will touch this stencil."

She went out of the room very mad. My husband and I was talking about how they don't know what they are doing. By that time, she came back in the room.

Nurse Chantel: "I told what you said and that you would not let me take it out and he told me just to leave it in."

"I knew you all could not take it out."

She then went out the room again very mad, we left the hospital, went to the drug store, and got my new medicine then we went Home.

This week my word is Self-Control.

Dictionary's View: Self-Control is when one has the ability to control oneself, in particular one's emotions and desires or the expression of them in one's behavior, especially in difficult situations.

Biblical View: To avoid letting resentment builds up toward an individual who hurt us. Remembering if one let oneself be consumed with resentment, one can become as helpless as a fish on a hook. If one allows someone else to one's thinking and emotions. No one should avenge themselves because vengeance belongs to God.

So, this reminded me if I let my emotions be beneficial which will enable me to develop warm friendships. If I let my emotions become unrestrained, I will let it become destructive, not only to me but also to those around me.

This is how I keep surviving by standing up for myself and making sure things are done right. I am not mean, and I am not being ugly I am just a Survivor!

JANICE HOLLIMAN

Controlling My Self, Controlling My Life

Control is keeping my head together; it is not letting
anger take, over me or my life. It's when I keep my head
on tight and keeping it straight,
It is for me not to let myself become full of hate.

Controlling myself is for me to be in control within
my inner self that means having control of myself,
is being aware of what is happening when
someone says or do something that may hurt my feelings.
I am in control, whenever I take control of my life,
I will be in control of how I see, how I view, and
how I handle others in all my dealings.

Controlling my life can be a great thing to deal with as long as I
remember I am not the only one in my life.
I really need to remember controlling my life is not so easy at times
because I cannot control the way others act,
the way others think, the words that may come out of their mouth
because they may not think what they do or say can cause a strike.

Controlling myself is very, good for my health, and it makes me feel
like I have more than commonwealth.
By me controlling my life, I will be controlling my
strife, by controlling my strife,
I am controlling my life.

⌒ *Chapter 16* ⌒

MY DEALING WITH THE CENTERS FOR DISEASE CONTROL

After I went home, I had to make my appointment with the CDC because I needed to change my medication for my staff infection. So, I made it for the next day I went in to have my medication change from what I was taking because it caused me to have a side effect. She brought the medicine I was going to be giving as an IV infusion.

"Can I please read about the medicine before you give it to me?"

So, she brought the information to read after I read it, I had to tell her I could not take that medication. She went to tell the doctor which told her to still give it to me because I could handle it.

"What! I am telling you I can't take this medicine really."

CDC Tech Mindy: "I went back and told her what you said again, and I was told to give it to you."

"I am telling you that I can't take this, and I am tired of telling people what I can take and not take, and I am forced to do what they want. Since you'll are trying to find something for me to take and I don't know what will happen if I don't take it."

So, she hooked the IV up and then she went back to the front desk. I was setting there within two minutes I start itching, then my heart start racing, then I couldn't breathe by that time I turned she was watching me and when she saw the look on my face, she ran over to me and pull the IV out as fast as she can.

CDC Tech Mindy: "I am so sorry I wish I would not have done the IV, but I had to, let me go and get the doctor."

"I told you what was going to happen, and you all wouldn't listen to what I said."

CDC Doctor: "What happen to you why did this happened we never had anyone to react to this medicine before we are so sorry."

"This is what I have been telling people all the time ever since I developed Crohn's disease my immune system dropped, and I can't take medicine that I may have took yesterday. Because before I found out about my Staph Infection, I took penicillin all my life."

CDC Doctor: "So we have to find something that you can take."

I learned later the medicine they gave me in the IV infusion when I had to go to my ear, nose, and throat I was losing my hearing in both of my ears.

I survived this round! So, I am a Survivor!

The Ear, Nose, and Throat Doctor

As I was saying earlier, I am losing both of my hearing and I do need hearing aids, but I don't use them for one thing because of the cost and I feel 'they will cramp my style,' I am just being funny, no, really, I wonder if they would mass with my nerves. Anyway, the reason why I went to see this doctor was because through the years I was losing my voice sometimes no sound would come out, I had a nice voice to sing with but now I can't because I have lost my voice.

After Dr. Ryan did the hearing test it shows I was losing my hearing in both ears, but the right one is worse than the left.

"How could that be happening?"

He asked me to have I been somewhere there was a lot of noise, I told him "No" then he said maybe, it was some medicine that I took. He said plus that was not my only problem he wanted to check you to see if you have something on my vocal cord.

"Is this the reason I lose my voice and sometimes it sounds like I am in a cave when I talk it sounds like an echo bouncing off the cave walls?"

He told me he wanted to have me take a certain test. When I got home and I began thinking about all my medicines that I had taken I began reading up on all my medicines, I came to the IV infusion that the CDC gave me. I read the side effects and there it was in black and white.

When I went back to see Dr Ryan he said,

Dr. Ryan: "Mrs. Holliman the test shows you have a module on one of your vocal cords. I will have to remove it, but you will not be able to talk for two weeks because of the healing time and then you will need to take vocal therapy."

Willie: "You are not going to make it. You cannot stop talking for two long weeks."

"Watch my blue smoke, I will show you I can, and I will show you what I am made of."

Willie: "Doc she is not going to be able to do it."

DR. Ryan: "In order for the surgery to work you cannot talk for two weeks."

"I understand what you are saying, and I will not talk until you tell me."

I had the surgery, and I proved my husband wrong I had a plan it was that I was going to use this time to do a deep mental cleaning and it will give me a great time giving thanks for all the things I have being through, and I will take the time to really look at all the beautiful things I can see out my bedroom window.

Willie: "I will be so glad when you can talk because I am not good at you signing with your hand it's driving me nuts."

"Writing and saying I am showing you and myself I can do anything if I put my mind to it and just do it and I am doing now."

When I went for my check-up Dr. Ryan asked me how did I do by not talking?

Willie: "I can answer that, she did very well because she has not had a sound come out of her mouth."

Dr. Ryan: "Great now you can start therapy now."

I did my therapy with the therapist; I still can't sing now every now and then I can carry a tune. I survived this round also plus, I proved to myself I can do whatever it takes for me to keep living. Even though I am no better than anyone else!

How Would I Feel If I Can't Hear A Sound?

*Sounds are when I can hear beautiful music, hearing
someone singing, being able to hear words that sound so
beautiful that won't leave my ears ringing.*
*I love hearing someone whisper thinking no one can hear
them say, something that they may not want anyone else
hear what they say for whatever the reason it is,
it's okay!*

*How would I feel, if I can't hear a sound, I will feel like no
one is around?*
*It can feel like I am not on common ground, or will
it make me feel like people may not want me
around because I cannot hear a sound?*

*When I hear voices that is calming, that is so peaceful and
so great, because there is so many things or people that
can cause a great big debate.*

*Wait, I can't hear, what did you say, what did they say?
I can't hear a word that's coming
out your mouth, I can't hear a word
that's coming out of their mouth, I
feel all alone every day.*

*It makes me feel like I am in a dark forest with
all the trees around me and I can't hear a sound.
I don't know which way to go because it is so
hard to find my way out, because I am afraid, I
hope I am not lost.*

I don't know which way to go, looking around
in the sky all I see is all these trees that have a
lot of moss.

If I can't hear, I will need to learn to read lips, I will need to
learn to read faces. To get myself out of this woody, lonely and
dark place or would it be places. Since I can't hear, I will have
to learn how to find my way out of all dark,
cold and strange places.

How would I feel if I can't hear a sound?
I have come to realize, if I am losing my hearing,
I feel I will survive because I will find a way to get around.
Even if I can't hear a sound.

Let's see what my word will this week be, Wow! Its Peace.

Dictionary's View: Is used as a friendly greeting. It is used as an order to remain silent. To leave.

Biblical View: True peace is much more than a dream; God's promised peace goes far beyond anything that this world can imagine. In a Biblical sense, real peace involves not simply a cessation of hostilities but also health, safety, and well-being.

Peace, peace, peace how will I use this word this week. I know peace is not a dream it is a promise which mean I need to go way above and beyond being nice to others. I need to see and understand what a person is feeling because they may not have a nice day and not realize what they are doing that may hurt me or me them. I must keep in mind they are human just like me and I must treat them the way I want to be treated. Yeah, that's what I will focus on this week, I am looking forward to peace.

∽ *Chapter 17* ∽

WHEN I WENT TO SEE MY HEART DOCTOR

After I got out the hospital and dealing with the (CDC) I went to see my heart doctor and he sent me to another kind of doctor. When I went to see him, I asked, and he examined me to make sure everything was okay with me and my health. Remembered I said my heart became enlarged well I asked my heart doctor, Dr. Weeks.

"If your heart become enlarged it don't go back down, do it?"

Dr. Weeks: "No, it doesn't ever go back down but yours did that's new."

Then he told me that he wanted to send me to a hematologist his name is Dr. King, he will be able to tell you everything you need to know about your blood clot. I went to see him he examined me, and he did some blood work and told me to come back in two weeks. Willie went back we was talking when Dr. King walked in the room and said,

Dr. King: "Mrs. Holliman, I don't know why you are here?"

At hearing that I said to myself,

"Why I'm here? It's to get the result of my test, oh my goodness he meant why am I alive."

Dr. King: "You had the worst case I ever seen, you had fourteen blood clots from your legs to your lungs. You do not suppose to be alive if you have one more, just one more will not have that three-hour window again, you will die. I am going to put you on blood thinner you will have to take two shots in your stomach every day for the rest of your life. And if you must have any kind of surgery, you can only stop taking your shots 'only one day before and you must go back on it the day after.' Because if you, don't you will have more blood clots and die."

I just found out the type of blood clots I have It is called DVT.

Deep vein thrombosis
From Wikipedia, the free encyclopedia

Deep vein thrombosis (DVT) is the formation of a blood clot in a deep vein, most commonly the legs.[2][a] Symptoms may include pain, swelling, redness, or warmth of the affected area.[2] About half of cases have no symptoms.[2] Complications may include pulmonary embolism, as a result of detachment of a clot which travels to the lungs, and post-thrombotic syndrome.[2][3]

Risk factors include recent surgery, cancer, trauma, lack of movement, obesity, smoking, hormonal birth control, pregnancy and the period following birth, antiphospholipid syndrome, and certain genetic conditions.[2][3] Genetic factors include deficiencies of antithrombin, protein C, and protein S, and factor V Leiden mutation.[3] The underlying mechanism typically involves some combination of decreased blood flow rate, increased tendency to clot, and injury to the blood vessel wall.[2]

The rate of DVTs increases from childhood to old age; in adulthood, about one in 1000 adults are affected per year.[6] About 5% of people are affected by a VTE at some point in time.[4]

Signs and symptoms

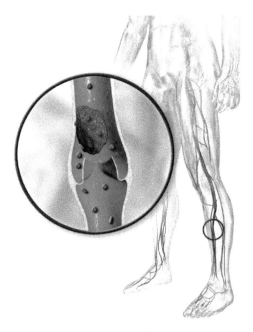

Illustration depicting a deep vein thrombosis

Common signs and symptoms of DVT include pain or tenderness, swelling, warmth, redness or discoloration, and distention of surface veins, although about half of those with the condition have no symptoms.[7] Signs and symptoms alone are not sufficiently sensitive or specific to make a diagnosis, but when considered in conjunction with known risk factors, can help determine the likelihood of DVT.[8] In most suspected cases, DVT is ruled out after evaluation,[9] and symptoms are more often due to other causes, such as cellulitis, Baker's cyst, musculoskeletal injury, or lymphedema.

[10] Other differential diagnoses include hematoma, tumors, venous or arterial aneurysms, and connective tissue disorders.[11]

Phlegmasia alba dolens and phlegmasia cerulea dolens occur when a DVT is very large and causes significant obstruction of the veins (complete or near- complete occlusion). In the former, the affected leg is white and painful as the congestion is so severe that the arterial blood supply is reduced. In the latter, the arterial supply is reduced to the point that there is a blue tinge and venous gangrene may develop, generally with severe pain. Surgery may be required in this setting.[12][13]

Causes

The three factors of Virchow's triad—venous stasis, hypercoagulability, and changes in the endothelial blood vessel lining (such as physical damage or endothelial activation)— contribute to DVT and are used to explain its formation.[14][15] Other related causes include activation of immune system components, the state of microparticles in the blood, the concentration of oxygen, and possible platelet activation.[16] Various risk factors contribute to DVT, though many at high risk never develop it.[17]

Acquired risk factors include the strong risk factor of older age,[15][17] which alters blood composition to favor clotting. Other important acquired risk factors include major surgery and trauma, both of which may increase the risk because of tissue factor from outside the vascular system entering the blood.[14] In orthopedic surgery, venous stasis may be temporarily provoked by a cessation of blood flow as part of the procedure.[16] Cancer can grow in and around veins, causing venous stasis, and can also stimulate increased levels of tissue factor. Pregnancy causes blood to favor clotting, and in the postpartum, placental tearing releases substances that favor clotting. Oral contraceptives[b] and hormonal replacement therapy increase the risk through a variety of mechanisms, including altered blood coagulation protein levels and reduced fibrinolysis.[16]

The disease term venous thromboembolism (VTE) includes the development of either DVT or pulmonary embolism (PE).[20][21] Genetic factors that increase the risk of VTE include deficiencies of three proteins that normally prevent blood from clotting—protein C, protein S, and antithrombin—in addition to non-O blood type and mutations in the factor V and prothrombin genes. Deficiencies in antithrombin, protein C, and protein S are rare but strong, or moderately strong, risk factors.[14][16] These three thrombophilia[c] increase the risk of VTE by about 10 times.[22] Factor V Leiden, which makes factor V resistant to inactivation by activated protein C,[24] and the genetic variant prothrombin G20210A, which causes increased prothrombin levels, are predominantly expressed in Caucasians.[14][d] They moderately increase risk for VTE, by three to eight times for factor V Leiden and two to three times for prothrombin G20210A.[22][25] Having a non-O blood type roughly doubles VTE risk.[16] Non-O blood type is common in all races, making it an important risk factor.[26] Individuals without O blood type have higher blood levels of von Willebrand factor and factor VIII than those with O blood type, increasing the likelihood of clotting.[26]

Some risk factors influence the location of DVT within the body. In isolated distal DVT, the profile of risk factors appears distinct from proximal DVT. Transient factors, such as surgery and immobilization, appear to dominate, whereas thrombophilia and age do not seem to increase risk.[27] In upper- extremity DVT, the most important risk factor is having a central venous catheter, and thoracic outlet syndrome also increases risk.[20]

This why I must keep my legs up and moving. They sometimes wake me up at night.

I don't like giving myself shots in my stomach every day and doing it twice is double the pain. Just thinking about me having to clean the area, pulling my skin and stick the needle in me it can get very sore.

This happened in 2010 when I started taking blood thinner shots. Three years ago, when I went to get it refilled, I told my insurance was no longer going to pay for my medication. They wanted me to change to a different brand I did, and I had a reaction to it I couldn't breathe, my heart begins beating fast plus I started breaking out.

I called Dr. King I told him what happened, I needed him to let my insurance know that I cannot take that new medication they switched me to because I am allergic to it and let them know I can only take the one I am on. They did but it didn't work so that meant I couldn't get my medication it was a good thing I had two more boxes before I ran out.

I set down one day to write them to let them know how serious my medication was for me that I tried what they wanted me to take and the side effects. I told them I took what they changed me to take that I could not take that medication. I explained to them about my illnesses, how I am allergic to so many medications.

I have become allergic due to me having Crohn's disease, which causes my immune system to drop I asked them to please look at my records to see how many medications I am allergic to, how many times I have gone to the ER due to allergic reactions. I told them I could not take that new medication, I wrote all my side effects, how I had fourteen blood clots while I was in the hospital from the blood clots the doctors put me on another medication, and I ended up in the hospital again and my medication were changed.

Now that they changed my medication, I was afraid that if they didn't put me back on the medication, I was on I could end up dead. I then asked them what they would do if that happened to them, I also said how my life depend on that medication. When I find something that work, I don't like to change it, I also said if it's not broke why fix it?

They wrote me back and let me know that they were going to give me another year. The year came and I had to do it again I wrote the same them the same letter and they gave it to me again but this time I had to tell them that I could not keep doing this every year because it may come to the point I may run out if medication while I am waiting on their approval. I told them I wish they will approve it for good; here we go again this year; I was not looking to having to deal with this.

I have had to write them for other medications also, it's no fun dealing or fighting with my health insurance to save my life. When it comes down to the point that my life is in the air and being out of medication that my life depends on in order to save my life and keep my health in good check to save my life.

I wonder what do this make me am I a Survivor or am I a bully? As I see it, I have to say whatever or do whatever it takes for me to keep living. A Survivor is a person that go above and beyond normal things to fight to live or have the will to live.

My word for this week is Patience.

Dictionary's View: Patience is the ability to endure difficult circumstances such as perseverance in the face of delay; tolerance of provocation without responding in annoyance/anger; or forbearance when under strain, especially when faced with longer-term difficulties. Patience is the level of endurance one can have before negativity. It is also used to refer to the character trait of being steadfast. Antonyms include hastiness and impetuousness.

Biblical View: It conveys the thought of waiting calmly for something, manifesting forbearance or strain. The patient person remains composed; the impatient one becomes hasty and irritable. It does not indicate weakness or indecisiveness; it bears the insignia of strength and purpose. Patience enhances one's personality, it costs other fine qualities with a varnish of permanence. It makes faith desirable, peace long-lasting, and love unshakable.

I wonder what I need to do to strengthen my faith, which will help me be patience. I know I need to focus on benefits that I personally have received, by doing so I will increase my appreciation for patience.

❧ *Chapter 18* ❧

THE NIGHT MY TOES START CURDLING

This happened one night while we had a family staying with us. I slept well that night, all I knew I woke-up screaming because my toes start curdling. The first thing Willie said to me was,

Willie: "Janice you need to stop screaming before you wake everybody up."

"I don't care who hear me this really hurt."

I went back to sleep then I woke up saying,

"Ahh..."

Willie asked me.

"What now?"

"It's my feet they are cuddling up and I can't stop it from hurting. Can you get me some water please?"

He got me the water I was able to sleep again. That morning came, "Ahh..."

Willie: "Let me see what you are talking about."

"See it won't stop at all I can't walk it's still happened Oh my goodness here goes another hard pain."

Willie took me to the ER they examined me. The ER Doctor ran some test on me they told me I was very dehydrated to the point my kidneys were cracking and they needed to admit me in the hospital to hydrate my body it would take days to hydrate me. I told Willie he should go Home before the bad snowstorm hit. He did make it home in time which was good. The doctor came in to see me to tell me something.

Dr. Gain: "Mrs. Holliman we have to tell you that you have Gallstones."

'"Gallstones I will pass those right?"

Dr. Gain: "Yes that's what will happen but since you have Crohn's disease, you will not be able to pass them because they will tear your intestines and that will be very painful."

I thank him for telling me and I would connect with my (GI) doctor. I was in for three days, and the hospital called me a taxi to bring me home, they do that when the weather is bad. That was the rudest person I ever seen. He took me and another patient Home that day. The snow was coming down hard and he was driving extremely fast.

The Other Patient: "Can you please slow down; you are driving too fast I can't take you driving like this."

Taxi Driver: "If you don't like it that's your problem and you can get out right now. They hired me to take people Home and I have done so for years."

"Do you realize you can cause her to have a heart attack?"

Taxi Driver: "Like I said she can get out and so can you."

As soon as I walked in my door I got on the phone and call the hospital and reported him. They said they didn't know he was talking to the patient like that this will be his last trip with the hospital. As time passed, I begin to suffer from the Gallstones, so I had them removed.

This is what happens when my feet start to twist before it hit my toes a week ago.

This is a very painful thing; I don't wish this on anyone. To be awaken by severe pain is no fun believe me it really does hurt to the point to make me scream oh man how painful it is. This remind me of the time I need a tooth pull it bothered me all week, the night before I got it pull, I went and bought some libation to drink to ease the nerve at 9:00p.m. it started, and I drank by 11:00p.m., the feeling came back it hurt so bad I stuck my face to a gas stove turned it on and said just let me die.

I was so tired from hurting that week I just didn't care anymore. I finally went to sleep after 4:00a.m., when I woke-up I got ready and when and got it pull. I survived that week I guess I was stronger than I thought, if I survive that I guess I can survive more than I think. I wonder is this person a Survivor; I hope so even I wanted to give up I didn't even when I was weak, I became strong.

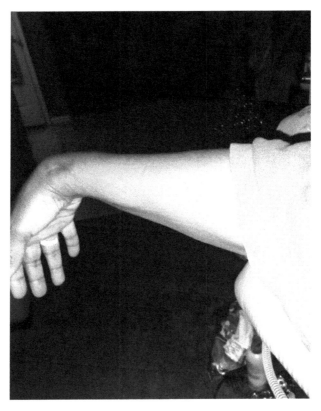

Sometimes, my hands curl-up, it can get worse than this.

Oh, The Pain Will It Ever Stop

Pain is a somatic sensation of acute discomfort
that we as people we want to avoid, it's
bothersome, it's a physical hurt.
It is a disorder, it can cause an emotional
anguish or make a person miserable, it causes
severe bodily suffering, the pain can really,
really hurt bad, but it can also be an alert.

Pain is when we hurt someone's feelings no matter what's the
reason is, or we do what we do because we want to, we must stop
bringing hurt to people if it's physical, or if it's emotional.
This emotional distress is a fundamental feeling
that we as people need to avoid, pain is like
being on the cold arctic ocean.

Pain is when we feel something hurt if it's with our
body, heart or if it's our brain. Either way it's pain,
sometimes it feels like hard cold rain.
It feels extremely hard or sharp which can hurt or
stick us with every drop, it can really make us feel like
we are going insane.

Oh, the pain, Oh the pain, why do it hurt so bad am I going mad?
No, I am not going mad, it can make me feel this way
because it hurt so bad.

Will it ever stop? How long will it hurt? Oh, the pain,
I feel no relief.
Yes, it will stop. It will hurt as long, as my
nerves feel it. There is relief but I can't see
it when it happens it may be brief.

The time will come when it will stop
hurting, I just need to hold on until it does.
I must hold on like I am sticking
with glue. Yes, the pain will stop,
whenever it wants to.

Yes, it will stop if we stop doing the things we do.
Oh, the pain! Oh, the pain! It doesn't have to be painful when it hurt.
But you know what? Thankfully, pain keeps us alert.

∽ *Chapter   19* ∽

SCAR TISSUES REMOVAL

This time around for my scar tissues removal which I have moved over the years since 2001 every sixteen-eighteen months. I have them removed because the pain gets so intense even with my high pain level it seems like it would feel like a fifth-teen not the top which is a ten.

I went to see my surgeon because he had to remove my scar tissues again. This time things have changed I have become allergic to new medications the day of my surgery we talked. I have become allergic to new medications which I gave the list to the nurse.

Dr. Homes told me not to worry he would not give me anything but antibiotics.

"That's what worry me I have become allergic to antibiotics I don't know which ones I am allergic to at this time."

Dr. Homes: "I have to give you an antibiotic to keep me from a bacterial infection."

"I guess you know but I really which you don't."

I had the surgery, and it was time for them to awake me which I did but not my body.

Nurse Ann: "Mrs. Holliman it's time to wake-up, Mrs. Holliman, Mrs. Holliman!"

I said this in my mind because I couldn't talk.

"I hear you; I am awake. I can't breathe, why can't breathe?"

Nurse Ann: "It's been forty-five minutes and she won't wake up."

Nurse Evelyn: "Did you try touching her.

Nurse Ann: "Yes but she won't wake-up."

I am laying there saying to myself.

"But I am awake. Am I still asleep and I am dreaming about this? I can't still breathe I have to get this pipe out of my mouth because it's choking me. Somebody is trying to kill me, yeah, they really trying to kill me. I bet you they were trying to kill someone else, and they mess with the wrong tube of oxygen they messed with mind instead. I must stop this poison from flowing through my tube. I know what I am going to do, I am going to clamp down on this tube in my mouth to stop the oxygen from coming through my tube."

Nurse Kim: "How long has it been since she been in recovery?"

Nurse Ann: "It's been about two hours."

Nurse Paul: "I think we need to get the doctor in Here to examine her to make sure everything is okay."

"I am awake, look at me, see me moving, I'm awake."

Dr. Little: "How long has she been like this?"

Nurse Ann: "It's been about three hours."

Dr. Little: "She is very tired the surgery took a lot out of her keep an eye on her."

"It's been that long I have holding the tube with my teeth for hours. I need to move, and I need to remove this tube because my jaw is getting tired. Can you all see the tears running down my face, can you see me crying. Why can't you'll see me batting my eyes I am letting you'll know I am awake."

Nurse Ann: "She is a very strong woman from me reading her record."

Nurse Paul: "Have anyone told her husband what's going on?"

Nurse Kim: "No we have not."

Nurse Paul: "Mr. Holliman we just want you to know she is doing very well."

IC Unit Nurse: "We are getting her bed ready now we will call you when we are ready."

"Wake-up Janice, wake-up now I can't go up there, because I will not ever come out of there. This is what the person that put something in my oxygen tube thinking they are trying to take someone else out, but they have the wrong person. It's been hours since they removed the tube, and I still can't move what's wrong?"

About one and a half hour later my body began to wake-up.

"Yeah, I can move finally."

Nurse Paul: "Mrs. Holliman, you are awake it's good to see you wake-up. I will call your husband and tell him we will be moving you to your room shortly after I cancel IC unit because we were going to send you there because we didn't know what was going on with you."

"I know everything that was said or done all day."

Nurse Paul: "You really heard everything Wow! How could that happen?

"Yes, I did!"

They put me in my room around 6:00p.m. And about 7:00a.m. the next morning a big brass doctor came in and talked to me and I told him everything that happen, what was said, and what was done.

When I got out of the hospital and I went for my follow-up.

Dr. Homes "I sorry about happen to you."

"Yeah, me too. How did the surgery go and what all did you give me?"

Dr. Homes: "It went fine but I did give you an antibiotic because I didn't want you to have an infection."

"Oh, my goodness, so no one tried to kill me you gave me something that could have killed me. So, you see when I told you not to give me any antibiotics because what could have happened this was what I meant."

Dr. Homes: "Yes, I really see I will never do it again."

I survived another round of illness, sometimes I wonder how much more can I take then I decides it don't matter just focus on the one that is in front of me at that time because I have already dealt with the pass other one as they happen, I put them in my brown paper bag and put them in my mental drawer until it's time for me to handle them.

This week's word is Love.

Dictionary's View: Is abstractly discussed; it usually refers to an experience one person feels for another. It often involves caring for, or identifying with, a person or thing, including oneself. Love change greatly over time. The best and worst thing about love is that it cannot be expressed in words. When one truly loves someone, it may be hard to express those emotions, through words.

Biblical View: Love is the real key to true unity. Everyone needs help from others to accomplish what one wants to do, so it is very imperative to learn a pleasant way to get that cooperation. A person should remember what they need and in what order they need it. It is very imperative and important not only others understand how to help but also imperative and important to know how to accept their help graciously.

I must remember love manifests itself by a friendly smile, by kindness and gentleness, by being cheerful and having warmth. It means I need to meditate on my blessings like being faithful because it will strengthen me to endure, and for me to see my joy plus it will bring love to help keep me be unselfish, because "love... does not look for its own interests."

So, for me to have good communication with others I must be lowliness of mind and have empathy for them. Above all my unselfish love will help me be successful in reaching the heart of others.

This will be a great way to survive and be a Survivor!

⌒∼ *Chapter 20* ⌒∼

ETIQUETTENESS

This means I care how I carry myself, why I am the way I am, and my purpose is because I feel like I was meant to help people smile and help them feel better about themselves. This is the reason why I find myself helping others, because I love people, and because this is also part of my why, my how, and my purpose. This really means to me and for me, which is how I keep surviving, and why I can honestly say I am a survivor. This is me giving back to others, by showing them they can be happy no matter how things look in their life even when things look dark, when we have wind knocked out of us. Just know that it is not the end if life when life gives us lemons make lemonade.

I love lemonade, I love it tart so when life have a bite to it and it bite me, I then know I am alive and I have something I can have faith in, hope, which brings me joy, which helps me have endurance, and which helps me have and show love.

I know life can be dark, but I chose to focus on the positive. I chose to look at the good, life can offer me as long, as I handle it in the right way with the right frame of mind, with the right heart. With a purpose, with a reason, with joy, with kindness, and unselfishness. This is what makes me feel like the person I am, the person I have become which is a happier person, a giver, a sharer, and a person who truly love and who cares.

Just because I am this person it does not make me bourgie is when a middle-class person with materialistic capitalist attitudes. Being obsessed with the finer things in life, in the South it is ultimately exists as a synonym for uppity and pretentious and it carry as racially tinged historical context.

Or I am seen as boujee which is high class literally or figuratively, or one of lower class trying to be high class. One who has or possesses swag. Elite, rich and are with foul words that not me in any way, shape, or form. These two words comes from the dictionary, so these are not my meanings, but I know these are not me or who I want to be. Anyone who feel like this is their chose of life, for them who am I to tell them how to live it, or for me to push my view on the way they want to live their life?

In the dictionary a Diva is a famous female opera singer, or of popular music. A diva is a self- important person who is temper mental and difficult to please typically used of a woman. In modernity, the expression Diva is used to address a woman who is glowing with beauty and such a shining beauty is often termed as 'Goddess of beauty!' A diva is a female god or a woman who is worshipped; there is some male also called divas. This spirit requires deliverance in human beings because many have taken on this word as a fad to describe a woman who is godly or is supposed to have it going on a Prima Donna; I never want to be connected to any of that but who ever want to be this type of person that's their life. Please, do not call me a diva or think I want to be called a diva.

By the way I don't like being called Bougie either because according to urban dictionary if you look up Bougie-B****, one of the top definitions is: A completely bougie/snobbish person who looks down on people below him/her. Typically involves a full look up and down at a person and then a scowl. I would never ever call anyone that and I wish no one call me one either, besides, I am not a female dog, which I would not call any one either.

This week I pulled the word Patience.
Dictionary's View: Patience is the capacity to accept or tolerate delay, trouble, or suffering without getting angry or upset. A person with great patience is a person who can control his or her emotions greatly. That person knows his or her inner essence and respects 'Time.' He or She knows that 'this time will pass soon' and he or she never bothers to struggle for what he or she will surely after some time.

Biblical View: Patience is more than simply putting up with a trying situation. A person with godly patience endures with a purpose. That person sees beyond his or her own needs and considers the welfare of the one causing a disagreeable situation. This is the reason why, when a patient person is wronged or provoked, will refuse to give up hope for improvement in the disturbed relationship.

So, this means I must focus on this especially important word this week because if I really wants to be a person with patience I must endure with a purpose. My purpose is being a person of peace, a peaceable person, a person who will raise above any anger or unease state of mind. Am I this kind of person? What do I need to do in order to do what I need to do and be peaceable with everyone?
Believe me I am not perfect in any form, but it does not mean I cannot work at being the best person I can or the best person I would love to be. Besides, I want to treat people the way I wants to be treated.

I must do what I need to do to survive. This really makes me want to be a Survivor!

✐ *Chapter 21* ✐

YOU CAN HIT ME ON MY HEAD WITH A HAMMER I WOULD NOT CARE

I remembered setting in my chair in my bedroom watching TV and my husband was setting in the Livingroom reading. I said,

"Hey Willie, 'you can hit me on my head with a hammer I would not care' I really mean it."

Willie: "What are you talking about?"

"I feel so tired, and I don't have the strength to stop you."

It was about 9:30p.m., our son was supposed to come over about 11:00p.m., that before they went home but he did not come. I guess it was about 12:00a.m., when my husband got ready for bed.

Willie: "Janice it's time for bed are you going to go now?"

I didn't move. He called me three times no answer, then he asked,

Willie: "Janice don't you have to go to the bathroom?"

I got up and paid my 'water bill' then I came and set back down in the chair. I learned months ago I have COPD and Sleep Apnea and I got my CPAP machine just three months before that night. I have not had time to show my husband what to do if anything happens to me besides, I had no idea how severe I had it.

Willie: "Janice are you coming to bed?"

"What?"

Willie: "Janice do you hear me?"

I did not answer, he kept calling me for a while then he got in bed, but he said he couldn't get me up, but before he went to bed, he ironed some clothes for me to wear for the next morning.

Willie: "Janice I ironed two out fits for you to wear which one do you want to wear? They are hanging in the bathroom."
I got up out of the chair and went to the bathroom and I looked at them as I was paying my 'water bill.'

"I'll wear this one."

I set there for a while, then I said,

"I think I need to go to the ER."

He helped me up and put me at the foot of the bed, our mirror was facing me, and when I saw myself.

"I am black as suck, I am dying."

As I said that our son came in and saw me.

Ramono: "Daddy, Momma eyes are orange she is not getting oxygen she is dying. We need to get her to the ER now."

Willie: "I know I am trying to get her dress now."

Ramono: "No we need to call 911 now and then get her dress as they come."

That was the last thing I remembered. The next thing I knew they had put me in a room, and I was out again I don't know for how long, then I realize I was being rolled somewhere.

ER Doctor: "We need to get her in the IC Unit she is dying and there is nothing we can do for her."

"You are lying because I am not dying."

I went out again then I woke-up in the IC Unit and I began praying and talking to my Grand Creator.

"I know I said I don't want to die, and I will fight even if it takes me to pull myself by my elbows. But I am so tired, but I am at peace and so serene, I am at peace with my Father, and I am at peace with my neighbors. I am so tired and peaceful I am going to let go after this last breath."

As I took in that last breath, I start feeling my life leaving me everything was turning white. 'I Do Not Believe' saying of the White Light!' Remember, I said white, and I was feeling serene, and as that was happening, I said,

"Janice wait a minute last year you crawled all the way around your car and you flatline three times. You are a fighter; you can fight this! Father, I am not ready to go my family needs me, I am not going!"

The next thing I knew was my son and his then wife came into the room, and I heard them.

Shane: "Ohhh... she looks bad, she is dying."

Ramono: "Don't say that because she can hear you." Shane: "Know she don't."

Ramono: "Yes she does, you never speak over someone if they are unconscious or in a coma."

Shane: "Oh really sorry!"

Ramono: "I need to go get my dad."

She then said she would stay with me until he comes back. When they came in the room and she left, I was out at this time. I was in the IC Unit for about three days. Then they moved me to a room and here I am. After I got home my husband kept apologizing to me.

Willie: "Janice I am so sorry I didn't get you to the hospital or called 911 that night."

"It's okay stop beating yourself up about it."

Willie: "But I am so sorry I didn't think. I couldn't think."

"I know you didn't know what to do it's okay, it was a good thing you couldn't get me in the bed because if I would have laid down, I would not be here today."

He said he stayed awake and kept praying for me all night I told him that was the best thing he could have done for me that's what kept me alive. He said he should have known better why he didn't think of doing that while it was happening. I told him,

"It's not your fault that you did not think about calling 911, it was mine's for not teaching you what to do or how to put the CPAP machine on me if anything happens to me."

Willie: "I couldn't get you in bed at all no matter how hard I tried or what I said to you to get you in bed."

"You got me up to go to the bathroom but instead of me getting in bed I went back to the chair and that's what saved me by setting up all night."

Willie: "But I know I should have call 911."

"It was a good thing our son didn't come until that morning instead of the night before when he was supposed to have come."

Willie: "You are right! But I should have gotten you to the hospital."

"Okay! Stop beating yourself up about it."

He kept saying the same thing for about a year, he just kept beating himself up. The reason why I hadn't showed him how to work the CPAP machine, was because I had noticed some changes in his memory. He would not remember things like how to do some of the simple things at times or he didn't understand what I would ask him to do or have him to do, that was in the year 2011. And he has been going down since then so for me to have showed him how it works would not have been an easy task.

I was right because it happened again, but I did show him what to do by this time which it took a few tries for him to get it right, but he did get the mass on my face. He was holding it and trying to get it on me with me getting the oxygen from the CPAP because he did turn it on, I woke-up and I helped him clamp it on. After that he always ask me every time, he think I am asleep.

Willie: "Janice do you have your CPAP on or don't forget your CPAP."

So, whenever I am with my friends, I always tell them if you see me a sleep and you can't wake me up call 911 and then go get my husband.

I only fall off to sleep setting down listening and being still, but I do not fall off while I am driving because I am doing something plus, I will never get behind the wheel if I am tired. I am very sure of that because I make very sure I am not sleepy while driving. Again, it only happens if I am setting still and just listening to a talk or if I am watching TV if I am having that feeling of 'I don't care if someone hit me on the head with a hammer.' I know this because again as I have said many times this is the reason why I had to learn about myself, about my body again to learn how to save myself.

So here I go again working hard to survive, is that a Survivor? Does it make me a Survivor?

What Does It Feel Let to Be Hit Over the Head with A Hammer?

A hammer is a very cold piece of iron that can kill a person
if someone hits you with it.
It will crack your skull, but I don't care because I don't have the
feeling or strength,
in my mind or with my arms because it makes me
feel like I have no arm length.

My strength is fatigue, my will is fatigue, it feels like I lose all my
strength and because it makes me feel so very, very fatigue,
It makes me feel like an antique, I know that's me and
it's not true because I am not unique.
It makes me feel very weak, it makes me feel
like an antique.

So, hitting me over the head with a hammer I
don't care!
You can hit me with a hammer while I am setting in this chair.
Crack, crack, I do not care even if you take and drag me by my heels.
It's incredibly sad to feel this way, it's incredibly sad
to hear myself say,
yes, you can, you can, hit me over the head today.

I may feel like I wants to be hit on my head with a hammer,
at that time, I am thinking like a person that using very, bad grammar.

Really, I am not wanting to die because I have the strength to survive,
see I really wants to save my life.
I really wants to stay alive.
So, I must do whatever is needed to stay alive;
I must do whatever I can, to survive.

JANICE HOLLIMAN

What must I do to survive? I must pull from deep inside to save
my life.
I somehow must reach deep inside of me and pull out whatever
it takes, even if I must use my survival knife.
As long as I do what it really takes to save myself and to save my life.
I will survive yes, I will survive, because I keep myself a
survival knife.

I will tell you this, hitting me with a hammer will not do,
because I will fight back and pull myself through.

Wow! My word is Faith let's see what I can learn this week.
Dictionary's View: Faith is one of those words that is difficult to tie down to one simple definition. According to a modern dictionary, faith is "unquestioning belief that does not require proof or evidence."

It's says some feel this not true they say, "Faith must have adequate evidence, else it is mere superstition." Faith is not the opposite of fact or of scientific knowledge. They say the evidence of faith may operate differently than those of science, but they are there.

I ask what do you think?

Biblical View: Faith I described in the Bible is not something blind or irrational, or a leap of as some have called it. And it is not credulity. Rather, it is something you have thought through carefully resulting in trust in God and his Word, which is firmly based on reason.

If you are to reason properly, you need accurate information. Even the most powerful computer programs designed on solid principles of logic will come up with some very strange conclusions if they are fed inaccurate data. So, it's the quality of your faith will depend greatly on what you hear or on how dependable the information you feed your mind proves to be. Appropriately, the Bible says that "faith follows the things heard."

So, a fundamental requirement for faith is "an accurate knowledge of truth." The Bible says only "the truth will set you free" free from misleading beliefs, whether they are scientific or religious. The Bible warns you not to put faith "in every word." It says "make sure of all things" or test out the things you hear before believing them.

This is deep as the Bible admonishes us to "test the insides expression to see whether they originate with God." By me doing this I will be in a position, even when my beliefs are challenged, "this makes a great defense before everyone that demands of me a reason for the hope in me."

This is truly me because of what I have faced and still facing so many challenges in my life, and I sure hope people see I have a lot of faith in me.

Chapter 22

I JUST KNEW I WAS GOING TO DIE

A few years later I start noticing how bad I was feeling and how bad it was getting, I noticed how I was gaining weight I gained 50 pounds in three months. I didn't have any clothes to wear, I couldn't walk three feet without having to lean on the wall I couldn't breathe, I turned very dark, every time we went out, I would have to lay down in the car and take a thirty-minute nap. This kept going on for months and I was getting worse. I was not eating, and I kept gaining weight, but I did I were busting out of my clothes.

So, one day I decided to call my surgeon Dr. Homes office was the doctor who did all my scar tissue removal surgeries in the pass years. I called and said I need help if something not done to help me, I am going to die. They asked me if I could come in next Monday? I said yes and they gave me the time.

When I got to the doctor office and signed in. When the doctor came in remember this is the same doctor that gave me the antibiotic which I asked not to give me. I went to him because he has been my surgeon since 2002 and he has done many of my surgeries since then and I know he knows me, and my body. I feel if it's not broke why fix it and I have trained him over the years.

Dr. Homes: "When I saw your name last night when I was going through my patients for today, I said I hope she is coming in for the gastric bypass surgery?"

"No, I am here to get help because I am so sick, and I know if I don't get help Now, I will not be here long so whatever you can do I will be so happy all I ask you is just don't leave me on a bag."

He asked me was my scar tissues again. I told him,

"I don't think so it's very different this time, I have gain 50 pounds in three months. I can't walk but three feet before I must stop and lean against the wall because I get very tired and can't breathe. Plus, when I am out no matter what I am doing I have to stop and take a thirty- minute nap, and I have turned very dark. I don't eat much, and I throw-up most of what I eat."

Dr. Homes: "Wow you are dealing with a lot, and it does sounds different than before so let's see what we can do. I still want you to think about having the weight loss surgery."

"I have said in the pass I will never have a bypass, but I realized when I really came down sick and feeling like I do I am willing to do it. So, I am telling you to do what you must do, again just don't leave me on a bag please."

He told me what he wanted to do he also said he will also have to look in my stomach and see what's going on.

So, the procedure was setup and done. He came to me to tell what he found

Dr. Homes: "When I looked in your stomach and I saw some corn in there."

"Corn! I ate that six weeks ago!"

Dr. Homes: "And I saw some greens also with some other things."

175

"Greens! I ate that eight weeks ago. What is going on with me?"

Dr. Homes: "Your food is not breaking down and dumping it's just setting in your stomach the way you are eating it. It's called Toxic Gut Syndrome there is no cure for it but what I going to do is bypass that area of your stomach by cutting it out and reattach it to give you a fighting chance. Because it is not working, I will have to cut and bypass that area it will make you have an exceedingly small stomach. You will always have this problem but at least we will be getting rid of the food that has poison your system."

"So, you are saying I am being poison by my own food?"

Dr. Homes: "Yes, it is, and it will continue doing so, so that means you will need to be incredibly careful with what you eat and how you eat it. Plus, you need to meet with the others that is having weight loss surgery and watch the film about it so you will understand what will happened and you will be given information on how to eat and what to eat and what not to eat."

I had my surgery when I went for my two-week check-up, he told me,

Dr. Homes: "You lost forty-two pounds that's the most I ever seen anyone lost in their first two weeks, I am very proud of you let's see how everything goes with you I will see you in a month."

I was thinking I lost that much weight in that short period of time. I didn't do it for the weight loss I did it to save my life. The next month I lost forty-five pounds. The third month I lost forty-five pounds the reason why I was losing so much weight was because I was throwing-up everything I ate or drank. So, on my fourth month he set up for to have my stomach checked out, so I had to make an appointment with my (GI) doctor.

"I am here because I am having problem with my stomach, I can't really eat or drink anything."

Dr. Downy: "It sounds like I need to go in and pop the whole in your stomach, I have to order the part and we have to set a date to do the procedure."

"Why it has not already popped?"

Dr. Downy: "You know things don't go easy with you, I'm joking I don't really know we have to look and see let's set it up for three weeks from now."

The weeks went by the day before I went to have my procedure, I felt something pop. But I didn't say anything about it, I had the procedure done. Dr. Downy in and saw that it has already popped.

"I thought so, but I was not sure that's why I didn't tell you that I thought it popped so I let you do what you did to make sure."

Dr. Downy: "That's good but you still have to be careful of your eating habit."

In six months in I stop taking all five of my diabetic shots a day. I also stopped my high blood pressure pills also because of the weight loss.

Then three months later my Hematologist cut my blood thinner from one hundred & thirty units down to one hundred units a day. I was and am glad to not have to stick myself everyday by cut the numbers of shots a day from seven hundred & thirty to three hundred & sixty-five shots a year.

I took two thousand & ninety shots in three years. As of now in the past six years I have taken the same two thousand & ninety shots, so it has been cut in half. Just think about a snowball rolling down a hill picking up snow on the way down getting bigger and bigger. But with losing weight it's the opposite as I lose weight it feels like a snowball that is getting smaller and smaller. I will wake-up wearing, one size and before I go to bed, I feel myself losing weight so I can never know what I am going to wear because what fitted me yesterday will not fit me today.

If I do any housework or walking, I feel my weight dropping. I can be setting down or laying down, and I even notice standing up the snowball effect of getting smaller and smaller.

I lost a total of two hundred pounds since 12/20/2012, I may gain anywhere between five to ten pounds and that's because of my fluid buildup. This year will mark my seven-year anniversary this December.

Losing Weight Was Not on My Mind

What's on my mind, is to live as long as I can,
what's on my mind is to fight as hard as I can, to
use all my strength
to fight with both tooth and nails.
What's on my mind, when I am giving myself, a
shot is, this really hurts I just want to really let out
a lot of wails.

I can't because that will not help, besides, I have to remember I have
to get use to all these
shots to save my life until I wouldn't need them anymore.
I can't let them become a bore, I am so glad I don't
have to take four,
just thinking about it if I had to take four shots a day
that will really make me want to hit the floor.
Not only that my stomach would be very sore,
each and every time I stick a
needles in my body or pore.

Losing weight just came with the package of
saving my life, even though it came at a
remarkably high price.
The price of not being able to eat or
drink, it is awfully hard to deal with it in
everyday life, and
I am still paying this extremely high price, to save my life.

Losing weight was not on my mind but
saving my life was it was the package that
came with saving myself it is not easy to
deal with it every day.
I know what I have to do in order to save my life,
I have to eat and drink the way my
body tells me this is what I must eat if
I really want
to live or feel good this day, so I must eat
this way.

It's like a song that keep playing in my head,
this is the way,
if I want to really live or feel good this day.
This is the way if I want to really live or
feel good this day!
It's like a song that keep playing in my head,
this is the way,
if I want to really live or feel good this day.
This is the way if I want to really live or feel good this day!

The word for this week is Peace and I am going to view it this way.
Dictionary's View: Peace is used as a friendly greeting. It is used as an order to remain silent. It's a state of security or order. It's also a pact or agreement to end hostilities between those who have been at war or who have had unfriendly words.

Biblical View: Peace is a sincere apology that has an effective way to repair a damaged relationship. Having a heartfelt apology which will never let a person (me) be too proud to swallow their pride, apologize, and it (I) will seek forgiveness for a sincerely humble person apologies are not difficult for me to make.

So, I am going to let my focus be that I will let my words of apology help make me a better person of peace. I will admit my mistakes and I will assure others; knows I am apologizing for the damage I have done. By doing so I know I can open opportunities for us to have open constructive discussions.

Now that's an idea to have, what a way to make and keep peace which will make me a peaceable person. I will see how hard it will be this week, focusing on me to keep peace.

Wow! Having peace to survive, it will make me a peaceful Survivor!

⌒ *Chapter 23* ⌒

SKIN REMOVALS

After I lost over one hundred and fifty pounds my skin begins to hang like water waves. It turned red and it begin to burn it really hurts. I tried everything I can to stop the pain I found out it was infected, so I had to find a skin removal doctor surgeon what do you call them? Oh, I know they are called plastic surgeon. I had him to remove skin from my bottom part of my stomach first. I had to call to let them know I was having a problem with my right side it was swelling they asked me to come in the next morning I did when the doctor came in.

"See what I mean I think it's infected my skin is tearing toward the back, I am pulling the fluid off ask I was told."

Dr. Jenkins: "Let's look at it and see what we can do. You are right it is tearing back here let's do this and cover it up and let's pull the fluid off two more times a day along using this cream I am giving you and I will see you in a couple of weeks."

It starts to heal but I notice my right side is not flat like it was before the infection even now, but it heals up well that's what really matter to me. Then my right thigh was done it went okay it heal well.

"Doctor this leg is much bigger than the left leg it has a lot of loose skin on it. I think you should remove a quite a bit of the loose skin on it."

Dr. Jenkins: "No I am just going to remove so much and if we have to go back and remove more I will."

"I am really telling you what you say you are going to take of will not be enough I will still have quite a bit of loose skin I'm just telling you."

Doctor this leg is much bigger than the left leg it has a lot of loose skin on it. I think you should remove a quite a bit of the loose skin on it."

Dr. Jenkins: "No I am just going to remove so much and if we have to go back and remove more I will."

"I am really telling you what you say you are going to take of will not be enough I will still have quite a bit of loose skin I'm just telling you."

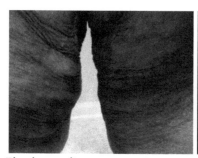

My Elephant. (I am not going to say what this is.) My skin is Inflame.

My Flying Squirrel (my arms.)

My Ugly Body, this is the top part of my stomach.

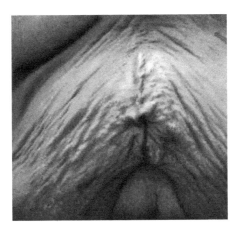

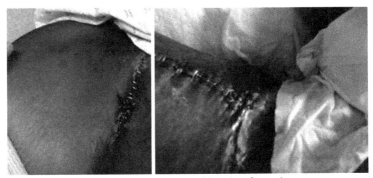

These pictures are pictures of both of my legs.

This is after it began to heal.

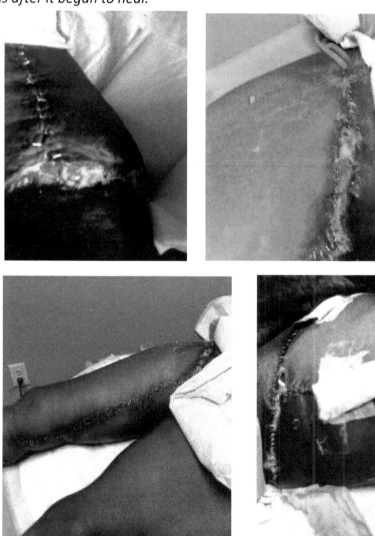

When it start to heal after a hard time. This is what they look like now.

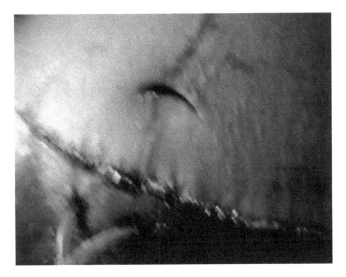

This is my very first skin removal, which is the bottom part of my stomach.

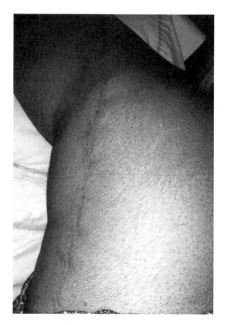

This is what it looks like now.

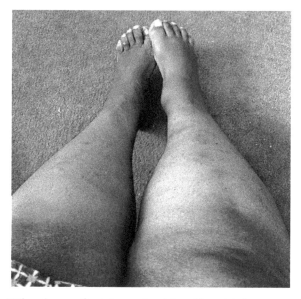

Why do my feet keep looking like this?

◦◦◦ *Chapter 24* ◦◦◦

HERE IT GOES AGAIN "OHHH... NO!"

As I was healing one Sunday my son came to set with me while my husband was out. We were watching TV we were not talking. I began feeling very funny and something told me to check my blood see if I can pull fluid into the ball that they had on me it came out in clots the little that I could was very clotted. I became tunnel vision my mind went on something that my hematologist told me in 2010 if I have one more blood clot I 'will not' have that three-hour window and I 'will not' be here. So, I gave myself two shots of my blood thinner medication.

"I need you to get my clothes out of my drawer while I call 911."

Ramono: "What's wrong?"

"I am having a problem with blood clots."

He asked me why I didn't tell him, and he took the phone and he said,

Ramono: "My mom is having a problem she is acting very funny she have a problem with blood clots."

911 asked him was I responsive? He told he didn't know because I was not saying anything, I just looked very funny. They asked him was my mouth twisted, he said "No." I heard every word I felt my mouth twisting, he didn't really know what he was looking at because he never knew what a twisted mouth looked like.

I was thinking about the words my doctor told me, I was feeling like I did before, and the words kept repeating in my head.

"You will not have that three-hour window if you have one more blood clot." So, I gave myself two more shots because it has been over an hour when I start feeling that way. The ambulance has not arrived yet, and I knew, I had to save myself I couldn't let it get worse. So, I gave myself two more shots, then the ambulance showed up they took me to the ER.

The ER Doctors ordered some test on me, the tech came in and did the test. After she finished, I asked her what was going on. She told me I then told her the reason why I was there, I told her.

"I have had 14 blood clots before at one time and I was told I would not make it if I have just one more clot. So, I gave myself a total of six shots to stop the clots and now they say they don't see anything."

The Tech: "Wow you save your own life by taking all those shots. I have seen people helping themselves doing what they think is right."

"I knew what was happening and I knew that I didn't have that much time. So, I had to do it and I am glad I did because I cause it on myself by me stop taking my blood thinner shots eight days before I should have, I knew better. I was told by my surgeon office and the hospital to stop it nine day before it was a must, I knew better so this is one of the reasons why I am here now."

"She told me she was glad I was still alive." After I got out, I went to see my hematologist.

"I did something I knew I should not have done. I stop my blood thinner shots eight days before my last surgery instead of one."

Dr. Jenkins: "I told you can only stop the day before any procedure you cannot 'ever' stop for that long. If you want to live you must not do it on more than a day."

I learned the hard way; I will never do that again. I went back to see Dr. Jenkins, I told him what happened and the reason why it happened I told him I will never put my life in jeopardy like that again.

"You didn't tell me, but your office kept insisting for me to stop I will never, do it again."

Dr. Jenkins: "I am sorry, I am glad to see you are still here. Now what are you going to do next, I think you need to do your breast next because they are so red, I can see the infection in your skin. Let us see how much you have to remove. Mrs. Holliman your insurance will not pay for this because you have to have a certain amount left and if I remove this you will be flat like a boy meaning you won't have any breast.

"You mean to tell me I have lost all my weight and now my 'headlights' are only skin and hanging like flapjacks? And my insurance refuses to pay for the surgery because of a certain amount is needed before they will pay? So, this means I have to come up with the money for them I will let you know when."

I Will Never Let Anyone Stop Me for Being Strong

*Being strong is having the strength to know myself, to
never let anyone make me do what I know is wrong.
Being strong is having the strength to stand-up, to what
I know is right no matter how hard things get, no matter
how people proceed me, keep my mind focus and be
head strong.*

*Never stop standing up for what I know, never stop
fighting for my life because on one knows me, like I
do on this earth better than me, so I will not
let anyone stop me for being, strong.
Know this there is nothing wrong, knowing I am not a
bad person when it comes to me having to fight to be
strong, no one should never blame me for being strong,
plus I am not wrong.*

*I will never let anyone tell me I am wrong, because I
love my life enough to do everything I can to save
myself or my life.
I will never let anyone make me feel bad, because
I am a person that live the real-life when things
become like cutting a tomato with a butter knife.
I will never let no one tell me or stop me for being
strong, I will never let no one or nothing
stop me from saving my life even
if I have to use a steak or wilderness knife.*

JANICE HOLLIMAN

I will never let anyone stop me for
being strong because this is what
makes me a Survivor.
Even if it means sometimes, I may have to use a flat head or a spiral
ratchet screwdriver.

I will never stop being strong, even if it hurts, I am not wrong.
I will never stop saving myself or my life when
I am in no way wrong, I keep fighting to be strong.
No, I will never let anyone stop me from fighting and stop me
from being strong.
I will fight with all my might to survive, to be a
Survivor, fight to be strong because I know I
do belong.

My word this time is Kindness, let's see how and what I can learn from it this week.

Dictionary's View: Kindness is the practice or quality of being kind. A kind act; favor. It's having kind behavior. t's having friendly feeling toward other and having a liking for them.

Biblical View: Kindness involves taking a genuine interest in welfare of others an interest that is expressed through helpful words and deeds. Kindness is more than a vender of politeness and courtesy. True kindness is motivated by deep love and empathy. We as humans, are created in God's image, we are capable of reflecting the quality of kindness.

So, this week I will imitate God and broaden the reach of our kindness beyond those related to us. I am going to show by taking an active interest in the welfare of others by doing more helpful acts and having considerate word. This means I need to be friendly, gentle, sympathetic, and generous, and have a considerate attitude toward others. I can do this just thinking about it brings a smile to my face.

⌒ *Chapter 25* ⌒

THE SUMMER OF 2015

This was in the spring of 2015 that summer I hurt myself. By falling when I hit my back on the corner of a wall. I hit so hard I felt a hard punch that came into my stomach, and I also felt my neck snap. There was no one around I called out for help, but no one heard me, so I had to get up on my own. I got up and went inside my apartment, Willie asked me what was wrong I told him what happened, I was in so much pain I went and laid in bed. The next day I asked him to rub some cream on my back as he was about to rub my back, he told me.

Willie: "You have a big bruise on your back."

"Please take a picture for me so I can see."

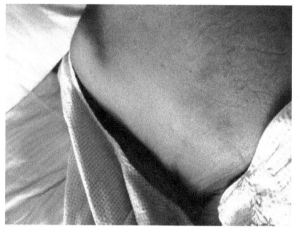

Picture of my back see the red spots this is where my is broke, in two places of the marks

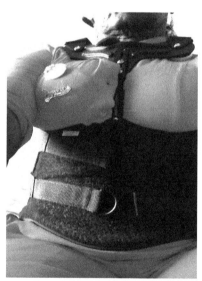

Me with my back brace, sometimes I still need it, but I don't have it now due to the mold and losing everything

I was in pain for days, a few days later I couldn't take the pain anymore, so I went to the ER. When I got there, I told them what happened the ER doctor told me I just springe my back and it will heal in about six months. He said that without taking any test or x-rays, he gave me some medication and sent me home.

I was in pain for months about two months later I was sleep, I woke-up screaming in the middle of the night. I took a pain pill I found myself hungry so I got a banana and went in the Livingroom and laid hanging over my ottoman with the banana in my right hand I would find myself waking-up and taking a bite of it. About 5:00a.m. that morning I went and got back in my bed.

I laid in bed until about 12:00p.m., I looked over at my birds and they looked at Willie like they were saying 'will you please take her to get help.' Funny because he saw their look also, he then said he was going to take me to the ER. When I got there, I end up with the same ER doctor and nurse from months ago. He asked me why I was there when I told him he told me that was an old case and he was not going to look at it, so he gave me some medication to have filled. The nurse rolled me out to my car after I asked her for a braf bag because I knew I was going to throw-up. As Willie pulled the car up, I did braf, in the braf bag, I looked at it, I was shocked to see it felt smooth and look like black tar. I said I would look at it when I get home after we go to the drug store to get my medication filled.

When I got home, I went into my bathroom I opened the bag and looked at it, that was when I really notice what it looked like, I called Willie in to look at it when he agrees with what I saw I told him we were going back to the hospital. When I returned that time, they had changed shift, this time I had a female doctor I told her what happened she asked me what did I want her to do?

"I want you to run all the test you need to in order to find out why my back was still hurting me even worse and to find out why I feel the punch in my stomach, plus the snap in my neck."

She examined me and she ran tests and blood work, hours later she came back in the room and told me what she found.

ER Doctor: "Mrs. Holliman, did anyone tell you that your back is fractured?"

"What! No, they didn't, when I first came here months ago the doctor who examined me did not do anything."

ER Doctor: "Matter of a fact you fractured your back in two places. How are you walking with your back broke in two places?"

I looked at her and told her I am not doing it on my own it all comes from above. She then told me that I needed to go and see a (GI) doctor to make sure I have not messed-up any of my organs or knock them out of place.

I went to see my (GI) doctor he examined me, and he ordered some test to make sure everything was in place and not damage. He told me what I threw-up was black blood. I knew what I threw-up was blood from the last few months about two months before. I was bleeding for a while enough to make that big ball, come to think of it I did I throw-up something so big maybe it was because it was like rubber and it was smooth and flexible, so it shape itself on the way out.

I needed to find someone to look at my back and my neck. I found a doctor whose name is Dr. Brown, when I first went to see him, he told me that he didn't see anything wrong with my back or neck.

He then read the report and said oh it did shows different from my test from a year before.

So, he told me that he wanted me to retake the MRI to make sure it was right, I did I saw there was a big different, but he wanted me to take it again because it was something, he was looking for directly, so I did and when I went back in January of 2016, he told me this.

Dr. Brown: "Your broke in your back is in a good place that it could most likely heal in time. But as for your neck it's not a matter of if, it's a matter of when you are going to become paralyzed, so you really do need to have neck surgery."

"Can I have it done in March because there are things, I need to get done first that was very important to me?"

He told me that would be okay, so I did everything that I needed to do then I called his office and told him in the middle of February that they could schedule me for surgery. The office called me back the next day and told me it would be on February 28, 2016. I went to South Georgia to pick-up my mom so, she would be with me when I have my surgery.

It was two days before my surgery, I began to have cold feet because I never ever wanted anyone to cut on my neck if you remembered how, I turned down the last surgery many years before.

I did some hard thinking on the pros and cons of the surgery, then I prayed, and I said,

"This is a time-consuming matter because of the time frame, I was told it was of the case of when, not if, I will become paralyzed so if it is that serious, please let me know please."

I went to sleep when I woke-up the next morning I couldn't move I still can hear myself,

"Oh, my goodness this is what being paralyzed feel like I can't move anything from the neck down. This is what I have been feeling for months 'oh my goodness', I get it I do need to have this surgery thank you for answering me I really see and understand why I need to have it done and I will."

What Can Make Me Become Paralyzed

What makes me paralyzed is it my words, or is it my thoughts
Sometimes I get frozen with my words because
they may not come out easily as I wish
I wish things may come out as smooth as butter on a dish.

My thoughts are so busy, I never can get a rest because
my mind keep running, it is full of things
that I may want to say.
But some time no matter how hard I try it just don't
come out the right way till this day.

I want to think about all the nice and wonderful things
when I can because there is so much hard and bad things
in the world that always keep getting in the way.
I am going to think of things that maybe real, true
because I can become paralyzed with my thoughts
any or many times a day.

Being paralyzed don't always mean it's with my body, it also can
mean it could be my thoughts, and my mind by being stuck with
never, wanting to change or never stop hating.
Not wanting to bend, by letting myself take
everything others say or do, f I keep looking and bending
for the good in people and knowing people may
not do things the way I may want them to do,
sometimes it can be frustrating.

What can make me become paralyzed is something, I
really needed to be wear of and I did realized.
Anything in life is something, that really
can make me become paralyzed.

What can make me become paralyzed?
Life itself it can paralyze me.
That's if I let it happen or just let it be.

My word for this week will be Faith.
Dictionary's View: Faith is when you have confidence or trust in someone or thing. Having faith in another person ability.

Biblical View: Faith is vital that we put faith in the One who can really help. Paul reminds us that God is "the one who can, according in us, do more than superabundantly beyond all the things we ask or conceive."

Faith is having to know my limitations, to trust my blessing of my outcome. I have the faith to look beyond all my trails and hardships. I am going to endure adversity like I just did, this makes me feels good about myself I am going to focus on how the rest of my week will go.

⌒ *Chapter 26* ⌒

MY OWN CAR RAN OVER ME

Remember I have a broken back and neck, while I was waiting to go back to see my doctor about the result of the MRI. On 12/11/15 at 12:00p.m., this seems strange, but it helps me remember. It was on a Friday we went to the bank downtown in an area where the traffic goes zoom, zoom, zoom. The bank is in a place where we must pay for parking with the arm that goes up and down.

I went in the bank they give me a sticker, so my parking is free. That day and at that time as I was paying with my sticker and ticket the machine would not take my ticket. I put the car in park I open the door without knowing my huge purse had a long strap on it setting on the arm in between the seats. After I took out some money I tried paying for my ticket because the person that was working in the booth was not there, so I had to pay. As I was paying my money drop to the ground, so I bend down to get it but as I did my car door was against this big yellow concrete poll, I was hanging out the door as I was pulling myself up, I felt something and thinking.

"I can't breathe, I am being crush, my car is moving."

As the car kept moving passing the poll my door swung open and I was thrown out, I landed on my stomach and the car ran over me on my left side from my middle back down to my toes which four of them was broken.

Willie was sitting on the other side not knowing anything because he was looking out the right- side window. As the car threw me out and ran over me, I pulled myself out of the middle of the driveway so the other cars could get out. I was not thinking of myself as I saw my car rolling out into a terribly busy street. All I can see is the 'The Red Sea' so I screamed to Willie.

"Hit the brakes! Hit the brakes! Hit the brakes!"

The reason I say 'The Red Sea' is because those cars was going zoom, zoom, zoom both ways with no letup. Less than a blink of an eye the lights just stop as the car rolled out into the street no more car moving. I saw him turning around and seeing what was happening, he climbed over the seat as I saw him being safe, I laid my head down. Blood was gushing everywhere, a lady got out of her car and said she would help me get my stuff, like my family air loom ring, my left earring, my other stuff and money.

Just as Willie got the car into the right lane 'The Red Sea' the cars went zoom, zoom, zoom again. I pull back in the parking lot ran over to me saying.

Willie: "Is she dead? Is she dead? Is she dead?"

By this time, the parking attendant came out saying some one need to go and get a blanket. Wait a minute, where are they going to get a blanket, as Willie came up, I told him to get the blanket out of the car. The reason why I have one is because I am prepared for anything. He got the blanket, brought it to me, and covered me up, the ambulance came they put me in the ambulance they ask me about cut my clothes I asked them not to cut my new hip slip, but they did. I told Willie to do something for me.

"I need you to go out there and find my ring, don't come to the hospital until you do, find it."

About two hours later he came but he said he could not find my ring, which meant someone took my ring. As I was waiting for the

ER doctor, and when he came in to examined me, he told me that I had sprung my toes...

"No, I know what broke toes feel like. He just threw everything I said to him as if it was nothing.

Until I said,

"Wait a minute did you hear what I said I told you I was thrown out of my own car and then it ran over me?"

I showed him where it ran over me, then he said,

"Oh, my goodness! I didn't realize what you were saying."

He ordered test; he stop the bleeding from my earlobe which split at the hole it was just hanging.

"Doctor, will I still be able to wear pierced earring again?"

Because the blood was gushing out, he fixed me up and sent me home we got home about 7:30p.m., by 9:00p.m., I was bleeding again so I asked Willie to go in the kitchen to get me some flour.

The reason why I said flour because that was what we use when I was growing-up it was flour or spider-webs. Who was going to look for spider-webs? So, flour was the best thing. I then said no I think we should go to the ER; I took a whole roll of paper towel with me I used the whole roll.

Willie asked for help in the waiting room, but they took their time blood start running everywhere. I made a statement since I have lost so much blood I could pass out and if I did, they would come running then I said that because I began feeling lite headed because of the blood lost.

They came and got me after I made that statement, I told them I just knew my head was bleeding not my ear. They clean it and said no it's just your ear I told them there was no way all that blood was coming from my ear. The ER doctor put glue on my ear, which didn't stop the bleeding, he then went to get the cauterizer to cauterize my wound. When he did it didn't stop the bleeding neither, he began to talk to himself I asked him did he said something about a blood thinner and he said yes so, I told him yes, I did.

He calls a nurse in, and he told her to stay with me and hold my earlobe. He came back in and he did something to my ear it stops bleeding we got home about 2:30a.m., I woke-up about 7:30a.m., to go to pay my 'water bill' I went back to bed I saw all the blood, but I was not thinking clear, because I said to myself, I will deal with this when I wake-up and I went back to sleep after I laid my head to the side out of the big blood spot. I woke-up about 10:00a.m. that Saturday morning.

Willie: "I am going to get your medication filled but you need to know your pillow is all bloody."

"I know before you go, can you to please help me clean-up so I can put the flour on my earlobe."

He helped me with the clean-up, he gave me the flour I rolled-up some tissue I put flour on it then clamp my earlobe, I got the rolled paper towel laid against my ear then I wrap it with a wrap.

Blood was all over my hair had dried it was a mess the blood made my hair so brittle I could break it if I touched it. I looked down at my pillow it was bloody, when I removed it and looked the second one was bloody also, I removed that pillow it was on my sponge mattress, and my mattress.

I wrap my head and keep it there for three days I had no more bleeding when someone from the hospital called to check on me. I told her what happened then I told her what I did, I also asked her why I lost so much blood? She told me I have a large blood vessel in my earlobe and that was why I bled so much. At hearing that it made me think of the reason why I am still here is because about a year my hematologist told me that.

Dr. Jenkins: "You have two extra pints of blood you should donate it someone."

"No, I am not I may need my own blood one day."

They didn't want this to happen, but it did, and I am so glad I kept all my blood I lost about three pints of that day. I survived that day by not giving up on myself by going old school by using what I learn as I grew-up. Surviving is fun it is teaching me I am a person who have the right to live.

This one after the first hospital before. This is the next day after I stop the bleeding, after the second hospital visit.

Let's see what I am looking to do this time 'Wow' it's Joy.
Dictionary's View: Joy is the emotion of great caused by something exceptionally good or satisfying; keen pleasure; relation.

Biblical View: Joy is a heart that is joyful does good as a curer, but a spirit that is stricken makes the bones dry.

This shows when I am discouraged in the days of being distress, I need my power will be scanty because discouragement can sap my energy, which can make me feel weak and vulnerable with no desire to change or to seek help. I am not going to let discouragement affect me. I am not going feel worthless because I will not feel that I can never enjoy a good relationship so I can be blessed. I must remember I have to cultivate balance in how I view myself, this week will be fun 'what a joy this will be.

⟡ *Chapter 27* ⟡

WHEN I HAD SURGERY ON MY NECK

The day came for my surgery after my soulful prayer, I was ready to have them cut on my neck. Dr. Jenkins put a rode and two plates in my neck, the surgery went well I was in the hospital for ten days, laying there and not being able to move with a neck brace on my neck which they had to make for me. On day eight the therapist came in got me up to walk to the restroom she wanted me to set on the portable toilet as I was setting.

"This toilet legs are very rocky you'll need to change it before someone fall out of it."

But they didn't because the next day that evening the nurse gave me a laxative, the doctors always order one for all patient the day before the patient go home. I was sleepy because of my medication I was given. After I took the laxative, I had to go I saw the portable toilet setting next to the bed and a nurse standing at the door I saw hew looking down the hall. I asked her to help me to the portable toilet, it was the same one I sat on the day before so I could pay my 'food bill' meaning I had a bowel movement. Anyway, as I was leaning to clean myself for the third time, I saw myself falling, and as it was happening, I was thinking.

"If I fall and hit my head, I can break my neck and become paralyzed or I can die so I have to stop this from happening."

I took my hands and put them in a position to break my fall. As I was falling the nurse put her right foot out to help but it looks like she was saying.

Nurse Tina: "Look at my new hooker heels."

It taps me on my forehead I don't like no one shoe touching me because I don't know where they shoes been. I fell then I set myself on the floor, she calls for help a male nurse came in the room he picked me up and threw me on the bed. I asked did I finish cleaning myself and please give me something to clean my hands, he told me I did. The next thing I knew I was fast asleep about 9:30p.m., they came in and put me in a new bed to make me feel more comfortable. I went back to sleep than about 12:30a.m., the two of them came and told me they were moving me out of that room and moving me closer to the nurse's station.

I was so sleepy, I was not thinking to ask any questions like what the reason was they doing all of this, and why they did not call anyone to come a examined me. The next morning, they all came running in my room they ran some tests and they said nothing went wrong, then they told me to check out and go home.

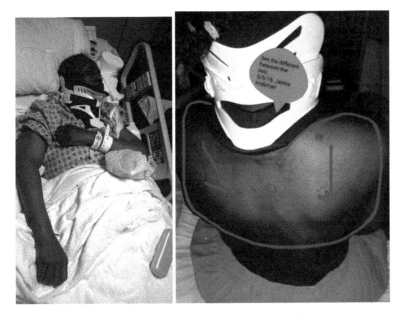

I was in the hospital.   *Over a month late*

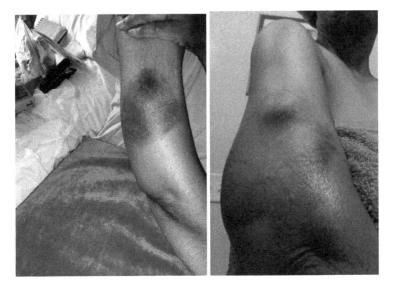

I can't tell you why this happened, wow seventeen days later, and it still pops up till this day.

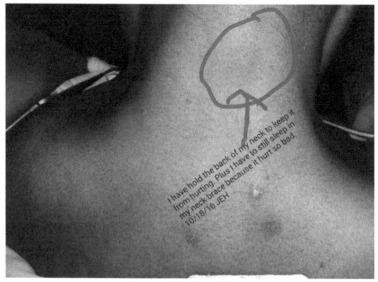

This really do still hurt

Examining the Things, I Have to Swallow

Swallowing can be hard if it's food, or something I may need to drink
or it could be any or everything I swallow, it even could be
what I am facing in life,
because life can be hard and not easy to chew and swallow.
Swallowing things in life is a big problem, whatever I
face in this world it can really hurt, sometimes I can't
get it down or I have
to throw-up because it really hurts
going down and it really hurts when
it's coming back-up.
When this happens all, I can do is finish and clean-up.

When I am examining my life, I see how things can
really hurt especially when I try to take life into my hand.
I keep looking around me so I can do my best
to understand what's going on in my life.

Why is it so hard to swallow the
things I am facing, I ask is it due to
the fact I see things the way they
are, or is it because
of the way they stand?

Swallowing things in life do have sharp edges
that can stick my throat while it is going down.
I have to lean to the left to stop the pain or
to help it to go down, I know as long as I
keep doing everything I can, I do know what
I need to do, to make sure, I will not drown.

Examining the things, I must swallow it is very necessary
to keep living.
Partly I have to be forgiving, be a good caregiver, it is very fitting,
I realized life can be very chilling,
and it can be very unforgiving.

My word for this week is Love.
Dictionary's View: Love encompasses a range of strong and positive emotional and mental states, from the most sublime virtue or good habit, the deepest interpersonal affection and to the simplest pleasure. Most common, love refers to a feeling of strong attraction and emotional attachment.

Biblical View: By showing love, we upbuild others and ourselves, as is implied: "There is more happiness in giving than there is in receiving."

At this time, I will focus on the fact how love is simple, yet strong, positive, I am going to let it show my deepest feeling, but I will show my emotion of love to bring pleasure to all.

∞ *Chapter 28* ∞

THE BIG CHANGE THAT HIT US FOR THE SECOND TIME

I already told you the way our lives change back in the 90's when my husband got sick at work. Which change our family life turned it upside down. I thought that was the worse time in our life, but we pull through. I never wish that on anyone, and I never wanted that to happen to us again, but it did.

About four years ago I began seeing a change in my husband. It was very subtle, but I notice little things happening. He began not remembering things, see he had a particularly good memory I would always ask him about things.

I would ask him to go to the store and get something he would forget the main thing he went to get. I noticed as time passed it got worse and more difficult dealing with him and his driving, I would let him know, he would become very offensive. As time pass, he starts driving on the wrong side of the road and I would have to let him know what he was doing. He starts to blame me of doing the same thing which was not true remembered a time we were riding on a four- lane highway the next thing I knew he was driving in the turning lane which was only for the other side.

"You are driving in the wrong lane."

Willie: "I am not driving wrong and besides, You, have done the same thing."

"No, I have not because that is for the oncoming traffic."

Willie: "You have, and I know what I am doing."

"Okay do what you want to when you are by yourself not when I am with you because I love myself and my life so don't do it when I am with you, please."

Willie: "You drive the way you want to, and I will drive the way I want."

"Not with me in here you are not, you can drive anyway you want to when I am not in here, I mean it, don't you see that oncoming traffic?"

These conversations begin to happen more and more so I would drive most of the time to keep peace and to save our life. I will never forget when I was sick, and he had to drive the whole time because I couldn't because I went to see my doctor and he was driving, I looked down and as I looked up, I saw him into the oncoming traffic when he was making a left turn.

"You are in the wrong lane hurry and get out of it because this is for the oncoming traffic."

Willie: "No I am not!"

After I told him to look at those yellow lines, and said they are for the other side not for us so hurry before we get hit. He told me we were in the right lane I know, and I asked him was there something wrong with him. I told him how he keeps fighting me every time I brought it up, I said I was only trying to help him, but he won't let me, he told me.

Willie: "You think you can drive that well you have drove in the wrong lane also."

"Okay maybe I have but I don't keep doing or blame someone else for the same thing."

Willie: "It's because I don't want to keep hearing how I keep driving wrong."

"You mean that you want me not tell you when you are about to kill yourself, us or someone else is that what you want?"

Willie: "No!"

One evening we was going to the most important day of the year, we picked-up two friends he was making a left turn he end-up in the wrong lane again. The three of us screamed.

The Three of Us: "You are driving on the wrong side of the road."

"That's it I am sorry, but you can't drive anymore."

He doesn't remember doing it because a few months ago the subject came up and I ask him about it. That was when he said it didn't happen so I had to called one of my two friends and asked her did she remember that night if so, could she please tell him about it. She did and he stated he didn't remember it.

Back to year 2016 that year I kept telling him something was off with him, and he would get offensive so I would drop it each time, but I would keep an eye on him. He stayed sick, every time he turned around that year, he was sick. His memory was getting worse, he would sleep all the time he stayed home because how bad he felt.

By that August we were in the bedroom I was setting on the bed on my computer. I saw out of the corner of my eye he was looking like he was fainting I called to him he would not respond he was foaming at the mouth. I called 911 and they ask all the questions they supposed to ask.

I told them my husband was having a stroke, they asked what's going on? I said his eyes was rolling back in his head and he was not responding to me. I had to call his name.

"Willie, do you hear me? Do you hear me? Look at me."

911: "Ask him to say this."

"Can you say ...? No, he can't."

They asked me was his mouth twisted. I told them yes. They told me to keep him calm help will be there shortly telling him not to move. I told him to,

"Stay steal don't move. No! No don't move."

The ambulance came they knocked on the door. I went to let them in and then we went to the bedroom, but he was not there he had gotten up and came into the Livingroom. They check him out and asked him questions, but he couldn't answer any questions.

They took him to the ER. I drove my car, but I was so hungry, so I stop off at Taco Bell to get myself a Taco Pizza, plus I was supposed to have a sleeping study done that night which was two blocks away. I went to the center and told them.

"I just stop by to let you'll know that my husband is in the hospital and I will not be able to do the test."

I went to the hospital with my food, I got there within minutes of the Ambulance getting him there. I told who I was there for they said he just got here, they saw my food and they asked me about it I told them.

"I did plus I made another stop before coming here."

ER Desk: "Wow you weren't wasting anytime."

They called me back, to his room.

Things Do Change Us

Things do change us but it's up to us which way we go.
It's up to us, to teach others what we know.
Change comes with time especially if we use it to stop crime.
It can help us be a good person
when we show people what's on our mind.

When we help people change their minds, to do what's right.
I wants to help people fight for right, I want to
bring what is in the dark, I will help bring
whatever it is to the light.

Change comes when I reach out to help others make a smile.
I love making smiles for all of us that brings joy to me and
whomever wants to change their lifestyle.

Meanwhile life may not be as good as it can be
because it is full of all kinds of hostility.
I hate seeing people being treated with hate or anger, as I see it everyone is
worthwhile and should have in
their life tranquility.

A change comes when we least expect it,
a change come to us all no matter who
we are, or no matter where we live.
It's no misgiving about our fear or our
doubt as long, as we keep striving, be
forgiving, and do whatever we need to
do to survive.

Even though changes do change us;
we must always remember we can't ever, let our
change makes us treasonous

This week my word is Mildness.

Dictionary's View: Mildness is a person who is not aggressiveness. It is having the amiably gentle or temperate in feeling or behavior toward others.

Biblical View: Mildness is a person who has a mild temper and who can have a calming effect. It can even soften the attitude of a person who is hostile.

Mildness can be hard to be now days because so many things goes wrong. People can really get on our nerves, they can really make us mad, make us upset, so keeping our cool and keeping this mild attitude can be hard. Well, let me tell you how I did, remembering if we live with anyone or deal with anyone who may have an illness it really can be trying to work with the word mildness.

This week there was an issue that came up with my husband if you don't remember he is dealing with a stroke, seizures, fluid on his brain, he having TIA's, lost has a lot of memory, a bad back, headaches, dizziness, he can't walk far, he can't use his hands like he used to, because he fractured his left shoulder in five pieces when he was seizing, he loses his balance all the time, he have bad moments about 70% of his day.

Chapter 29

HOW MUCH MORE CAN WE DEAL WITH?

When I have to deal with all of this everyday it can take a total on me. Specifically, when I have all my own illnesses to deal with, but I have to keep going, I have to do all the housework, I do all the driving now because the doctor told him he can't drive, this was sad but also funny.

Willie: "Dr. Calming, when can I drive again?"

Dr. Calming: "Let's see in forty years."

I start laughing to myself without him knowing but he doesn't want me to tell the doctors anything about him. He gets terribly angry all the time, but he doesn't remember anything. I know it is hard on him because he is so use to doing so many things all his life. Now he can't do much and this makes him terribly angry. I know he don't like it when I say he do not remember but he turns right around and ask me things that I was trying to help him with.

This is where mildness comes in play for me, I must remember what he is going through, I know and understand it is extremely hard on him. I hope he realize and remember I can only help him if he let me. Sometimes I just get quiet, or I may start singing songs that up-building I sing my songs to focus on how I need to keep calm. Just the other week, was one of those days. I know we should never go to bed without talking but sometimes I must keep quite because no matter what I say or how I say it, it will set him off.

I do understand but I am only human, and I do have feelings. So, to keep us both mild temple until he feels okay not better, I just say nothing. I just keep signing and praying for him to feel better.

This is where mildness is really needed, I think I did well, I know I can do better. I do wish I handled it a little better by being aware what may happen by keeping my suite of armor shined. The meaning of mildness is not letting people or things make me get upset or angry.

We used to pull these nine important words together but for the past two years I can't get him to do so. It's okay the word I pull, I pull it for the both of us, but it means I must work harder with each word. Because it's like working with a person who have Bipolar, Dementia or Alzheimer. I do understand him even if he doesn't think so, he may not even remember what he does or say most of the time. I only want the best for him and for us. It can be awfully hard for me especially when I am not feeling well myself, it can take all I have to focus on myself, but I can't.

Remember we still staying with our son, I like to do everything myself just to keep peace. But he wants to do things to help so I let him, I can ask him to do something, and he will get it wrong and when I asked him.

"What did I asked you to do?"

He gets truly angry with me so many times no matter what or how I would say it. But I don't take it personal, I do understand even if he doesn't think so. At times I will just let him vent his feelings because again I know it can be hard, sometimes it can be extremely hard. He is not a bad person; he is just sick which he didn't asked to be, just like the rest of us.

"I will tell him this is the reason why, I rather do it myself to keep peace."

I ask him at times, what do he think about Bipolar, Alzheimer's or Dementia he hates everything I say or ask. I have tried to tell him he need to change his insurance so it can cover all his payment because we do not have the money for his doctor's visits, but he will not. He is not getting the proper help he needs to help himself, and I can't keep filling out papers for him and dealing with things that I should not have to do. Because if I do, I cannot do my own paperwork I am only one person I get mentally tired at times, and it can set off my anxiety.

This is the reason why, I focus on my words each week they help me a lot, they help me save my life, in all ways like my mind, my body, and my inner self. Besides, I would want him to do the same for me if I was in his shape. This is what love and marriage is all about when we said our 'I Do's' it was and is not for us to find an easy way out because this is a threefold-cord union not a twofold-cord.

A threefold-cord is much stronger than any old twofold-cord. He is a good person, people love him, he loves to give hugs, and I know he love to get hugs also, that stems from his growing-up he was a momma's boy, which nothing is wrong with that because it helps makes him a good person because she raised him right the best way she could, she did good by all her kids.

You Are Not the Person I Married

Who are you? Do I know you at all? Are you the person I married?
Are you the person that I said 'I Do' too?
Do you know I use to see you as standing tall?
During hard times some people wonder instead of being married,
they may say why do I feel like I am being buried.
Wondering if your mate is saying they feel like they are being buried.
Hey, no one is perfect, are you?
We should never say we shouldn't get married.

You are not the person I married, knowing we was
young and as time goes by, as we go through changes,
we see things, become for better or for worse.
Things do have an adjective reaction that is opposite
to our direction. It sometimes becomes contrary to
our interests or our welfare we need to reimburse all
our adverse.

Why are you not the person I married, I really do know
and I really, do understand all about you and what you
have gone through?
Please tell me I understand I have changed too, please tell me if I mean,
do I treat people the way you do?

Do I have Alzheimer's or Dementia which can make me mean?
Do I hurt people feelings, or do I make sure they see
me as a person they can feel really good to be around especially when I
fix them a fine cuisine?

You are not the person I married, neither am I, we both
said we are going to grow old together with
one another,
and we are going to take care of each other.

For better or for worse but you are not the
person I married.
As time goes by do, we both, feel like we
are being buried?

We are going to do whatever it takes to loosen-up and
clear-up all confusion,
the conclusion is we need to come, and we need to make sure we don't
cause a contusion.

Who are you?
Are you the person I said 'I Do' too?
Do I know you at all?
Do you know I use to see you as a person standing tall?
Are you the person I married?
Love being married, I never will feel like I am being buried.

I am going to continue to work the word Mildness this week also.
Dictionary's View: Mildness is the quality or state of being mild; as mildness of temper, the mildness of the winter.

Biblical View: Mildness is when a person who have mildness is happy because they clothed themselves with mildness.

I know mildness can be hard a mild attitude can be hard. We all have bad days, by keeping my cool. When living with others or just dealing them can be very trying. To work with the word mildness is a word we really need to think about, it helps me see the goodness in people even when what we may not want to feel like doing.

Chapter 30

WHILE WILLIE WAS IN THE HOSPITAL

As I said earlier Willie was foaming at the mouth, we got him to the hospital he didn't know what was going on, he didn't know where he was at first, and he didn't know why he was there. It was because I called an ambulance because of what he was doing. When the doctors came in, they had me to step out so they can have some x-rays done.

As I was standing at the desk, I saw a paper explaining about TIAs it talked about every minute or minutes it said how many hours some brain cells will die and the longer there is no help some of those cells will never regenerated in the front lobe.

The doctors kept coming in and they all kept asking him the same questions and he answered them. The doctor came in and told him that he had a TIA, then the next day he came back and told him there was nothing wrong with him besides the fact they saw fluid on his brain, which he would have to go and see another doctor from another hospital to take care of the fluid problem.

"Wait a minute You walk in Here and keep asking him the same questions and he gives you the answer you wants to hear. He gives the answer because he has become hip to your questions, why don't you ask him something you have not asked him. When you come in here and tell us one thing and then you come back and change it, it don't cut it for me. I know what TIAs are, and I know what strokes are and that was him. You walk in here for two days like you know him, and you don't. I have been with him for thirty-nine years, so I know when something is wrong with him, and you don't. Because you keep coming in here with different things, you are showing me you may not know what you are saying."

The next day his neurologist Dr. Calming came in he asked the same questions he gave the same answer I suggest he asked him something different he did, and Willie couldn't answer him, but he should have known the answer, but he just didn't remember.

Dr. Calming: "I see what you mean he is not okay."

I was asked to have the doctor's name Dr. Douglas have a certain test done. I asked nurse Gloria to asked him could he please do the test. He come flying in the room and said,

Dr. Douglas: "I understand you want this test done if I wanted him to have that test, I would have ordered it I am not doing it."

I didn't say anything at that time but because I was terribly upset after he left, I called our GI doctor Dr. Downy because I needed to talk with him. We were talking Dr. Douglas came in and start talking.

"Dr. Downy do you hear him?"

Dr. Downy: "Yes I do."

He kept talking and saying what he wanted to say I again asked Dr. Downy did he hear him, and he said yes! Ask Dr. Douglas kept talking I was asking Dr. Downy for the third time about him hearing what he was saying. By that time Dr. Douglas realized I was on the phone he goes.

Dr. Douglas: "Oh I didn't know you was on the phone."

He left the room with this funny look on his face after he have showed out. When he left, I asked Dr. Downy what he think about that he said.

Dr. Downy: "Listen Do Not Let Anyone Send Him Home if You Do Not feel like he is ready."

You make sure All Your questions are answered and he is out of danger."

"Thanks, I will do that."

Dr. Douglas came back in the room about two hours later and said,

Dr. Douglas: "I am going to let him go home today."

"Oh No He is Not!"

Dr. Douglas: "Yes he is because there is nothing wrong with him."

"He is not going Home because You keep coming in here with something new each time or different. He is not going Home because I know something is wrong with him and don't treat me like I am stupid because I am not. If he goes home and something goes wrong, I must bring him back or if something happens and he don't make it back what do you think I should do? No, he is not going Home."

He left the room again then he came back not along he had two more doctors with him that Willie will have to go and see for the fluid on his brain after he leave this hospital, plus he had nurse Gloria with him.

Dr. Douglas start talking, I stop him by putting my hand up and I said,

"I have Nothing to say to you because I have already told You what I had to say to you."

One of the other Doctor name was Dr. Ramson from another hospital came to do rounds like they always do.

Dr. Ramson: "I understand to are not going to let him go home today."

"No, he is not."

Dr. Ramson: "What about tomorrow?

"No as long as I can't get the right help for him, he will not be going home."

Dr. Ramson: "I understand what you mean I probably feel the same way as you do. The reason why we are having him to come to the other hospital is because they do not do this kind of surgery in this hospital."

"I can understand what you are saying but that will have to wait until they find out what is wrong with him here now."

She thanked me and then they left. About forty-five minutes later nurse Gloria came back in the room.

"I am sorry that you had to see me say the things I said but he acts like he doesn't know what he is doing so I had to let him know where I am coming from."

Nurse Gloria: "No, you did nothing wrong, you did the right thing. It was so funny I was thinking about my dad I had just started working here and my father became extremely sick. I let my family talk me into letting us send my dad Home when he was not ready to go home. I knew better but my sister said let the doctor do what they need to do, they did then they sent him home and he had to come back two more times. What was so strange was we never make rounds we always go into a room and go over all the cases. This is the very first time this happened I wonder why."

I thanked her for saying what she said after I told her it was meant to happen the way it did, and it was out of man hands.

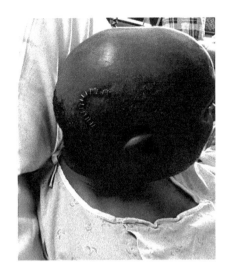

Willie after having head surgery

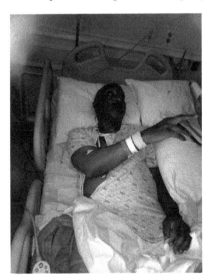

Willie is in the hospital from having his seizure.

⌁ *Chapter 31* ⌁

FINDING MOLD IN OUR APARTMENT

This happen during the time of hurricane Irma, when my mom came up when Irma was coming. This were during the time when Willie had got out the hospital from his TIAs he was about to have surgery to have a shank put in in head for the fluid on his brain. This was also the same time my sister found out that she had pancreatic cancer.

My sister was living in Miami Fla., or months no one could find her because she did not let us know what was going on with her. I had to call fourteen hospital and I couldn't still find her, so I text her again she did respond and told me she was in the hospital, and she told me what was going on with her. Hurricane Irma was on its way to Miami I told her to get out of the hurricane area and she told me.

Cynthia: "If I have pancreatic cancer, I'm not going anywhere."

"Don't think like that get yourself Home where your family is and because you are all alone there and don't think just because you may have pancreatic cancer you can just give up on life because every minute counts."

Willie had just got out the hospital about three weeks ago and was about to have surgery on his head having a tube running from his head into his stomach so the fluid can run from his brain into his stomach.

His surgery was to be that coming Thursday and hurricane Irma was on its way it was also headed to South Georgia where my mom lives in my hometown. So, our son Ramono went to get her for me while I got the guest room ready which was also Willie's man cave. Willie was asleep as I was finishing cleaning he woke-up and asked me what was I doing? I told him about my mom was on her way and as I was saying it, Ramono showed-up with my mom.

Willie: "Who is that? What are they doing Here?"

I told him and he still didn't remember anything, I saw something wrong with him that night, so I recorded him plus I asked him some questions to see where his mind was, I recorded the whole conversation. The next morning, he had a doctor appointment he asked me again about why my mom was here, so I played the recording.

Willie: "I don't want to hear anything."

"Why because you didn't remember your own son? Or was it because you didn't remember our wedding anniversary or the year we got married?"

Willie: "No I don't because it makes me look like a fool."

"I recorded it because you always tell me I was lying so I decided to let you hear for yourself."

My sister came home after she was let out of the hospital, I told her to come home she had a friend that was going to drive her home but that morning they was to leave her friend decided not to come so my sister Cynthia drove all the way home as sick as she was by herself. No one could go and get her because they wouldn't let anyone in Fla., she made it home.

Why Are My Walls Wet?

The night Irma hit I went in the guest room where my mom slept, we lived on the first floor of three floors. I went in the room where my mom was to talk to her. I saw out of the corner of my eye, and I saw my walls, I asked myself.

"Why is my walls wet I don't have a roof?"

The next morning, I called the complex office and made a report, maintenance came to check it out. When he came to checks the walls in the rooms and then he checked the closet that was when he said.

Maintenance: "Mrs. Holliman, your walls and carpet are wet we need you to empty your closet so we can fix it."

It was just a few days before Willie was to have his surgery. My mind was on that and not the walls or closet. I asked my mom to stay here with me for a few days so she could stay with our birds while Willie was in the hospital his surgery was that Thursday she stayed until that Monday when Ramono took her back home after the storm.

Why are my walls yet?

That Saturday Ramono and his now ex-wife Shane came over to help me clear out the closet. Sandy and I was in the Livingroom when I heard.

Ramono: "Momma, I need you to come here."

As I get in the room, he said,

Ramono: "You got black mold I know because when I worked for our apartment, I had to take a class on mold, and this is what this is."

As he was talking, I said I had to get out of there because the smell was so bad. I ran in the Livingroom he came out and asked me if I had a mask, I gave him one. The smell went all over the apartment, I heard him coughing and then he came out of the room and said he couldn't take it. He also told me to hurry and close your bedroom door to protect the birds.

I call the office to report the mold problem it took them about four hours to come after I called a total of three times and Ramono went to the office to report it also. I couldn't breathe, I was dizzy, and I had a big headache I was getting extremely sick. We had to open the door to the Livingroom so I could breathe. Hours later Mindy from the office came to look at the room after the maintenance man came in to check things out, he went outside to call her. She came in the apartment, and she went into the room I was so dizzy I stayed in the Livingroom. Mindy and Ramono was in the room talking I overheard her so I mustered-up some strength and went in the office that was off from the Livingroom and I talked with her. She told me to just close the door and wait until that Monday.

"I can't stay in here don't you smell that odor coming out of this room. There is no way I can stay here."

Mindy: "There is nothing wrong with you staying here if you close the door."

"There is no way I can, or I am going to stay here with this smell. You need to do something."

Mindy: "Can you stay with your son until Monday?"

"What if I didn't have no one to stay with then what?"

Mindy: "Can you stay with your son?"

I asked my family could I come and stay with them for a few days, they said yes so, I gathered up some stuff very quickly and left with the birds. Remember Willie was still in the hospital after having his surgery when we found the Mold.

Again, why are my walls wet?

See how the box is wet, well this because water was coming in for years.

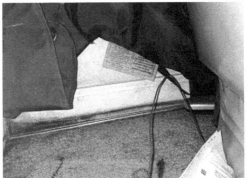

This is what my son found when he was cleaning out this closet because of the wet walls.

This is when they tore out the walls

This is in the master bedroom and dining room. Years earlier we had mold problems a few times see around the plug in the master bedroom. They used a machine when they cut the wall from the first-time years ago. You can see where they cut around the socket. And the other picture is the dining room, see the mold in the corner.

These two pictures are of the living room by the patio door. The one on the left is before I pulled back the carpet and the right one is after I pulled the carpet back to see how bad the mold is in this spot.

This report teaches us something about mold. I pulled it up just the way it is from this website.

https://www.medicinenet.com/mold_exposure/article.htm

Source: Getty Images

What is mold?

Molds are various types of fungi (singular = fungus) that grow in filaments and reproduce by forming spores that can travel through the air. The term mildew refers to some kinds of mold, particularly mold in the home with a white or grayish color or mold growing in shower stalls and bathrooms. Mold may grow indoors or outdoors and thrives in damp, warm, and humid environments. Mold exists in essentially any environment or season.

The most common types of household mold found indoors include Cladosporium, Penicillium, Alternaria, and Aspergillus. Stachybotryschartarum (also known as Stachybotrys atra and sometimes referred to as "black mold") is a greenish-black indoor mold, although it is less common than the other types of mold found in homes. Black mold grows on household surfaces that have high cellulose content, such as wood, fiberboard, gypsum board, paper, dust, and lint. There are types of mold that can grow on substances as different as foods and carpet.

Molds reproduce by forming tiny spores that are not visible to the naked eye. Mold spores are very hardy and can survive under conditions in which mold cannot grow, such as in dry and harsh environments. These spores travel through outdoor and indoor air. When the mold spores in the air land on a surface where moisture is present, mold can then start to grow.

Outdoors, molds play a role in the decomposition of organic material such as dead trees, compost, and leaves. They are most common in damp, dark areas or areas of decomposing plant life. People often find mold indoors in basements or shower stalls. Indoor mold in residential areas has the potential to cause health problems and can destroy surfaces and objects where it grows.

Where does mold grow in homes?

Although bathrooms (particularly shower stalls) and basements are typical moist areas prone to mold growth, any moist area in the home can be moldy. Drywall, ceiling tiles, carpets, furniture, ductwork, roofing, paneling, wallpaper, under sinks, and the areas around plumbing pipes are examples of areas in the home that can harbor mold if the ideal growing conditions are present.

Mold spores from the outdoor air can enter the home through open doors, windows, and vents. It may also become attached to clothing, shoes, and pets and therefore be carried indoors.

Mold can have many different colors (including brown, green, and black) and sometimes appears as spots. Additionally, a musty odor may be present. Mold growth may hide underneath carpeting, on the backside of wallpaper, and behind drywall or wall paneling. Mold thrives in saunas, greenhouses, and construction areas.

What are the health risks of mold exposure? What are symptoms and signs of mold allergy?

Molds produce irritating substances that may act as allergy causing substances (allergens) in sensitive individuals. Furthermore, some molds produce toxic substances known as mycotoxins, but mold itself is not poisonous or toxic. The term "toxic mold," therefore, refers to the fact that certain kinds of mold can produce mycotoxins. The conditions under which some molds produce toxins is not understood, and the presence of mold, even a mold that is capable of producing toxins, does not always imply that toxins are being produced or that a health risk or problem is present. Mold may not cause any health problems, or it may lead to allergy or other symptoms in people, including adults and children, who are sensitive to molds.

Allergic reactions to mold are the most common health effects of mold and are therefore the greatest health risk related to mold. Allergic reactions may happen immediately or develop after a period following exposure. Both growing mold and mold spores may lead to allergic reactions. Symptoms and signs of mold allergy may include sneezing, runny nose, coughing,

Allergic reactions to mold are the most common health effects of mold and are therefore the greatest health risk related to mold. Allergic reactions may happen immediately or develop after a period following exposure. Both growing mold and mold spores may lead to allergic reactions. Symptoms and signs of mold allergy may include

1.sneezing,
2.runny nose,
3.coughing,
4.wheezing,
5.watery eyes,
6.redness of the eyes,
7.itchy eyes,
8.skin irritation, or rash.

Mold or mold spores may cause asthma attacks in people who have asthma and are allergic to mold. Even in some nonallergic individuals, mold can cause symptoms of irritation in the eyes, skin, and airways. For example, the "black mold" Stachybotrys, along with some other types of mold, produces toxins known as mycotoxins that can cause irritation of the skin and airways in susceptible individuals.

Sometimes, people may develop severe reactions to mold exposure. Symptoms of severe reactions, which are uncommon, include fever and difficulty breathing. People with compromised immune systems or patients with chronic lung disease can develop serious infections of the lungs due to molds.

It is not possible to predict the degree of severity of the health risks associated with mold in the home. Allergic individuals vary in their degree of susceptibility to mold, and any symptoms and health risks also depend upon the extent and exact type of mold that is present.

In 2004 guidelines update in 2009, the Institute of Medicine (IOM) reported there was sufficient evidence to link indoor exposure to mold with upper respiratory tract symptoms, cough, and wheezing in otherwise healthy people, although the report stated that was no evidence that mold causes medical conditions like asthma, bronchitis, or other respiratory conditions. Mold also worsens asthma symptoms in people who have asthma. Mold was also reported to be linked to hypersensitivity pneumonitis in individuals susceptible to this immunologic condition. This uncommon disease is similar to pneumonia and can develop in susceptible individuals after brief or prolonged exposure to mold, but there has been no conclusive evidence to prove this relationship.

Chapter 32

WHERE DO WE GO FROM HERE?

As I was saying, Willie was in the hospital having surgery, I was all alone. My son Ramono had to work he came after he got off from work, it was hard being by myself doing the surgery it was a little ruff for a minute with him, but they got things under control.

One good but sad thing that happened while I was waiting on Willie to come out of surgery. A friend called me, and we were talking I told her about my sister just finding out she had pancreatic cancer. She asked me what her symptoms was I told her, she then told me that she was having some of these symptoms she said that she was going back to the doctors and insist they do more test like my sister. She did and she found out that she had ovarian cancer and she died within two years.

I had fourteen things on my plate at that time. Out of all of them I only like to four of them which was my faith, my family, my friends, and myself. But to live I had to eat the rest when needed to survive. Sometimes we must do what we need to do to survive even if it means we don't like everything we have to eat, but to stay alive we must eat it. That's what a true Survivor will do!

Let's see some of them, I had nowhere to lay my head, no I had no pillow to lay my head on. Willie was in the hospital from surgery, I was sleeping on my son's sofa which I am still doing at this very time.

My husband went to rehab for rehabilitation after he left the hospital, my sister dying from pancreatic cancer just got back home and she was in the hospital about forty-five miles from my husband. Not knowing where we going to live.

That Monday Mindy called and told me that they were going to put a machine in our apartment to pull the moisture out of the air. I asked her to please have them do an air quality test before they do anything, she said she will.

That night I got a call from one of my neighbors about 10:00p.m., she asked me what was going on, where am I? I explained everything to her, she then told me that she saw two men hanging around my apartment. And that my curtains were open, and my lights was on, and people can see everything in my place. I got upset and said I was on my way she also called the police we both got there at the same time. I unlocked the door while they went in and then they let me in when I walked in there not only was lights was on but the door to my bedroom was open and that mean the smell and the mold had gotten in the other end of the apartment.

I had a freezer in the guestroom it was full of food like stakes, lamb shops, and other kind of meats and other food like cakes which I baked homemade, and other foods. As I entered the guestroom not only was the air machine not running and they unplugged my freezer. My stuff was ruining because of the mold spores flew everywhere that Saturday and by them opening all my doors they ruined everything. I was upset because the way they disrespect my stuff.

That next morning, I went to see my husband in rehab and after I left there, I went to see my sister in the hospital downtown in the city. By the time I left my sister's side I had a severe headache and I needed to eat and sleep, but I also needed to handle my business about our apartment. I went in the office to speak with the office manager, and she didn't like me coming in and talking to her.

I asked her what they were going to do about where we were going to stay. She told me that I could stay in the apartment I told her.

"How could we stay in that apartment when all that mold was in there?"

Office Manager Keisha: "Mrs. Holliman you if you feel you can't stay there then you can move upstairs in another apartment."

"How can we move into another apartment upstairs when we live in a handicap apartment, you know we can't live upstairs, and besides what are we going to sleep on?"

Keisha: "You can move your stuff in there?'

"Are you crazy with all that mold on it, we can't take that stuff, I had it closed off and your people went and opened everything and let the mold go on and into everything. I don't think so!"

Keisha: "I have been dealing with mold for many years and I know my job."

"I asked Mindy would you'll please do an air quality test and she said you all would, I also asked her if you all not touch anything until it is done, and she said you all would. I come down last night to find out about the mass that was done to my place and how my stuff was handled. Then to find out that they have went and cut the wall out without doing the air test."

Keisha: "It's our place and we can do whatever we want to and how we want to do it."

"Yes, but as long as my stuff is in there and we are paying the rent I have the right to protect my stuff. Did you all get the air test done?"

Keisha: "Yes we did let me go and call him and see what he found."

When she came back, she told me that the man said he did not do the test because he only does it when he is told, and they did not tell him to do one.

"I need to know what kind of mold it is."

Keisha: "Mrs. Holliman, you just need to know everything."

"No, I don't need to know my doctor told me to find out what kind of mold it is."

She then said that everyone got problems and my problems is no different from anyone else. And I need to stop needing to know everything.

"Let me ask you, what if it was you wouldn't you want to know what kind of mold it is?"

Keisha: "No I wouldn't!"

"That's your problem, and as for me having problems like everyone else, that's their problem because right now I don't care about them because I need to take care of my problem and the problem is the reason is why my husband is in the shape he is in now."

She looked at me and said,

Keisha: "Well, what do you want us to do about it?"

"What are you going to do about it?"

Keisha: "You needed to tell us what you want to do."

"We need somewhere to stay."

Keisha: "We will put you all up in a hotel."

"What about food because all our food was in our apartment, and it were ruined."

Keisha: "We will call and make arrangement for the room."

The next day I told her will wait until my husband come out of rehab because he will need somewhere to sleep. As she was saying something, I told her I had a headache, and I don't do business with a headache I will get back with her later.

That Thursday Willie had the rehab call me so he could tell me that he wanted, out and for me to come and get him tomorrow. I was thinking what to do and how I was going to do it because we did not have a place to lay our head or clothes to wear. I called the apartment office and told them Willie was getting out the next day so I will need that room.

When I got to rehab to pick him up the first thing, Willie said to me was,

Willie: "You are acting just like Betty Jean your dad's wife because you didn't want to come to get me out of here."

I looked at him for thinking like that when I am working hard as I can to get things done for us both and for him to compare me with her was not fair. No, I didn't let it get to me because I start singing to myself by tuning him out.

I brought him to our son's house to see the birds, then we went to the hotel to check in. A week later we got our checkout bill under the door about 4:00a.m., I called the apartment office to see what was going on no answer, so we packed everything up and put it on the cart and we were about to checkout then the office called to update our stay. About four days later it happened again, I had to call for the same thing. Then days later this time, I put everything on the cart and took it to the car then as I took the key to the front desk, they said my complex called and extended our stay.

Again, this time I asked the hotel could they hold our stuff until we come back so I went to the office and asked what was going on and we were told that everything was ready, and we can move back in our apartment. Now we were told that they were going to clean everything and at this time we were told all we must do is clean. I told Mindy that day that we were not going to move back in that apartment because of my health she told me.

Mindy: "What do he know he have not been in the apartment, and he don't know anything about mold."

"He knows me, and he knows my health and when he told me that I need to leave everything there and start over because of my health meaning I cannot take anything with me."

Mindy: "We are not going to do anything else for you guys, beside Keisha is not here so I can't okay anything."

"You know what I am not going to let you all kill me don't even worry about it we will just go and get our stuff."

We left and stop at the mailbox, and we went back to the hotel to get our stuff and take it to my son's house. I walked in the hotel going to our room it was right behind the front desk as I was walking to the room, I spoke to the people that I saw without really paying attention Willie came in behind me, I heard someone say.

Mindy: "Mr. Willie it's so good to see you we have been so worried about you how are you doing?"

"Mrs. Holliman see, I am here to extend your stay."

"Oh, did she give you the gift card also?"

Mindy: "I have not spoken with Keisha."

"Oh, really okay!"

We went to the room as we were talking, we both said to each other.

Willie & Janice: "You see how she lied about her not being able to do anything without Keisha's okay? Yeah, and Here she beat us to the hotel."

Just think all those hoops we had to jump just for them to do the right thing. Let me tell you how we have paid rental insurance for years, I had our insurance company to send someone to come and check the apartment. I waited in the apartment for about two hours I was wearing a hazard suit from head to toe plus hazard mask and glasses. The mold got me even wearing what I had on, I passed out from the mold.

When he got there, we looked and talked about the apartment, he said that he needed to see them in the office to find out what cause the damage to the apartment. I waited for days for the report and a check. I made two calls before I could speak with him, he told me that Keisha said that they got everything and that means they wasn't going to pay anything.

That made me so mad I asked him.

"You mean to tell me that for many years we paid for rental insurance and when it comes down to it you mean to tell me they end-up being your client instead of us?"

You tell me what would you have said, what would you have done? I wrote the main office and told them what happened with Keisha, that she had no right telling my insurance company not to pay us anything. I let them know how angry I was and need them to handle the situation.

They wrote me back to we given an apartment, but I turned it down, they said our apartment was ready to move back in, but I refuse to do that also. They were not going to handle anything any different.

So, I wrote them back and I told them this.

"First of all, I did not refuse anything, what she offered was an apartment on the second floor and we could not go up the steps because we were living in a handicap apartment so there is no way we can live upstairs. And as for us moving back in the same apartment, I am waiting on a report from housing, plus my doctor told me that I had to move and start over because of my health."

Why I Could Not, No Can Not Wear Any of My Clothes?

I remember the first few days I was at my son's house while my husband was in rehab I went and got some of my clothes. I put them in the downstairs closet and my son told me the next morning that I had to take my clothes out of his house because the mold was so strong, so I had to take them out by putting them in a plastic bag and put them in the garage.

"Keisha I can't wear any of my clothes."

Keisha: "All you had to do is wash them."

"90% of my clothes is dry clean only."

Keisha: "Give them to me and I will have them clean."

I had thirty pieces of clothes it took about two months before she called me about the clothes finally, asked.

Keisha: "Should I put them in the apartment closet?"

"Why, are you going to put clean clothes back in mold?"

I knew I could not wear those clothes because mold bed themselves in all fabrics and I had tried to wear some of my clothes I had after the mold, I found out I was very much affected by being in the mold.

It didn't matter if I wore hazarded suits from head to toe, I still cannot wear any of my clothes. It also affects my husband he can't be around mold at all either, each time we put on anything with any kind of mold on it we react to it badly and each time I got back in the car Willie would have a bad reaction.

My reaction range from itching to can't breathe. There are some days I can look like I am dead, my skin breaks out, it turns dark, it burns, it's dry, having bruises and more. It also ran my blood pressure up which I had gotten off my blood pressure medication because of my weight loss. But since the mold I notice it keeps going up until one day I had the worst headache. As I was driving, I got extremely sick.

"Willie, I have to pull over to the fire station to check out how my high blood pressure is."

When I got there, they took my blood pressure. It was extremely high to the point they took me to the ER to get it down I had to end-up back on blood pressure medication till this day.

We had to go to pick-up our mail out of our mailbox and we would run into some of our neighbors from time to time. They would tell us that they had mold also and I would share with them what I found out. One of our neighbors told us that they put them in another apartment due to mold for two weeks. We told her what happened to us and how we were affected, how bad and dangerous mold is, I told her that she needs to wash their clothes again.

"We can't do that because of our health, I am having a problem breathing while I am standing here talking with you because I can smell and feel the effect at this time, we need to go because I am feeling dizzy."

After a month in the hotel, I were in the store, and I got a call from Keshia the office manager.

Keisha: "We are not paying for your hotel anymore."

She said it with a smart mouth way. After we left the hotel, we had to move in with our son and Shane. I didn't say anything because I was hungry, and I had another headache which I had for three days after I had to go back in the apartment for some especially important papers. Each time I came out of that apartment I had to take two baths from head to toe. I had to throw the clothes I had on in the trash, this shows I could never wear any of my clothes I had in my apartment which it was a lot.

They said they did an air quality test and it passed, they lied because they said that they did a test on our kitchen, and dining room inside and outside. Not true! Because there is no, outside to those two rooms because there is another apartment on the other side of my walls.

There are two Reports made: 'The one they had done. And the one We had done.' They were about five months apart.

Please look for them in the back of the book.

You will see the different between the two. You will if they had cleaned our apartment so well how could there be so much different between the two. You will be able to learn that what people say about cleaning mold is not totally true, especially for some people.

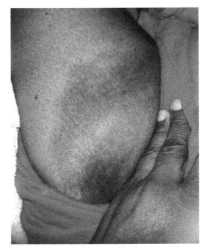

I have these bruises popping up times at any every were.

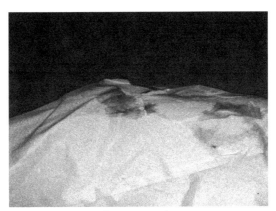

This comes from my throat at time

See how thin my hair is because of the mold.

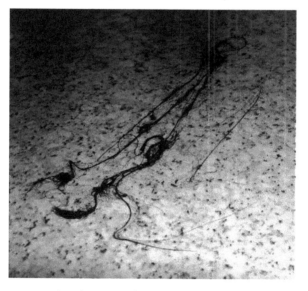

See how my hair is coming out.

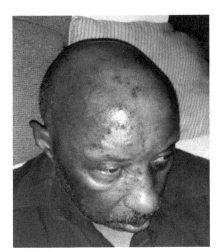 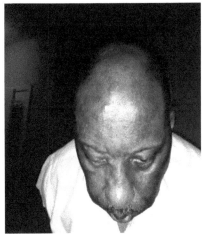

These two pictures are some of the things that was happening to his just like his skin and face changed so did he change. What was going on affect him both inside and outside? He felt worse than he looked.

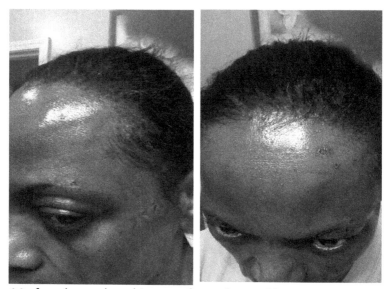

My face keeps breaking out from the mold anytime I come around it. This any type of mold can affect me.

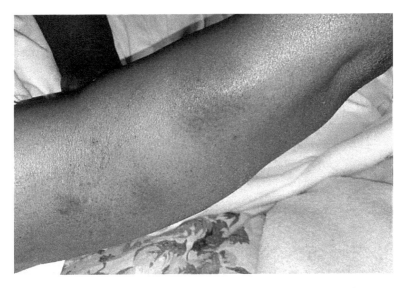

Bruise from the effect of any type of mold till this day.

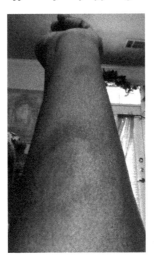

Bruise from the effect after the mold.

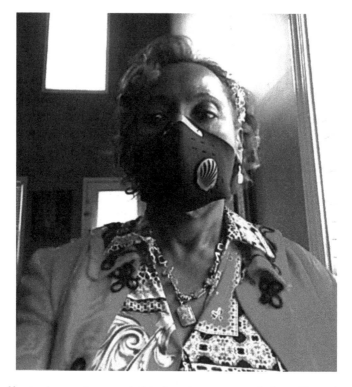

It affected me also, and this is what some of the effect done to me.

My word is Self-Control this time.
Dictionary's View: Self- Control is willpower, restraint, self-discipline, cool, coolness, calmness, self-restraint, self-mastery, strength of mind or will. The keeping of one's thoughts and emotions to oneself.

Biblical View: Self-Control is the proper emotional condition which promotes well-being. "Calm heart is the life of the fleshly organism." "A man of discernment is cool of spirit," controlling one's emotions.

Let me see how I will focus on having the will power control my emotion, to strengthening my mind, being calm at heart and treat others by mastering my emotions.

This were I sleep for the past 2 years because we cannot keep going up the steps in my son's house. After we had lost our Home and everything, we own due to the mold.

✐ *Chapter   33* ✐

LOSING EVERYTHING WE OWN

Five months had gone by and we still staying with our son and still paying rent for the apartment. We finally got out of our lease this was after I called housing to come and check out the apartment. They did and told me that we could not live there, and he said the walls was wet this was around October that year. We waited on the report, but we never got it, so I called them, they said that there was nothing wrong with the apartment by the supervisor of that department. I told her after she fused at me about the guy's report and I told her what he said, and I had proof of that which I made her very mad then I told her.

"You need to come and check out this for yourself."

We got a letter saying she was coming to inspect the apartment some time from 9:00a.m.- 1:00p.m. Which in December it was very cold snow was on the ground and we could not set in the apartment, so we had to set in the car from 8:45a.m. until she came. It was so cold we set there for hours then just before 12:00p.m., I wrote a note stating how cold it was and we have set and waited for hours as I opened the car door to take a put the note on the door, I got a call from the gate it was her. I let her in, and she came up to the apartment I got out of the car being incredibly careful with my cane because I couldn't use my roller walker on the ice, we don't get just snow we always get ice with it.

She got out the car I spoke to her, but she didn't say a word, so I dropped my keys on purpose. She came around me and then I walked behind her we both went up to the door as I opened the door, she said oh this is your apartment. We were in there for a while, and I had to stick my head out of the door after I showed her around the smell was so bad. We left then there was a letter sent to us and the office, but I didn't anything about it until I went to pay rent and we went to the mailbox, and I saw the letter which said we work had to be done within a few days which had passed.

I went back to the office and showed Mindy the letter.

Mindy: "We got ours two weeks ago."

"Mindy why you all didn't call us?"

They let the date pass and they have not done anything about the request. I told Mindy to call housing and let them know that I didn't know anything about the letter and so I could not do anything inspector supervisor wanted me to do. I told Mindy to call first thing the next morning and get things cleared-up. Even though she told me I had nothing to worry about I didn't trust her or them.

They did call them, and things got straight. They didn't get things done like they should so months later I received a call to let me know that they have another apartment for us on the first floor. We asked if we could see it, we they told us the painters were painting which was not true, because we went by, and no one was there they just didn't want us to see the apartment.

"Keisha housing told us to have the apartment air tested before we move in."

Which we did, and I had them to pay for it, I also had them to do an air quality test on the first one and I am glad I did.

"We didn't have anyone to help us move our things and we didn't have the money to put it in storage."

Keshia: "We will have movers there; you all just need to be there also."

I said that because I knew we could not keep anything besides, we could not find anyone who would help or wanted to help we understood, we don't blame them because we didn't want them to get sick. But it would have been nice if someone would have offered, before that month earlier we asked some friends if they could help us move something out so they could shampoo the floors only one person can help. Ramono help the day before because he had something to do the day of, we move a lot that day and we got rid of a lot too.

On the day we move, that was the day we lost everything, it was sad because when you see all your things going to the dumpster hurts. I was okay with that the only thing that really hurt was losing my clothes, see I since I have lost weight, I had new clothes mostly dress clothes, 90% was dry clean only.

They wanted me to show them what to move first, so I did but two minutes in the apartment I had to run out. I told them I could only be outside next to the truck as they brought everything out. The first items were my clothes I took pictures of everything they brought out. About fifth teen minutes later I noticed I could not breathe, and it was cool and windy, so I told them that I had to be fifty or more feet away from our things and I had to be up-wind. I see forty years of our life haul to the dumpster wow, wow, wow.

I learned something that day it's okay loosing material things even my clothes. It's only stuff and it don't really matter our life does. We had three trucks and two cars to load up from eight rooms and four closets. It took us all day to trips to the dumpster, but we don't think it all went to the dumpster. Because we overheard them say they was going to keep somethings plus they still had items on the truck when they came back for the second load.

When we were waiting on them to come back for the second load, I went to visit one of the neighbors the one that had a mold problem themselves. When I walked in the front door, I could feel the effect of the mold hitting me as I stepped in the Livingroom and I was going down to the floor, so I rush out and I told her I had to leave because of the mold that was still in there. I don't know what happened to them we have not talked in about a year I hope they got out.

I never told them about us having it done on the first apartment, the difference is amazing. We had it done months after they called themselves doing the remediation, see for yourself. This was months later, and the floors was still wet after they supposed to have clean them. The air quality person asks me why was the floors wet, it was so long I forgot they said they was going to clean the floors but that was about six weeks or more so they should have dried right?

As for the second apartment air quality test it was lower, and he said that could be to them working and cleaning. I set down and wrote a letter or contract that if we find any sign of mold no matter how small it was, we will be moving without any problems. One day we went in after we moved items in which was boxes because we didn't have anything else to put in there. We notice they did not put new kitchen appliances in as they promise so we went back and fore on that issue. They did not clean the apartment like they should the air vents was dirty and more like body hair in the bathroom which we had to keep after them about. I was not going to clean someone else's nasty mass.

One day I took some friends over to see the new apartment to see if they could smell the mold. As we were walking down the wall, I had to give them the key and I had to turn around and go back to my car.

Carol & Pam: "We didn't smell anything."

As they were saying that I could not breathe so one of them got my inhaler for me. After I got home one of them called me and told me they were sick.

"What are you feeling?"

She told me how she felt. I said that was the mold and I told her what to do. This showed me I was not crazy, or I was not trying to be mean I only was making sure we survive. By not getting any sicker but it didn't help because just walking up to the door made me sick.

One day when it was raining awfully hard, Willie and I stopped by the new apartment to check-up on things, we couldn't go in because the mold smell were so bad, we turn around came home and I set down and wrote a letter to let them know we were not going to keep that apartment, she let us out the lease with no problem, but the stuff that was in there we couldn't keep it either.

Again, please read their mold report and compare it to my mold report.

These pictures are from the day we move all our stuff out of our apartment of 10 years, after five months after we found the mold. These are just some of what we lost. These are some of the pictures and stuff we lost on moving day.

My word for at this time is Faith.
Dictionary's View: To have faith is to believe that (someone or something) deserves to be trusted. Kids want their parents to always have in faith them. We want them to say we have or had faith in us.

Biblical View: Paul wrote: "With the heart" one exercises faith. This is why Paul word that "faith is not a possession of all people." Even Peter urges us to 'supply to our faith virtue, knowledge, self-control, endurance, godly devotion, brotherly affection, and love.'

'As for me I want to have a receptive heart, so I will be on the lookout. I plan to show a waiting attitude toward everything and everybody that I come in contact.'

∽ *Chapter 34* ∽

WHAT IN THE WORLD DID SHE DO?

As you know about the mold issue well by my lung doctor sent me to the hospital to have a procedure done on my lung to see if they could find mold. While I was at the hospital, this is what happened the nurse was prepping for the procedure. I told her like I always tell everyone for whatever they do by saying.

"Do Not stick me in my wrist or the back of my hands because I have fibromyalgia, it is very sensitive with pain."

Which she said OKAY, she wiped my upper left arm and stuck me, but she couldn't get the IV needle in, then switched arms and she had the same problem with my right arm. I repeated to her.

"Do Not stick me in my wrist or the back of my hands."

IV Nurse: "I will not."

"Really Do Not stick me there."

She starts wiping down my wrist and the back of my hand. I told her again, but she told me.

IV Nurse: "I am not going to stick you in your wrist I am just wiping it down."

"Okay as long as you know."

I turn my head and I was about to say something to her the next thing I heard was a loud scream came out of me. I look down as I grab the bed with my left hand because of my quick reflex, because I didn't want to knock her out. Anyway, she didn't say a word she just pulled the needle out, and she just walked out.

"What in The World Did She Do? She stuck me it was in my wrist."

There were two more nurses in the room I asked them what her name was, one told me Emma. By that time, another nurse came in and she prepped the IV needle and she got it in on the first try. Then she checked my blood pressure and she said it jump about thirty points, so she had to give me something to bring it down.

They did the procedure I went home; days went by I was still in pain; weeks went by the pain was worse. It was over a month when I decided to call the hospital and let them know what happened and to see what they were going to do to help. When I called, they told me someone will call me back, it was days when that happened.

It was in December while Willie and myself was on the way to see my sister who was were in the hospital and they pulled fluid off her left lung. Someone called me but I told them I was driving, and I could not talk business at that time, and would he call me back at another time.

We Went Home to For a Funeral

Willie and I went to my hometown because my dad's baby sister just died her funeral was that day. Willie was not feeling well that day, but I couldn't leave him home because he could not stay alone because of the TIAs, he kept on; keep having.

We didn't make it to the funeral Willie went and laid down and went to sleep, while I was cooking, I then woke him so he could eat. He didn't know where he was, he asked so many questions I knew, he was having another TIA, so I called 911.

When they got there, they realized what shape he was in, so they took him to the ER I always say that hospital is only good enough to put a band-aid on its patient. I brought him back to the house the next morning when he was woken, because I needed to know what was going on, he was having a TIA at that time, I recorded our conversation so if I need to, I could play it back.

Two weeks later my sister died on December 25th, we had her funeral; I saw my brothers and sister from another mother whom I have not seen since we were kids for all of them except one. With this funeral I have had a total of nine funeral seven of them was within eight months.

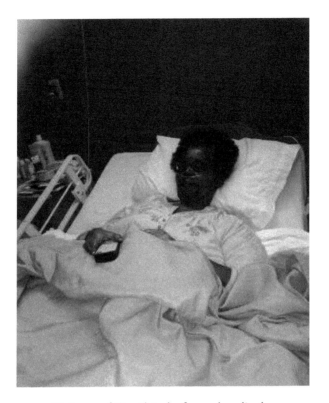

Picture of Cynthia before she died.

After the funeral I called again but I didn't get to talk to anyone, I called again the same thing no one to talk too. Because I was in so much pain, I decided that I needed help, so I called Dr. Calming office to make an appointment to have a nerve test done. Dr. Calming did the test, and he did find nerve damage, so he sent me to a hand surgeon name Dr. Watts.

The word is Goodness I wonder how good kind I be.
Dictionary's View: Goodness is the quality or state of being kind, honest, generous, helpful, useful, or effective.

Biblical View: Goodness also involves moral excellence and virtue, without badness or rottenness. Goodness is clear by its beneficial effect on others. It is an active, positive quality manifested in helpful deeds. For hardly would anyone die for a righteous man, though perhaps for a good man someone my dare to die.

Since goodness is a part of the fruitage of the spirit, is a positive quality. I will display goodness when I do good and let it be a beneficial act toward others. As long, as I enjoy peace and happiness, I have one standard of goodness and I know where I need to look for the knowledge of good and bad which I will do.

⬿ *Chapter 35* ⬿

HAVING NERVE DAMAGE

I really need to find out what she did to me, I wonder if she damaged my nerve. They haven't call me, so I had to call back I decided to call them back and I got the run around and I called again, and I got the run around again. I want them to do something about the pain but that did not happen, so I decided to go and see my own neurologist Dr. Calming. To have a nerve test done to let me know if it was nerve damage and it was, he sent me to see a hand surgeon his name was Dr. Watts.

I went to see him, and he looked at the test it did show I did have a problem that was very painful. Dr. Calming told me that I had Corbel Tonal in both of my hand, but the nerve damage had nothing to do with my corbel tonal.

Dr. Watts told me he would do the surgery I had the right hand done first because that's where all my pain was coming from and that was the reason why I was there it hurt so bad I was not myself. As I was waiting for my surgery that April Willie became sick, so we set my surgery when everything was cleared.

While he was in the hospital at the time, I found out the date of my surgery which was good because he would be in the hospital, and I would not have to worry about him while I had my surgery. But it didn't happen the way I planned. But I did have it at the end of May that year.

The pain was so bad when each time I went into the office I told him how bad my wrist was hurting. He told me what he was going to do with my wrist he said.

Dr. Watts: "I see the knot on your wrist, and it do show on the report that it is nerve damage."

"I know and it is very painful I have to wear a glove to keep anything it from touching it because when it does the pain run up and down my hand."

After I had the surgery it felt better, he had told me what he was going to do by saying.

Dr. Watts: "I am going to use a device to wrap that nerve."

"Okay I hope it will work."

During the surgery when he opens my wrist, he saw that I had enough fat in my wrist so he took some and wrap the nerve with my own fat the said because I am allergic to so many things, he felt it was much safer to use my, own fat because I would not be allergic to my own fat.

Dr. Watts: "I went to a convention this past weekend, and I talked about you I told them how much pain you were in and to see you know you are a totally different person because of the pain you had from your wrist. I know you had corbel tonal also, but you didn't care about that it was that confounded nerve in your wrist. I am glad you came to me this was lesson for me and the other doctors enjoy your story."

"Wow you talk about me and telling me that you felt that my nerve damage was a situation that they enjoyed and learn something from it, but I didn't tell you how bad it got, one day I was heating a cup of tea I open the door and stuck my hand in the microwave. When I did it knot me to the floor that pain was so bad, it hit me. Every time I got near the microwave it would hurt much more than usual and I would put my hand behind my back to stop the pain."

Dr. Watts: "The microwave was off, and it still made you drop to the floor. Wow I would never think a microwave being off cause that kind of pain."

"Yes, it did, and it really hurt so bad."

I did therapy for a while, about three months later I start noticing the pain was increasing I realized the wrapping it with my own fat did not work. I was supposed to have been getting ready to have my left hand done for corbel tonal also, but I couldn't until I get nerve damage done in my right hand. Until it felt better so I could use it while my left hand heals.

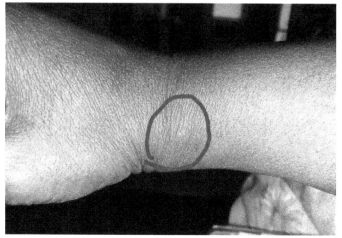

This is where the nurse stuck me in my nerve

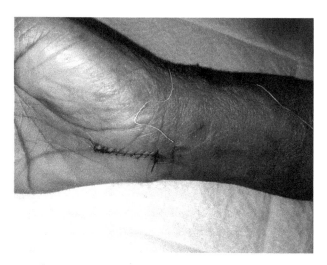

This is my right wrist after the first surgery.

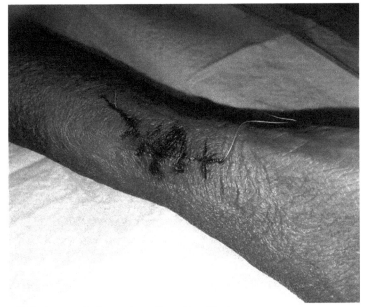

This is my right wrist after the first surgery, on my nerve damage.

I end up waiting until the next year to have my right wrist redone because of the severe pain. After many months we did set date to have the right wrist redone surgery. He told me that he would have to also cut my ligament in my thumb because if he didn't, he would have to go back in and cut it because I would end-up with scar tissue. He told me that he had to order a device made from pork. When he told me pork, I asked him would the pork mess with my blood pressure, he told me no it wouldn't.

I went home and it bother me the whole week when I went in for my next visit, I asked him again and he said no it shouldn't because a device and not food. I said OKAY, but I was not totally sure of that because if I eat anything like pork, watermelon, raisins, or grapes, they all will run up my blood pressure. I really do know how my body reacts to things and I should have listened to myself because it was warning me, but I did not listen. I went ahead and had it put in and I learn not long after how it really works.

I had the surgery and while my hand was healing, I ate some pork bacon. I could only eat one bite because what I feared came true it does run it up. I did tell him by asking him.

"Do you remember me asking you if that pork device would mess with my blood pressure?"

Dr. Watts: "I do, it won't."

"Sorry to tell you but you were wrong."

Dr. Watts: "Janice you are easy to have reaction to a lot of stuff this prove it to me."

So now I am learning how to eat pork again that mean I can only eat a bite or two before I feel my pressure rise. Sometimes it makes my head hurt every time I eat any pork or anything that cause it to rise, I really hate this which mean I have to be incredibly careful I was off blood pressure medication but due to the mold which caused it to rise.

Six weeks later I had my left hand done for the corbel tonal. As for my right hand I still have problem with it sometimes I still wear gloves, so the nerves won't cause so much pain. And as for the ligament in my thumb it hurts all the time, sometimes I can't use this hand like I wish. But I am doing my best to deal with it, the best way I can. Sometimes I can't cook which I love or typing on my laptop. I still remember the last words he said.

Dr. Watts: "Janice I was so glad to help you. Now that you have your surgeries done and they healed well if you need me, please let me know. And now that you have had your surgeries you can move on with your life."

Just thinking about those words made me think, this is me and my pain. I need to do what I need to do to move on every day I have to live with the pain.

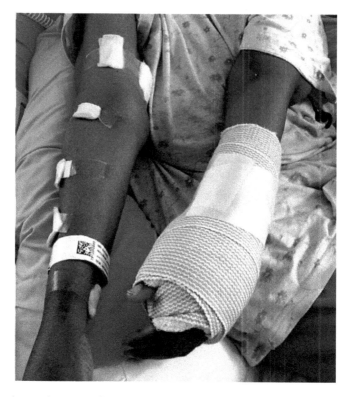

*See how they stuck me so many times for my left right hand.
And see how many times they stuck me because they could not
stick me in my wrist or the back of my hand.*

My word for the week is Love

Dictionary's View: Love is when the best and worst thing about love is that it cannot be expressed in word. When one genuinely loves someone, it may be hard to express those emotions, through words.

Biblical View: "Love builds up." When parents are generous in expressing love to our children we are, in effect, imitation our Grand Creator.

I am so thankful that I was an encouragement to our son because parental love and attention lay a firm foundation for my child as he grew it help him to develop and it made him responsible and mature adult to me that was and still is very important.

∞ Chapter 36 ∞

WILLING HAVING SEIZURE

In 2017 that April notice Willie acting strange he kept asking me the same questions over and over and he was not remembering anything. I look at him and I asked him to take an aspirin to help stop what was about to happen, but he wouldn't, and this is what happened.

Willie: "I am not going to take anything I am grown, and you can't make me take it."

"You need to take it because you are about to have another TIA."

Willie: "So what if I do?"

"Ramono, will you come down and ask your dad to take the aspirin so he will not have another TIA?"

Ramono: "What make you think I can make him take an aspirin when you can't, I am not going to do it."

Willie: "I told you I am not taking it; he can't make me take one either." "You are not helping him or me, he would still listen to you just try it."

Ramono went back upstairs and went to sleep, and Willie was still fussing so I looked at him and said,

"Okay do what you want to do if it happened, all I am going to do is call 911. Because I am not going to let you kill me, because you are hardheaded, I am not going to kill myself over you. Mark by words it is going to happen."

About 5:00p.m., Willie was setting watching TV and I saw him jerking, he was jerking so hard like a fish out of water. I called 911 and then I called Ramono down and said see what I was telling you, now I must go and set at the hospital. I was having a sleep test done on me again that day so I drove my car so I could stop by the office to do my sleep test, to let them know I would not be able to take the test and I got some food. As I was on my way to the hospital when I stop at the red lights, I would voice text some of my friends to let them know what happened. They asked him somethings he couldn't answer them because he didn't know what was going on all he knew was his shoulder hurt him very much.

Ramono, came in his car I had him to stay there to answer any questions the doctors may ask or make sure they take good care of him. While I went to call his family to let them know what's going on with him because my phone would not work where, we were at that time. As I return, they had brought Willie back and put him out in the hall, I ran into one of our friends came, he dropped what he was doing to be by Willie's side that was good for him because Willie love people and he is a hugger. As I have said before, he always became a hugger because of his mother showed all her kids real motherly love, so it made him show it to others.

Even though his stepdad was very abusive to them, so was a mom's boy in a good way. Which help him learn how to treat people most of the times, he is set in his ways, and he will not bend especially with his family. At times he became and acted like his stepfather, and I would have to let him know what was happening, and how he was acting. I was not use to this lifestyle growing-up, I lived in a household of sixteen people in a three-bedroom house. I do not remember to this day ever standing in line waiting to get to use the one bathroom in the whole house. I grew-up in a three-generation household and my grandfather was a mean man but he was not mean to his grandkids, he was known as a mean person in my hometown.

I learned some people handle things one way and others handle the same things another way, this is where we are different. He let any and everything get to him, and I have the I don't care attitude meaning I am not going to let anyone, or anything hurt me, or make me sick or kill me. I do care about people because I love helping people before I help myself, I have always been that way.

Willie kept telling us that his arm hurt, when the test came back it showed he shattered his left shoulder. They got him a room he was in the hospital for about a week, and no one came to see him which he began to ask, I notice it had troubled him, so we talk, and I said for him not to let it bother him. I understood how he felt because there was no one to give any support in anyway at that time. I was alone everyday dealing with everything myself by myself. This was what I was telling him about doing the things he needed to help himself and to help me.

When he was to have his surgery which the doctors changed that day of to two days later because the doctors wanted to make sure he had the full staff on duty. Everyone knew what was going on, but no one was there for neither one of us. I decided to stop sending out texts and focus on what was going on we prayed and talked to upbuild each other. Ramono was going through a big problem of his own, his twelve years marriage was ending. I had to also deal with that problem also because she didn't leave the house and moved on with her life, she stayed to torrent him for many months.

Willie had his surgery the doctors came to tell Ramono and myself that it was worse than he thought. He said thought Willie shattered his shoulder in three pieces but when he went in, he saw five pieces, and it was like a puzzle that needed to be put back together.

Dr. Jones: "We will have to wait and see how it will heal if it doesn't heal right, we will have to go back in and put a prosthetic shoulder in."

Ramono: "How will we know if it heals right?"

Dr. Jones: "It he can't raise his arm up high enough."

Well, he can't lift it up the way he should, but he says he is not going to have it done because he does not want to go back in the hospital.

While he was in the hospital, he developed four blood clots, he was bleeding inside and they didn't know where it was coming from, he end-up with and infection, his blood level was low, he had problem with his heart and breathing. They told him he needed a blood transfusion, wow when they said that something happened to him because he never wanted to die.

Willie: "I am not going to take any blood."

This went on for two weeks where they kept telling him he was going to die, he never let them change his mind. They came up with everything in the book, but he never gave in.

He was in the hospital for about three and a half weeks, then he went to rehab, this time he stayed there for a while to get better.

Willie have not been back in the hospital since, but it doesn't mean he still don't have TIAs because he does, it happens at any given time even when he is asleep. Just the other day I looked at him and I notice his face looked funny I asked him about it, he said he felt something happening that morning before he got out of bed.

I reminded him the reason why I don't like leaving him. Surviving is helping others as well.

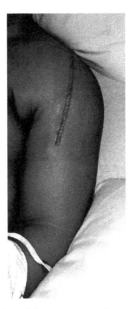

This is Willie after his shoulder surgery because of his seizure

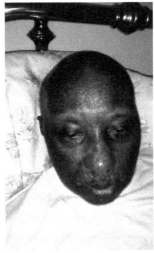

This is how Willie look during his TIAs episodes

My word for this round is Self-Control okay let us do it.

Dictionary's View: Self-Control is impulsivity, willpower, and ego depletion. Self- Control-or the ability to subdue one's impulses, emotions, and behaviors to achieve long-term goals-is what separates modern people from their ancient ancestors and the rest of the animal kingdom. It is primarily rooted in the pre-frontal cortex, which is significantly larger in humans that in other mammals with similar brains. It is typically called willpower which is what allows people to direct their attention, and it underlies all kinds of achievement. Ego depletion is one possible explanation for why individuals are more apt to reach whatever they crave and when they're feeling overworked.

Biblical View: Self-Control is controlling "our heart regarding whatever our hearts may condemn us in, we need to know God is greater than our hearts and he knows all things. It's like saying "As a city's water dam broken through, it is saying it is without a wall. So is the man who cannot control his temper." "Do not keep company with a hot-tempered man or get involved with one disposed to rage. So that we never learn their ways and ensure our self." "A calm heat is the life of the fleshly organism."

My emotions are like fire and when controlled, they're beneficial, when unrestrained, they're destructive. So, I need to do my best to keep my emotions in check, so I will not later think of what I said that I regret saying. I will be patient so I can learn to control my emotions, so my emotions do not control me.

⮿ *Chapter 37* ⮾

BRINGING HER FAMILY MEMBERS TO THROW US OUT

As I have said before, we moved in with our son and his then wife Shane, they are divorce now. Let me tell you what lead up to her calling the police. We move in with them when we found mold in our apartment to help them out, I did all the housework including cooking. We knew our son had did it all for the past twelve years, he got worn out for doing it all those years, he really spoiled her which was not a bad thing.

When the truth came out, she let her true self show, one day she brought her cousins to the house. My husband and I was out with friends, and I got a call about something someone said which was not me. When we got home, we found out she threw our clothes out the door in the front yard. But her cousins picked them up and put them back in the closet, they left and went to the hotel. They came back to the house Ramono was not home, Willie and I was watching TV and one of her cousins came down and spoke to us. She later started talking she asked.

Kelly: "Why are you'll Here? I know about the mold problem but why are you Here?"

"Because when we asked if we could come, they both told us yes, so this is why we are here."

Willie: "Why are you asking? What does it have to do with you?"

Kelly: "This is my cousin's house and she want you all gone so why don't you all to leave?'

Shane and Kelly's sister Missy was upstairs, and they start calling her and she said she was just talking to us. And they kept calling her the next thing I knew was she was standing over my husband and he stood up. Shane and Missy come running down the steps and told Kelly to come upstairs, she said that we were just talking. Before I knew Missy jumped in Willie's face and said he hit her sister; Kelly told her he did not hit her.

Shane and Missy: "He did hit you."

Willie: "I did not hit her; I didn't even think about hitting her."

"Willie, can you please set down?"

The three got Willie in a circle and they were pushing him. Even though he was sick and weak he was not going to let them push him down. I went to my purse and got my pepper spray and I tried to get him out he knot me down; he didn't know it was me. I got up and said if anyone touch me, I know something, meaning I was going to spray them.

Shane: "I am calling the police they are on their way."

I knew she was lying because I was watching everything, so I knew what she said. At that point I looked up I saw Missy pending Kelly up on the wall with her feet dangling in the air because Missy had her by the neck with one hand. I just set and looked at them it was crazy.

Shane: "Ramono, you need to come home and stop what's going on."

He came and he had a friend to come with him. The whole scene played out it boil to the point that Shane and Missy called Kelly a liar. When they got ready to leave, they told Kelly let's go but she didn't want to leave she was too busy saying he didn't hit me, and they kept saying he did, but he didn't. He was about to fall over but he kept himself up the best way he could.

Shane and Missy left Kelly at the house, and they said they was not going to come back to pick her up. Kelly told us that her cousin Shane was manipulator and devious, we all just looked at each other. I told my son that we should take her to the hotel, so he called Shane and asked her which hotel they were in she told him they were downtown. Because she didn't want him to know where she was, but he knew. We took her to the hotel and dropped her off and I asked her for the fourth time why do they believe her lies.

My husband was in the hospital fighting for his life and I had to deal with everything around me. Just think Willie's illness, My illnesses, the mold, our living problems, Ramono's problem and more. I was blame of using something of Shane's which I never touched anything of hers.

Months later Kelly came back she said to help Shane pack because she was finally moving. While she was here drinking as usual both times, she came she drank all my wine in the fridge. I Keep some in the fridge because I love cooking with it and each time, she came she would turn the bottle up to her mouth and drank.

One night while I was in the kitchen cleaning she came in and asked me why; do I use her cousin's stuff and I told her I never used anything of hers. I remembered my son would ask me why I don't use the crockpot I told him I don't know something just wouldn't let me. I knew because it was hers and I didn't want to mess with any of her stuff way before things came out. I knew she didn't want us here so I did as less as I could with any of her things. She loved it when someone wash her clothes and clean her bedroom.

For months I would tell Willie and Ramono I was not going to keep getting up and down opening, closing, and locking the door and garage. She had it so bad she just walks out and drive out the garage leaving the door open and the garage up anyone could walk in and hurt us she didn't care. Or she felt like we are her slaves and did everything for her. She never would ask or say please will you or can you do this or that. Then she would leave, and my husband would jump up and open the garage for her at any given time, me I would not move, and I told him he should not be doing it either like he is her slave that was the way she treated us, I am no one slave on this earth.

Repeatedly, she did this and she never would say thank you. Even though no one is speaking with you it still is nice to say please and thank you that's just courtesy.

While my husband was in the hospital and rehab, I remember her going out right after my son left home, she went out the garage and left it opened I did get up and lock and let the garage door down for my safety about fifteen minutes later she came back. She blew I didn't move, fifteen minutes later she blew again I didn't move, she did it again and I still didn't move. She called my son and asked him why I wouldn't open the garage for her he told her why she don't ask me herself. She blew again I never open the door, so she got out the car came in the front door; went and opened the garage to pull in her car. Why couldn't she do that all the time, I am not her slave, and I shouldn't have to stop what I am doing or wake-up to cater to her every demand no. I was very tired with everything, go on going back and forth to and from the hospital and rehab for over a month and dealing with my hand pain and my other illnesses.

I still had to take care of myself, I went to see one of my doctors and he changed one of my medication instead of giving me what I normally take, I told him I couldn't take it but who listen to me?

Anyway, I took the new medication, that next morning my son came down and asked me something about the door I declared I didn't get up and lock the door after she kept leaving it open. I really didn't realize what I did, it happened again the next morning something happened, I didn't remember doing it. I realized it was an effect from the new medication and I told him.

"You need to tell her to do things for herself like I have told you time and time again. Please tell her this because I was sleep walking and I don't want to end-up, going in her room and hurting her because of me sleep walking because I don't want to go to jail over her foolishness."

I stop taking that medication because not only did it caused me to sleepwalk, but I were also more tired than before, and I notice some bumps on my arms. He must have told her because she never blew again for me to let her in or her going out and leaving it open. When Willie came home, she started it again, but I put a stop to it.

"Please stop, no because you are extremely sick and all this getting up and down is not good for you what if you fall and hit your head then what?"

I meant he should no longer wash her clothes because she needs to learn how to do things herself. When she wanted us to hear anything, she would talk loud at times she would try to get Ramono to hit her by what she was saying and doing.

I later would ask him about why she was trying to get him to hit her, he would say he didn't notice her doing those things. I would say that's because you had gotten so use to her mouth through the years until you tuned her out which was good, he didn't he would just close his bedroom door.

Well, how about Peace?
Dictionary's View: Peace is a quiet, calm rapport, concord, truce; lack of hostility. It is the absence of war or other hostilities.

Biblical View: Peace is you would pay attention to his commandments! Then our peace would become just like a river. And our righteousness like the waves of the sea.

I know true peace is much more than a dream. It's a promise of peace that goes far beyond anything I can imagine. Like how long it's for, and who will be privileged to it, and it means a complete peace of mind.

∽ *Chapter 38* ∽

THE BIG DAY THE POLICE CAME

One Saturday, while we were out, she was home, and she called Ramono to ask him.

Shane: "Why did your parents took my clothes out of the washing machine and laid them on the dryer?"

Ramono: "Momma, Shane called me and said you all took her clothes out and left them on top of the dryer."

"No, We Never touch anything, I was in the kitchen cooking, and she came down on the phone laughing and talking loud, she took them out of the washer and set them on the dryer herself and she set there for about thirty minutes talking then she went up the stairs."

Then as soon as we got home, he came at me again because she said I did take them out. I told him I didn't touch anything besides that Willie asked me should he put them in the dryer, and I told him no he should not touch them because she is not helping him, she was using him, so he didn't touch them.

"Just like you both keep saying I am just trying to keep peace in the house. But you all are not what you all are doing is being her slave and she treat you all worse than that."

About ten minutes later Ramono came down and ask.

Ramono: "Shane said you stole a package that she was looking for in the mail she said where is it?"

Oh, I have had enough, and I said it loud enough for her to hear me.

"I 'Did Not Touch,' any package I am sick of being 'Blame for Something I Did Not Do.' I never seen a package and if the postman left it, I do not know anything about. Beforehand she would tell me that she was looking for a package and if we go out the front door to please make sure the note she wrote be in the door for the postman, which didn't happen. And I am not going to set here and say different."

Ramono and Willie start looking around the house to find it, Ramono went to the garage to look for it and I looked at them both and shook my head and said,

"You all don't believe me I am truly saying I 'Never Seen It', but you all are her slaves running around here trying to please her."

She came running down the steps talking out loud.

Shane: "I didn't call you a liar and say you stole anything and why are you talking loud?"

"You did call me a liar."

Shane: "No, I didn't!"

"Yes, You Did, when you said I did the things you say I did when I didn't say or do anything. 'I Am Not the Lair' you are because you been lying all this time about everything just because you got caught doing what you were doing, and you didn't like the fact I may have seen it."

Shane: "I want you'll out of my house now. I don't eat the food you cook."

"I am not going anywhere and stop spitting on me and back-up out of my face. And you have ate all the food I cooked because I made sure I cooked things you will eat mostly, and you stop eating after you got caught, I still cooked for everyone that's your problem if you not eating besides, you ate that cola chicken last week."

Shane: "I am going to call the police."

"Go ahead call the police."

Ramono didn't want her to call the police, but I told him let her call them. He then said at the end of the day 'he is the one who have to live here.' His dad told him when God is with you no man can stand against you, he does not talk much because of his illness. She called them, she kept going to the door then I notice she went outside in her robe, and she was out there for a while. I looked out the window and I saw not one, not two, but three police cars outside so I opened the door.

"Hi, how are you all doing come on in."

Officer came in and said,

Male Officer: "She called us to tell us she wants you all out and you all have to leave because this is her house."

"Officer we are not going anywhere because this is our son's house also and he told us to stay and besides, he is the head of this household."

Male Officer: "This her house and if she doesn't want, you all Here, so you all have to leave."

By that time Ramono came down to listen to what he was saying.

"Officer, tell me what do you know about some proprietorship?"

Ramono: "Momma, he doesn't know anything about that."

Which the officer said he didn't know, and I said I knew he didn't. The next thing he said was that it was going to be hard living a house with no one talking. I said no one talks to her anyway if the problem comes it's from her. He left and she came in the house and Ramono asked her what they told her?

Shane: "I Told Them to 'Write Down Everything!' and to put it on record."

Ramono: "Oh No, They Are Not! I am going out Here to talk to them about this."

Shane: "No, No, don't go! You don't have to go and talk to them about it."

He went to talk with the two female officers. While he was out talking to them, she started talking and saying.

"I just needed to know my options. It was just a misunderstanding we can get along as long, as we respect each other. I respect Willie when he is at the table studying or reading. We just should stay out of each other's way. He is going to need someone to stay here with him after I am gone, so you guys should stay here.

Ramono came back in and ask Willie and I to step outside. We all went in the back yard I looked up in the bedroom, she was looking out the window and she was on the phone with her family.

Ramono: "The officers told me they asked her did you all contribute to anything in the house she told them yes. So, they told her she could not put you all out, what she would have to do is file to evict you all with eviction papers and she will have to go to court and then she will have to wait on all of that plus it was going to cost her some money. Don't you all worry about anything she will be gone way before you all do."

She didn't say anything again to us about anything. She really thought she was smart like she always would tell Ramono, "At the End of The Day!" Whenever she tries to say something to hurt him.

She is gone after five months. I knew from the beginning, but he wanted to marry her, so I kept my mouth closed. No matter what I did for her she hated me and all I ever did was do things, make things, and buy things for her. But we didn't get into their marriage because it was not for us to do.

This week word is Joy how will I use it this time?
Dictionary's View: Joy is intense and especially ecstatic or exultant happiness, pleasure, or satisfaction, and to enjoy.

Biblical View: Joy is a joyful heart makes for a cheerful countenance. But heartache crushes the spirit. joyful heart is good medicine, or good for healing. But a crushed spirit saps one's strength. Joy do not depend on external things, it come from that deep inner satisfaction.

So, joy is not a mere personality trait that I am born with; it is part of "the new personality," I know joy is a heart quality, because it may also show my outwardly quality on occasion.

What Is Joy?

*Joy is a constant aspect which it's inward permanence as a heartfelt
feature of my new personality.
Joy is having hospitality, it is loquacity thinking and doing kindness,
joy is full of wonderful sounds that is total musicality.*

*There are times when my joy will be disturbed about something, or I
will become face with unpleasant conditions.
I will admit I will not like it, when someone or something take my joy
away because I will not feel happy I will not let anyone, or
Anything affect my joyful depositions.*

*I can still have joy in my heart when I remember "happiness is
when I am persecuted."
Because it makes me stronger knowing when I am made to feel weak,
I know I am not unsuited.*

*I will leap for joy since my reward is great, it is primarily my deep
inner satisfaction.
To know my joy, it can be a direct action, to what is said or done to
me, as long, as I don't let it become an overreaction.*

*I know I must stand firm when I am under trial.
I am going to do it with a great smile. It is joy that helps me to endure
while I am under tribulation.
I will do my best to endure all I am face without any confrontation.*

Chapter 39

HOW I LOST MY DAD

I lost my dad about seven months after I lost my sister, I remember telling my brother Emmanuel and my sister Cynthia before she moved to Miami, Fla. I told them I had a bad feeling that one day our dad is going to die, and we will not know anything about it until it's all over.

This is what really happened, our dad became sick a few years ago. His wife took him to the hospital, and she planned on having him committed in a way she could control It because she was a nurse before she retired, and her daughter is one also. He lived about five hours away from us so that was hard within itself.

The day Cynthia and I went to see him we were there the whole day; we spoke with the nurses and his doctor. His wife Betty Jean told us he had Alzheimer, Cynthia and I asked the doctor if he had Alzheimer and the doctor said.

Dr. Kindle: "No he does not have Alzheimer the only reason why he is here is because he has a kidney infection, and his blood sugar."

"Why would someone say he is in here because he has Alzheimer if he doesn't have it?"

Dr. Kindle: "I can't say why they would say but I am only d pressure, and his diabetes."

Cynthia: "So you mean to tell us, he is not in here because of him having Alzheimer?"

Dr. Kindle: "No he does not have it; I am treating him for what I told you he has and when he gets better from this he can go home."

The two of us went back into the room and we told him what the doctor said. The three of us talked about it among ourselves and we also called Emmanuel and told him what the doctor said. We realized his wife Betty Jean wanted the doctors to said he has Alzheimer so she could commit him. They called her to let her know that we were there so she, her daughter and granddaughter came.

Betty Jean asked us to have the doctor come to see him we said yes. She then asked us what did he say?

Cynthia & I: "He told us he didn't have Alzheimer."

Betty Jean: "That's not what I was told someone is lying. They said he have Alzheimer."

"That was not what we were told, not only that Dr. Kindle said his mind was intact and there is no sign of Alzheimer at this time no matter how we want to make it so it will not happen."

Betty Jean became angry we could see it was not what she wanted to here, we looked at each other and shook our head. Then the conversation switches over to something dear to him, his car.

Betty Jean: "I am going to get rid of that car because you don't need it and you can't drive it anymore."

Granddaughter Katy: "Yeah you are not going to drive it anymore."

Clifford: "You'll are not going to give my car away and I am going to drive it when I get out of here."

Katy: "We have told you are not going to drive it; I am going to use it to drive going to work."

Clifford: "You are not taking my car."

He was getting very upset; he was getting angry with them and what his wife and her granddaughter said. Cynthia and I set and listen to all that mess and seeing how he was getting. Betty Jean's daughter Mary walked out of the room because she knows what they were doing by working his nerves getting him upset. I got tired of the whole thing, so I had to say something. This was so disrespectful for that child to talk to him the way she was doing and the way her grandmother and mother was letting her talk to a grow man.

"You all need to stop upsetting him about his car. It belongs to him, and he should do what he wants to with it. It's about him getting well and only that at this current time. Instead of al trying to get and keep him upset and angry what you are doing is running his blood pressure up it is a shame."

Betty Jean got so angry she rolled her eyes at me. She then called Cynthia out in the hall to talk with her. But Cynthia said Janice come on let's see what she wants to talk about. She stood there saying what she was going to do before he comes home.

Cynthia and I went to him a few more times in the hospital. We realized Betty Jean didn't want him home she was making plans to keep him in the hospital. Cynthia had a five-bedroom house and she asked him did he want to come and stay with her. He would say yes then he would talk with Betty Jean and then he changes his mind, or he will say slow down. He would go back and forth on the matter.

Cynthia asked again she said if he don't come and live with her, she wanted to move to Miami, Fla. I finally told her to go and live her life and don't worry about him. Our brother Emmanuel lived about three hours away from my dad and he would go visit him when we were not with him.

About a month later Betty Jean had him move to a rehab and a nursing home. She had him moved and she fix it so we could not get any information on him. One day his case worker called me and told me what was going on and she also told me what I needed to do. I called Emmanuel and told him what was going on he and I did what she told me, and I called her back. When I got her on the phone, she told me her supervisor told her to stay out it and do not give me any more information. Emmanuel reminded me what happened to him when dad was in another hospital but the next day, he called her they told him she no longer works there.

Now after Betty Jean got him in the nursing home fix so that the only persons who can get information was, she and her daughter. The three of us tried to get some information they told us our name is not on the list so we can't get any information on our dad, I again told the two of them.

"That something is going to happen to him, and we will not know what's going on until it's all said and done."

They agreed with me on this matter because as they both said everything that is happening shows this is what she is doing. One day I decided to call her and ask her could she please add my name to the list so that as his child we will know what is going on she rudely said.

Betty Jean: "NO!"

"Why would you not add me to the list?"

Betty Jean: "Because I have enough people added on the list which is myself, my daughter, Emmanuel, Cynthia, and Linda."

"Can you take Linda's name off since she does not call or come to see what's going on with him?"

Betty Jean: "No I am not going to change it."

"I know you don't like me that's okay I still have no bad feelings against you even with the way you treat him and the things you do and have said."

Betty Jean: "No I don't like you because you put your nose in my family business, I don't put mind in yours."

"NO, you don't because I am not trying to do things underhanded. You do not have to like me you should not stop us from having any information why is this? Plus, you have not added any of my family to the list it's just you and your daughter is on the list."

Betty Jean: "Who told you their name is not on the list because it is you are just mad because I will not add you to the list."

I knew this was not true because I spoke with both of my siblings and they both said that she don't like any of us and our name is not on the that list, both of them said because I have called to try to get information on him and I am told the same thing you are told. Plus, Cynthia called the Home while I was on the phone and I heard them say,

The Nursing Home: "We can't tell you anything because you are not on the list to give information about him."

Cynthia: "Mrs. Jackson said I am on the list. Can you please tell me who is on the list?"

The Nursing Home: "It is only two names on the list which is Mrs. Jackson and her daughter Mary."

Cynthia thanked the person and hung that end of the called.

Cynthia: "You see she lied none of us is on the list, she is just trying to get you angry and want you to say something so she can use it against you."

"I know what she is doing, sorry I will not give her what she wants."

Way before Cynthia moved to Miami, Betty Jean gave my dad's car to my baby sister Linda just to hurt my dad which it did because he would talk about that every time, we called him. For my dad when someone did or said anything, he didn't like he would try to hurt the person by saying things like they are not my child. When he has more children than the nine of us which one was months older than me which I thought I was the oldest which I found out when we both became grown and married. My dad could be very mean, and he would say and do things to hurt his kids, I know it there was not one of us who didn't fall out with him about the matter, I never had a problem with him saying I was not his. But the three of us showed we forgave him and moved on and did the best we could toward him to help him find out he was wrong.

We all felt like he was brained wash and afraid of his wife. He at times called her daughter and her three kids his kids, see he raised her, but he never raised his own kids. We would tell him time to time we are not his kids they are, because that's the way he tries to make us feel. The last time I talked to him I even told him how I felt about feeling what could happened. He said he got that straightened out with Mary. I told him to stop letting her fool him because when it comes to it, she is going to take her mother's side. He would fight us on it I would tell him keep thinking she would do the right thing.

The Day We Took Him Out

Cynthia went ahead and move to Miami, but before she left, we both went back to see him this time he wanted us to take him to the bank. He wanted to see what was going on in his bank account when he got there, and they all know who he was they told him they could not give him any information about his own account. The reason why he didn't have his ID, it was because she took all his stuff, he kept asking her for it and she would never give it to him. On this very day my dad and Cynthia decided to go by the house to get some of his things.

I had to go and pay my 'water bill' I told them not to call her and asked her anything to give her heads-up. When I back in the car, I overheard them talking to Emmanuel about what they did, I said didn't I tell you all not to call her? Emmanuel said to call the police we all agree because no one wanted to walk in and face a gun in our face because there was a gun there my dad said.

We called the police; we parked a block away and waited on them to show-up. We then pulled- up in the driveway she closed the garage, I asked my dad; do they closed the garage, he said no it's never closed. I told him each time I would come up to see them it never has been closed My dad asked Cynthia what time it was. She told him, he said it's about time for her youngest grandson to come home on a special bus because he has special needs. I said so she is home, and she did all of this to cover up the fact of her being home.

As I was looking around, I saw someone looking out the bedroom window. The officer rang the doorbell, no one came, he walked around the house and no answer. He came back to the car and said he can only take the report down and she could make a complaint which she did. Days later she received a called from someone maybe another officer, this person told Cynthia she could not tell her anything it could only come from my dad when he had given her the okay to do so in front of the officer on the scene. Plus, the officer on the call said somethings Cynthia never mentioned. Cynthia concluded that this person had to speak with Betty Jean.

We took him to lunch that day, then we took him to get his hair cut because the Home did not take care of him the way they should. His nails needed to be cut, he needs new shoes because his feet were swollen and he could not wear his shoes, so he needed new shoes which he kept asking her to do but it was not done. He asked for new clothes because his clothes did not fit and most of the clothes was not his, and the ones he was wearing had holds in them. So, we got him somethings which he needed even a cell phone.

Over time things start missing, phone calls would not go through, and his address book went missing out of his drawer after over a year. He would find his wallet at the foot of the bed on the floor. My dad was a person who always made sure everything was in place, he always was that type of person all my life.

After Cynthia move to Miami, I still went to see my dad because I was the only one who was able see about him besides his wife and her daughter. I went and took him to get his Driver License, which he asked me to give them to him which I refuse because we didn't want her to get them. He asked me repeatedly at one time while my brother was there visiting with me my dad said I was just like Betty Jean. My brother Emmanuel told him not to call me Betty Jean because we are here to help you and for you to call her that name you should know better than that. When she is spending her time energy, and money to come and see about you and to make sure you're taken care of like a child should.

I am his POA, his Power of Attorney which I never acted on because I wanted to do the right thing by not causing any problems out of respect. I filled it with the state, so it is public in records. After my sister died Emmanuel and I talked about making sure we could find out things about our dad when we knew there was no way that was going to happen. I again I mentioned about something happening we finally got him to say he want to move where his kids were, Here in Georgia. But after Cynthia death he withdrew, and he would keep saying for us not to worry about him just take care of ourselves. I told Emmanuel, daddy was not going to be with us long, because he didn't want us to go and see him and there were times, we couldn't talk with him for weeks. I thought it was just me, but I found out Emmanuel had the same problem.

I made plans to go and see him on a weekend with my son, but he told me someone said I shouldn't go. I hate it up to this day I blame myself for not going, by not following my heart. By not doing the right thing by my father, I would never let anyone do that to me again. If I am wrong 'Great Day in the Morning' if problems happen because of it, I am willing to take it and deal with it to make it right. It hurts so bad to know I could have done what I should do to help my father. Yes, I blame myself because I will want someone to be there for me, if it shakes things up for the right reason so be it. It hurts me for not following my gut, sometimes, I wonder if I ask anyone would they want me to do what I can to help them, I wonder what would they say?

Sometimes I wonder if this makes me a bad person for not being there for my dad. I ask myself what I would do if it happens to my mom, would I do all I can, or would I let anyone stop me from doing what I know, or feel is right. Over the years this is what I lived by doing and saying what I feel is right by doing it in a peaceable way.

Late one night I received a call from Emmanuel, he said "Daddy is in the hospital." I asked him some questions he said he didn't know anything he only know Betty Jean called my dad's baby sister's son who seven months before died two weeks before Cynthia, called to tell him. I asked Emmanuel about the hospital information he didn't know that either. So, I got up the next morning, I called the nursing home, I began asking questions about our dad, I were told rudely.

"We Cannot Tell You Anything Because You Are Not on The List."

I again asked, can you please, tell me about my dad. She told me the same thing, so I said,

"You may not be able or want to tell me anything, because I am not on the list, but you are going to tell me where my dad is!"

The person told me to hold on and then someone came on the phone the person that gave me the information over a year before he died, she told me where to find him. I called and they connected me to the nurse who was his caregiver. After I told her who I was and why I called and asking her some information about him she said.

Nurse Tammie: "I spoke with his daughter Mary this morning."

"Mary is not his daughter that's his stepdaughter, I am his daughter and I need to know some info on him, so she told me. I asked her, her name and for the fax number so I could send her some paper about my dad I said they would speak for themselves. I went to the nearest Office Depot and fax info to the hospital, knowing she would let Betty Jean and Mary know about the papers. I sent her the Power of Attorney papers; I then went to the post office and I overnight Betty Jean her copy meaning she would get two copies."

Nurse Tammie: "She told me not to let him go back to hospice."

"What do you mean by hospice?"

I knew what she said and meant but I was in shock to hear her say something we didn't know anything about.

"What's wrong with him?"

Nurse Tammie: "He have pneumonia, bed sores, and kidney failure, he doesn't have long to live."

I said to myself I said it, I kept saying something like this was going to happened and here we are in a place I didn't want to be to say I was right. I called Emmanuel to let him know what I did, he said that was good because those papers had to be active before he died otherwise it would be no good. I told him I know he was right that's why I kept saying I needed to make them active, and I didn't until now. I told Emmanuel I was making plans to go up and see about him by this time he has move about fifteen hours away so I was the only person to go and see about him and to see what was going on even though I was told i should not get involved. That was a hurtful thing for someone to tell someone not to go and see about him.

The next morning Emmanuel, before I left the house that morning, he called to tell me our dad died early that morning it broke my heart, but I didn't cry. I had things to do, and I went to handle them I need to do as I see it, my life must go on plus I needed to make plans to go to the funeral. We all got a text from Linda saying where the funeral was and that we all were to meet that date and time at the place of service.

The Day of The Funeral
My husband just got out of the hospital and rehab, plus I just had hand surgery on my right hand two months before. I could not leave my husband because of his illness so I had to take him with me. We got to the funeral home I was the last one to arrive, I went inside were everyone was, and the first thing Emmanuel said to me.

Emmanuel: "Janice I am so sorry that your name is not on the program."

Then the rest on my siblings said the same thing along with my aunt who I have not seen for over forty years. We all talked, we said how dirty it was for us to meet at the funeral home as his kids. But to leave me and my brother by my mother names off was uncalled for, it was unkind and to put things the way it happened shows what kind of person that do things like that.

When it was about time to go in for the funeral we didn't walk in as a family my sibling and other family members decided to set in the middle of the room. When I walked in, I asked them what they were doing, that they have the right to set up front because we are his kids. I set on the front row along with my aunt and my brother James. Emmanuel decided not to stay inside because he knew he felt like he would had told them off. Then my baby brother Calvin got up in the middle of the program because he got mad with what came out of some people mouth.

Betty Jean and her daughter and grandkids came walking in while we are setting down. Yes, we should have come in the limo and walked in as a family, but we were not looked at as family. I never in my life ever seen a funeral like this one. As she was walking in and as Betty Jean got closer to the front and she saw us sitting she tried to let those crocodile tears try to come out, but they wouldn't come down.

"Look at those crocodile tears she can't even cry right."

James touch me and said be good. I was good it just came out but that was that. I set there with my legs cross because I must keep one if not both legs propped up because of health reasons. But instead of the preacher preaching about the person who was dead, he was preaching to us about how we need to be acting he go like this.

The Preacher: "You set Here with your legs cross and your arms cross. Letting your body language talk saying what you want it to say. When you need to be showing love to each other and not back bite anyone. You need to walk up to each other and tell them he wants us to get along."

He went on and on we all are setting there he is talking to me each, and every one of us was telling yourself that. But I told them he was talking to me because he was looking at me on the front row. The rest said no, he was talking to me. It was a big mess there where not that many people there for my dad to have so many friends as he claimed. Most all the ones there was family members, I say this because the preacher ask,

The Preacher: "Who all Here are no kin to the deceased, and we all looked around?"

It was not that many.

As we were going out the body was at the back and so that meant you pass the body as we went out. While we were in line near the casket one-man pants failed down, we all busted out laughing. When we got to the grave site and I was talking to him it's a shame to say this, but it was my own cousin my dad's baby sister's son. I have to say I have not seen him over forty years. It was good to see them again but not at that place and time.

After the grave site service part, the preacher said that the family wants to thank all for coming and everyone are welcome to come to the house to eat. None of us was going and we didn't we all went to a restaurant to eat before we all got back on the road. We set and ate and laugh and talk about the whole thing. They talk about how her grandkids got up there and said how he was a loving grandfather and loving father and husband. They talked about how good he was how much fun they had as a family which made my family up-set, I told them they just wanted to make us mad by saying they was a happy family, but we all knew what the real deal was. They talked about the picture they had of him on the back of the program to make him look bad. I let them know that they want everyone to see them as a happy family and to rub in our faces but please don't let that make you up-set. It's over now he is not in pain anymore and we don't have to worry about him anymore.

Emmanuel and I talk from time to time about him we realized when he told us that they put him in another hospital and how in the world could he be in the same hospital if he had the same number. It didn't hit us until we found out that he was in hospice of the nursing home close to a month. They knew he was dying for about a month and they did not let us know. Now do you see why I kept saying what I was saying about worrying about his life or his death.

I never wanted to be right but sometimes we are, even if it doesn't feel good. I do my best to see the best in people but sometimes that can't be found in some people and for those one I feel sad for them truly. I know I will survive this too because it will pass as time goes by. Now I want people to realize surviving don't just mean to survive illnesses, but it can come in all forms, from our enemies, our loved ones, our family and our friends.

This is my dad, my sister, dad.

This is the last picture of my and myself

Okay the word for this round is Kindness.
Dictionary's View: Kindness is not just the quality or state of being kind, it is a kind act. It is an endeavor to be kind even to people we do not know. It includes being gentle and considerate.

Biblical View: Kindness is one to the things we should clothe ourselves with which is the tender affections of compassion, kindness, having humility. And we are to continue putting up with one another and forgiving one another freely even if we or anyone has a cause for complaint against another.

Just to remember that if I keep my heart clean, to stay kind and to show kindness to all even my enemies. And to say I do forgive all and I also ask for forgiving from all because I can never truly forgive with the without the other, I need to, no I must do and ask for both. I always need to keep encouraging all, I meet with my words and my deeds, and always with sincerity from my heart.

❧ *Chapter 40* ❧

TWO CAR ACCIDENTS

This past February, at the beginning of the month Willie and myself was in the city looking at some houses. I made a left turned on onto the main street when the light was red on both ends for me to make that left turn. After I made the turn, and I went a few feet down the street I heard a horn blow then the next thing I knew was we got hit. It was a young lady she ran the red light; she came up behind me and then she must have realized what was going on. This was as I was in the left lane and as I had just put my right signal light on to get into the right lane, the next thing I knew was me saying,

"Oh no she didn't she hit me."

I asked Willie if he was okay, he said yes, I told him that I knew he was not okay because if I feel the way I feel, and she hit us on his side I know he was hurt. But he kept telling me he was okay, there was a person walking down the street when the accident happened and he called 911, I overhead him say she already called. My car was facing the other lane when the police came because we tried to get my car out of the road because when the lights turned green again cars from both ends began rushing down the road the eyewitness said.

Eyewitness: "Hey you'll need to slow down can't you see a car accident Here. You can't be rushing down the road passing this car like you are doing."

Man: "Can you pull your car over to the side if you can?"

By that time the police came and after she spoke with the young lady, then came to me and asked me what happened I explain to the officer what happened,

The Officer: "The young lady had the right a way even if she ran the red light if when a person makes a left turn in the state of Georgia, you will be the one that will get the ticket."

Should that be right, especially, if the light was red on both ends.

The Officer: "Can you try and move the car around the corner on the next street."

The officer called for an ambulance, which came and asked me did I want them to take us to the hospital. Willie told me he was okay, but I knew better. Besides, I called one of my friends Carol and asked her to come and take us to the ER, I wanted and needed to take pictures of the accident even though I could barely walk.

I took the pictures, on the way to the ER I asked her to take to get something to eat because I knew how they won't let us eat while waiting and plus we were hungry because we hadn't eaten. As we were waiting on our food, we were looking at Willie he was in the car and my friend said something is wrong with Willie by the way he was holding his head and the way he was acting, I looked, and I told her she was right.

When we got to the ER, they called us back, they examine us both and some test also. When they called me back to give me the result, the way the nurse was looking and acting I felt something was not right. As I was walking in the room, and I looked up and saw the doctor and the way he was looking at me I knew something was not right.

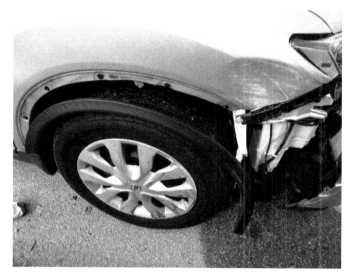

These are the from the first accident.

This is from the second accident.

Mrs. Holliman Your Test Results

ER Doctor: "Mrs. Holliman, your test results show you have no broken bones, you got whiplash."

"Good!"

ER Doctor: "We did find something that we were not looking for you have Lung Cancer."...

"Cancer, Cancer, Cancer!"

THIS IS NUMBER 91 ON MY LIST! We will see how it pans out!

He then told me not to get afraid and I told him I was not afraid I was just trying to wrap my head around what he was saying. He told me it was in my left lung, and I asked him if scar tissue be what they see? He said yes. I went out of the room and sitting waiting Willie came back from talking to the doctor. As I was waiting some of our friends came to the ER to support us and they were waiting with me and they asked what the doctor say, when I said what he told me the reaction was not what I was looking for at that time.

When Willie came out, he told us he had a concussion, so I decided to ask him how that happened if he said he did not get hurt. He then said that the doctor said he hit his head, I only said oh yeah, I thought you did not get hurt. He told me that he doesn't know how that happened, so I had to explain it to him.

When I got home and I was still thinking about myself it dawns on me, I hit my forehead and said dummy he said lung, not throat which I was thinking about because of my neck surgery years ago and I could not think clear when he told me what he told me. I made an appointment to see my lung doctor which I saw his aid Bill, I told him why I was there he ran test, and I went to get the test from the hospital he told me that he saw on the hospital test, but he didn't see it on theirs. He used the words it probably, was their machine but wait it didn't show up on Willie.

I saw my heart doctor and I told him about it, so he told me that he wants to send me to have a second opinion just to make myself feel better. It was twenty days later the day we were to get our car due to the accident which we were driving a rental, we were hit again, this time on my side. I called Ramono to come and get us, I prayed it was not me that cause the accident even though I knew I was not the factor. I got the report a week later to prove it was not my fault. We got up the next morning and went to get our car and then we went to the ER, and I asked them to do the test over again because I wanted to see if it was a mistake or not. And it was there so I made the appointment and they saw it on both reports. I must go back to see my first lung doctor because he gave me my CPAP machine.

I told him about the test he got rude and said that they didn't tell me that, when I told him they did he said they didn't, and they don't know what they were talking about. I just said to myself I am not going to fuss with him about this I will just wait to see the new lung doctor, name Dr. Upshaw. Which I did see her again and she ordered, Lung CT which I had when I went back, I spoke with her aid Gabby, I notice how she was asking me all these questions about my breast they are concern about Breast Cancer. Now I will have to now, deal with another factor to deal with. How much more can I take? With me having more to deal with I wonder how things are going to pan out. Meantime I am going to take everything I can to keep it down or stop it from growing. That goes for both of them.

THIS IS NUMBER 92 ON MY LIST!

Gabby ordered a Lung Biopsy for me to have done which I had a hard time to deal with and plus I had a severe-side effect while I was at the hospital and the next week and a half was hard on me, it is a wait and see thing at this time plus dealing with make an appointment with a new (OB/GYN).

THIS IS THE PICTURE OF THE LAST CAR IN ACCIDENT

*This is from the last car accident but, we weren't
in it at the time, it happened at the dealers.*

Yes, I did say another car accident, we were not in the car I had got a new car. I was waiting on my tag, but it hadn't showed up yet, so I went to the dealer, and they got things cleared up for me. They also filled the car with gas, and they wash and vacuum the car, as they were bringing the car around. The next thing I knew Ronnie came to tell what happened, he was the one who sold me my car. He came in and said,

Ronnie: "Mrs. Holliman I have some news to tell you."

"Is its good news or bad news?"

Ronnie: "It depends on how you look at it, as we were bringing your car around to you someone was driving in the parking lot hit your car, we are going to give you a new car."

"Oh, this is just a material thing, I am so glad we were not in the car."

I looked at Willie because he went with me that day which he never does because he hates riding in cars now. The reason why I looked at him because he was saying on the way to the dealer.

"I don't want to be in another accident."

With me thinking about what he said, and I said to him,

"At least you were not in the car accident like you ask for, but you didn't say anything about the car being in an accident."

He looked at me like I was crazy, but I told him you know I am right which he did agree. And we both thank our Grand Creator for us not being in the car at that time.

The next morning as I was leaving got a phone called from someone name Robert who said he woke-up around 2:00a.m., and he called me around 10:00a.m. He told me that he was worried about what happened with my car. He called to ask me if I could keep my car and they would give me some money for inconvenience. I ask him about the depreciation on the car. I was told it would not go down like that, I knew better so I told him let me think about it and I would call him with my answer two days later.

I told him thank you, but I will not take the offer I will do the new car deal because of what I was saying about the depreciation of the car. So, I got my new car after about two and a half weeks. Now I am waiting on my new tag.

Chapter 41

NOTICING THE CHANGES

As you know by now Willie have a lot to deal with himself, meaning all his illnesses which you just know of some. The ones you do know about is very hard on him. He is a person that do not handle things like I do we are totally two different people. He is a worry wart, and I am not; he is a depressed person, and I am not, and he is a person that always see the negative in everything where I see the positive.

He is a hard-working person, and he loves to show people how to make a person feel good because he is a hugger and I was not, but I am now because of him.

He had a hard life being raise by an abusive stepfather, but his mother tried to make up for that by teaching them how to show love to people. But he also picked up some of his stepfather ways which he didn't even realized he had until later in life.

With his illnesses with his brain caused him to change in a noticeably big way and it is not for the good. I am saying this not to hurt him or show no disrespect, but it is to show people how life changes and things do happen and it's not always for the best.

Willie always was a person that will make people laugh and he is a person that let his feeling get in his way. He hates being sick and not doing the things he use to do when he was young and healthy. He does not like being in a place where he can't drive anymore, go anywhere, do anything. I must do it by myself or with some friends. I won a cruise, and he don't want to go; No, I should say he can't go because of his health. His sense of humor is worse than ever especially with his family.

I keep asking him to notice things about himself and he refuse to do so. When someone ask me about him, when I tell them, they look at me like I have done wrong. I have asked some of my friends if something would ever happen to Willie would people talk to me or treat me the way they do now, and I was told "No" because they are intimidated by you. I don't know why because I treat them the way I would want to be treated; I know I do speak my mind when I really need too. Wait this is about Willie not me!

He is a very impatient person, but he will do anything to please a lot of people, especially his friends. He is a good person most of the times, but in the past few years as I began to see the changes in him, and I would talk to him about it he would get very offensive about whatever I say. Even when it comes down to talking to his doctors and nurses when he doesn't know the answer to the questions and they look at me for the answer and I would help him by telling them the answer, he will get very mad with me.

So, I decided to let him answer himself and he can't answer, and I say nothing he then asks me to answer for him or to help him. People let me tell you whenever you are dealing with a person that have had a stroke or have a brain problem look out and I hope the best for you. Because you can't say anything to them because they will take it wrong. It doesn't matter if you talk in an undertone voice, they will take it wrong. If you say, please they will take it wrong. If you ask them in a question form, they will take it wrong. They take things the way they perceive it, so it doesn't matter what you do they are going to take it wrong.

What about not hearing what you say to them when they can't hear? Or they hear the wrong thing when you said nothing close to what they think you may have said, they hear the wrong words. They get the wrong meaning of words, or the meaning of what you are talking about.

When you learned to ask them, do they remember things instead of saying you don't remember this or that, please forget it because you still said the wrong thing. Try this one if you decide not to say nothing, they still get mad and say you are the one that got mad and wouldn't say anything because of being angry. Just forget it, you are in the wrong, if you start singing to put your mind on something nice to keep your joy, nope that won't work either. What about this one every time you tell them something about them and they go, "You do too."

I guess you are asking why a person would want to be around anyone like that. Well let me put it this way why run from something every time there is a problem? What do it teach you, nothing but how to run away and never knowing how to help others or yourself? Will it teach you how to bend and give into others or do it teach you how to only think of yourself? What do the words 'for better or for worst' mean to you? Have the love cool off or have you lost it all together?

Ask yourself to do you want to be the person who always blame it on the rain? Can you take constructive criticism? Are you the type of person that never think you are wrong?

Is this a form of trials if not is it a form of illness? But wait if it because due to illness? What is a person to do? Let's see first let's not take it personal. Remember they may not know what they are doing. Even if you remind them of what is going on, they may lash out at you, in some of the most horrible ways. They may not even remember what is going on and they may never remember what they have said to you.

But do this give them the right to lash out at you the way they do? Would you be wrong if you throw-up your hands and say, "I want out " or do you say, "I am sick of you, I wish you will die?" "If you can say this to me, I can say the same to you." I heard these words being said to one's mates, it's sad and it's wrong.

I will have to say, No, Stop, and look at why those words are being said and who the real person is, none of the words you say, will help or make you a better person if you throw gas on the fire just walk away relax and think, then come back to deal with it. If they have a mental problem, they may not even remember what they say. Yes, those words do hurt, but what are you going to do about it is what really matters.

It doesn't mean that you are a weak person because you want to keep that person around you or in your life. Ask yourself this forgiveness starts somewhere why can't it start with you? Why do we have to be the one to look for forgiveness when we can be the one to show forgiveness it doesn't mean you are weak or a push over, it can show you want to be a better, kind and loving person.

I wonder if you are saying she is the stupidest person I ever met, or she is an abused person. I will answer this the way I see it "No I Am Not Neither." I am a person that looks for the good in people and believe me I will only take what I can take before I will tell you to back off, but I first will do my best to keep the peace and to bring joy to people. I see people as they may be having a bad day and tomorrow it may be a better day. Plus, I remember I am not perfect, and we do not live in a perfect world if we do someone forgot to wake me up and plus, they forgot to tell me.

Changes is in all of us, it is what we make of it and how we deal with it. Now compound this with me and my illnesses. Dealing with these things and more I must deal with the fact of asking myself am I a Survivor? Is this the way a good Survivor should be? Or will a Survivor good or not want to treat people or want people to treat them? As for me I am going to do my best, keep my joy, protect my faith, keep loving, and keep enduring and survive whatever life throws at me. Remember my poem What is a Survivor?

I received this!

Date, In private
Love, In private
Be happy, In private
Live, In private
That way, You can
Take your losses, in private
Maintain, In private rebuild yourself, In private.

This not the way I see it! Words are for the beholder, just like beauty are in the eyes of the beholder. This means everyone sees what they want and what they like. And it's up to each of us to see what we want to see. To hear what we want to hear, the way we want to hear it. What we read the way we see the words in black and white, we should ask ourselves is this truly what I see at is my eyes tricking me. It also goes for my ears too, was what I heard the real way the person said or is it how I take it? This private poem I see it in a different way, I say if one wants to be truly happy is what I will take from it, and this is what I got.

Why Not in Private

*To anyone that feel this way I must say I really am sorry for whom
ever feel this way.
I truly feel for you if you think you should never live your life
in a dismay.*

*Why date if you can't share your joy.
Unless it's not the real McCoy.*

*Love is above all else, it is to show, to feel, to give and to hold.
If you do feel that you must keep it private, your
world must also be cold.*

*When you are happy, no matter how life around you are
in a state of crappie.
You will fight to never let anyone take your joy away
and make you unhappy.*

*To live your life in private, that's sad to know you can't show how
you really feel That's like living on a pin wheel,
it's like living in fear, it's like living in a world that is unreal.*

*Loss is when you can't be happy, loss is when you can't share,
but the biggest and greatest loss;
is when you, let someone else tell you, they are your, happy life boss.*

*Why would you want to keep your life in private, what have you done
to cause you so much pain?
Stop letting people worry you, stop letting people pull your chain, and
please letting people keep giving a migraine.*

Yes now is the time to rebuild yourself, but not in private because to rebuild, is to get rid of the old and bring in the new let your new self be a person you will enjoy, when you can feel you are fulfill, if you do this then your life will be a great deal, and you will feel very thrilled.

Chapter 42

THE TYPE OF PERSON I AM

I am a peacemaker not a peace breaker, I learned over the years there are people that do not like what I do or the way I do things without knowing me or understanding me. There are people when I tell them something that they do not like they lash out at me and throw things in my face by turning what I have told them, they will try and turn it around to hurt me. With knowing this it does not stop them from saying what they say I said, this cause me to get quiet, and I don't say anything to keep peace with everyone. Someone told me I am evil even wicked which I am for from it. And once a person has been able as some negative no matter if a person knows better that when a seed has been planted, I will tell you are viewed that way no matter what, and that is a shame. But believe me I will never view anyone that way. I am not perfect; I don't like it when someone called me perfect because there is no one perfect on this given earth. If it is, I have all the money in the world, and I would not be writing this book because I would not have anything to tell.

Yes, it does hurt when I go and do things or buy things for them and they know that I am going to do it. Then take it and then later say are not going to use what I gave them. To me that like saying I don't want you to do anything for me. Why didn't you tell me when I told you I was going to do it, have you stop and though about the time, the energy I have wasted on help you from my heart. When I could have been focusing on myself or someone who realty appreciates my help.

That can make a person say I will never help that person again no matter what. Yes, feeling do have a big deal to do with everything especially when a person wants to help someone especially their family and friends. If you ask anyone how they would feel if that happens to them, they said they would be terribly angry, and they would not ever do anything for that person again. I can understand why they would say that because that mean that person who give you back your gift, they stop you for storing your treasures in a place where no rust or moss to grow. But it's okay at the end of the day I will move on without any anger in my heart in the long run and I will get to the point of feeling sorry for that person.

I did a personality test which shows me as an ENFJ-A IENFJ-T It said I have a Protagonist Personality Type. If you like to do one on yourself google 16 personalities test or quiz.

I learned a lot about myself this year, I learned there are sixteen personalities in the world. Which means there are sixteen slots of personality they put us in, some of the things do point to me, yes there are somethings that's right about me, but there are also somethings that are 'Not Me' at all. So please read this information and get an ideal of who I am and look at me as a person that always wants the best for everyone. Some people see me as this type of person and like me for being this type of person because they feel and are glad to have this type of person they can come and talk too. I will listen to your problem no matter how bad I may feel because I always wants to bring joy and a smile to anyone face that's just me.

Yes, people do say bad things about me I am okay with that because for me I say I cannot please everyone all the time and I can never please someone none of the time. Enjoy reading this!

I copied this from the website as read it I pointed out what applied to me in bold.

You can go to any 16 personalities websites to take the personality test. This will help you see how the world see or think about you, plus you will get look at knowing who you are, so if you feel like there are somethings you may need or want to change about yourself do it, because it is an eye opener you will go WOW!

What you see in bold writing which are me or not me!

A protagonist is the leading character or one of the major characters in a drama, movie, novel, or other fictional text. We are the main figure it one of the prominent figures in a real situation. We are an advocate or champion of a particular cause or idea. We are an active participant in an event. We are a leader, proponent, or supporter of a cause, some of the things a protagonist is an advocate, advocator, backer, booster, promoter, supporter, and a true believer.

ENFJ-A / ENFJ-T

A Protagonist Introduction
Everything you do right now ripples outward and affects everyone. Your (My)

posture can shine your **(my)** heart or transmit anxiety. Your (My) breath can radiate love or muddy the room in depression. Your (My) glance can awaken joy. Your (My) words can inspire freedom. Your (My) every act can open hearts and minds.

Protagonists are natural-born leaders, full of passion and charisma. Forming around two percent of the population, they are oftentimes our <u>politicians,</u> (Not in politics;) our coaches and our teachers, reaching out and inspiring others to achieve -+and to do good in the world. With a natural confidence that begets influence, Protagonists take a great deal of pride and joy in guiding others to work together to improve themselves and their community.

Firm Believers in the People

People are-drawn to strong personalities, and Protagonists radiate authenticity, concern, and altruism, unafraid to stand up and speak when they feel something needs to be said. They find it natural and easy to communicate with others, especially in person, and their Intuitive (N) trait helps people with the Protagonist personality type to reach every mind, be it through facts and logic or raw emotion. Protagonists easily see people's motivations and seemingly disconnected events and are able to bring these ideas together and communicate them as a common goal with an eloquence that is nothing short of mesmerizing. (This is me in a big way.)

The interest Protagonists have in others is genuine, almost to a fault- when they believe in someone, they can become too involved in the other person's problems, place too much trust in them. This trust tends to be a self-fulfilling prophecy, as Protagonists' altruism and authenticity inspire those, they care about to become better themselves. But if they aren't careful, they can overextend their optimism, sometimes pushing others further than they're ready or willing to go.

Protagonists are vulnerable to another snare as well: they have a tremendous capacity for reflecting on and analyzing their own feelings, but if they get too caught up in another person's plight, they can develop a sort of emotional hypochondria, seeing other people's problems in themselves, (Sorry not me.) trying to fix something in themselves that isn't wrong (Again, not me.) If they get to a point where they are held back by limitations someone else is experiencing, it can hinder Protagonists' ability to see past the dilemma and be of any help at all. (Not Me) When this happens, it is important for Protagonists to pull back and use that self-reflection to distinguish between what they really feel, and what is a separate issue that needs to be looked at from another perspective. (I am all ways making sure that I do not let myself get in the way.)

Protagonists are genuine, caring people who talk the talk and walk the walk, and nothing makes them happier than leading the charge, uniting and motivating their team with infectious enthusiasm. (Me!)

People with the Protagonist personality type are passionate altruists, sometimes even to a fault, and they are unlikely to be afraid to take the slings and arrows while standing up for the people and ideas they believe in. It is no wonder that many famous Protagonists are cultural or political icons- this personality type wants to lead the way to a brighter future, whether it's by leading a nation to prosperity, or leading their little league softball team to a hard-fought victory. (Me)

Protagonist Strengths

Tolerant- Protagonists are true team players, and they recognize that that means listening to other peoples' opinions, even when they contradict their own. They admit they do not have all the answers, and are often receptive to dissent, so long as it remains constructive. (Me!)

Reliable- The one thing that galls Protagonists the most is the idea of letting down a person or because (what) they believe in. If it is possible, Protagonists can always be counted on to see it through. (Me!)

Charismatic-Charm and popularity are qualities Protagonists have in spades. They instinctively know how to capture an audience and pick up on mood and motivation in ways that allow them to communicate with reason, emotion, passion, restraint- whatever the situation calls for. Talented imitators, Protagonists are able to shift their tone and manner to reflect the needs of the audience, while still maintaining their own voice. (Me!)

Altruistic- Uniting these qualities is Protagonists' unyielding desire to do good in and for their communities, be it in their own home or the global stage. Warm and selfless, Protagonists genuinely believe that if they can just bring people together, they can do a world of good. (Me!)

Natural Leaders- More than seeking authority themselves, Protagonists often end up in leadership roles at the request of others, cheered on by the many admirers of their strong personality and positive vision. (Me!)

Protagonist Weaknesses

Overly Idealistic- People with the Protagonist personality type can be caught off guard as they find that, through circumstance or nature, or simple misunderstanding, people fight against them and defy the principles they've adopted, however well-intentioned they may be. (This is absolutely true for me.) They are more likely to feel pity for this opposition than anger and can earn a reputation of naivete. (I may become hurt but not hate and I am not a naivete.)

Too Selfless- Protagonists can bury themselves in their hopeful promises, feeling others' problems as their own and striving hard to meet their word. If they aren't careful, they can spread themselves too thin, and be left unable to help anyone. (I may spread myself thin, but the rest is not me.)

Too Sensitive- While receptive to criticism, seeing it as a tool for leading a better team, it's easy for Protagonists to take it a little too much to heart. Their sensitivity to others means that Protagonists sometimes feel problems that aren't their own and try to fix things they can't fix, worrying if they are doing enough. (I may worry to that point.)

Fluctuating Self-Esteem- Protagonists define their self-esteem by whether they are able to live up to their ideals, and sometimes ask for criticism more out of insecurity than out of confidence, always wondering what they could do better. If they fail to meet a goal or to help someone, they said they'd help, their self-confidence will undoubtedly plummet.

Struggle to Make Tough Decisions -If caught between a rock and a hard place, Protagonists can be stricken with paralysis, imagining all the consequences of their actions, especially if those consequences are humanitarian.

Protagonist Relationship

People who share the Protagonist personality type feel most at home when they are in a relationship, and few types are more eager to establish a loving commitment with their chosen partners. Protagonists take dating and relationships seriously, selecting partners with an eye towards the long haul, rather than the more casual approach that might be expected from some types in the Explorer Role group. There's really no greater joy for Protagonists than to help along the goals of someone they care about, and the interweaving of lives that a committed relationship represents is the perfect opportunity to do just that. (Me)

I'm a Slow Walker, but I Never Walk Back

Even in the dating phase, people with the Protagonist personality type are ready to show their commitment by taking the time and effort to establish themselves as dependable, trustworthy partners.

Their Intuitive (N) trait helps them to keep up with the rapidly shifting moods that are common early in relationships, but Protagonists will still rely on conversations about their mutual feelings, checking the pulse of the relationship by asking how things are, and if there's anything else they can do. While this can help to keep conflict, which Protagonists abhor, to a minimum, they also risk being overbearing, or needy Protagonists should keep in mind that sometimes the only thing that's wrong is being asked what's wrong too often. (I feel this may happen, but I don't have a problem with it.)

Protagonists don't need much to be happy, just to know that their partner is happy, and for their partner to express that happiness through visible affection. Making others' goals come to fruition is often the chiefs concern of Protagonists, and they will spare no effort in helping their partner to live the dream. If they aren't careful though, Protagonists' quest for their partners' satisfaction can leave them neglecting their own needs, and it's important for them to remember to express those needs on occasion, especially early on. (This Is me all the way.)

You cannot Escape the Responsibility of Tomorrow by Evading It Today

Protagonists' tendency to avoid any kind of conflict, sometimes even sacrificing their own principles to keep the peace, can lead to long-term problems if these efforts never fully resolve the underlying issues that they mask. On the other hand, people with the Protagonist personality type can sometimes be too preemptive in resolving their conflicts, asking for criticisms and suggestions in ways that convey neediness or insecurity. Protagonists invest their emotions wholly in their relationships and are sometimes so eager to please that it actually undermines the relationship- this can lead to resentment, and even the failure of the relationship. When this happens, Protagonists experience strong senses of guilt and betrayal, as they see all their efforts slip away. (I do see this happening but what can one do about it?)

If potential partners appreciate these qualities though and make an effort themselves to look after the needs of their Protagonist partners, they will enjoy long, happy, passionate relationships. Protagonists are known to be dependable lovers, perhaps more interested in routine and stability than spontaneity in their sex lives, but always dedicated to the selfless satisfaction of their partners. Ultimately, Protagonist personality types believe that the only true happiness is mutual happiness, and that is the stuff successful relationships are made of. (True!)

Friendships

When it comes to friendships, Protagonists are anything but passive. While some personality types may accept the circumstantial highs and lows of friendship, their feelings waxing and waning with the times, Protagonists will put active effort into maintaining these connections, viewing them as substantial and important, not something to let slip away through laziness or inattention.

This philosophy of genuine connection is core to the Protagonist personality type, and while it is visible in the workplace and in romance, it is clearest in the breadth and depth of Protagonist friendships. (Yes!)

All My life I Have Tried to Pluck a Thistle and Plant a Flower Wherever the Flower Would Grow...

People with the Protagonist personality type take genuine pleasure in getting to know other people, and have no trouble talking with people of all types and modes of thought. Even in disagreement, other perspectives are fascinating to Protagonists- though like most people, they connect best with individuals who share their principles and ideals, and types in Diplomat and Analyst Role groups are best able to explore Protagonists' viewpoints with them, which are simply too idealistic for most. It is with these closest friends that Protagonists will truly open up, keeping their many other connections in a realm of lighthearted but genuine support and encouragement.

Others truly value their Protagonist friends, appreciating the warmth, kindness, and sincere optimism and cheer they bring to the table. Protagonists want to be the best friends possible, and it shows in how they work to find out not just the superficial interests of their friends, but their strengths, passions, hopes and dreams. Nothing makes Protagonists happier than to see the people they care about do well, and they are more than happy to take their own time and energy to help make it happen.

We Should Be Too Big to Take Offense, and Too Noble to Give It

While Protagonists enjoy lending this helping hand, other personality types may simply not have the energy or drive to keep up with it- creating further strain, people with the Protagonist personality type can become offended if their efforts aren't reciprocated when the opportunity arises. Ultimately, Protagonists' give and take can become stifling to types who are more interested in the moment than the future, or who simply have Identities that rest firmly on the Assertive side, making them content with who they are and uninterested in the sort of self- improvement and goal-setting that Protagonists hold so dear. (Not Me)

When this happens Protagonist personalities can be critical, if they believe it necessary. While usually tactful and often helpful, if their friend is already annoyed by Protagonists' attempts to push them forward, it can simply cause them to dig in their heels further. Protagonists should try to avoid taking this personally when it happens and relax their inflexibility into an occasional "live and let live" attitude. (I do understand this, and I do work hard on this part of my life, not making any problem for a person worse because am I want to make people happy.)

Ultimately though, Protagonists will find that their excitement and unyielding optimism will yield them many satisfying relationships with people who appreciate and share their vision and authenticity. The joy Protagonists take in moving things forward means that there is always a sense of purpose behind their friendships, creating bonds that are not easily shaken. (True!)

Parenthood

As natural leaders, Protagonists make excellent parents, striving to strike a balance between being encouraging and supportive friends to their children, while also working to instill strong values and a sense of personal responsibility. If there's one strong trend with the Protagonist personality type, it's that they are a bedrock of empathetic support, not bullheadedly telling people what they ought to do, but helping them to explore their options and encouraging them to follow their hearts.

Protagonist parents will encourage their children to explore and grow, recognizing and appreciating the individuality of the people they bring into this world and help to raise. (True, True, True Wow!)

Whatever You Are, Be a Good One

Protagonist parents take pride in nurturing and inspiring strong values, and they take care to ensure that the basis for these values comes from understanding, not blind obedience. Whatever their children need in order to learn and grow, Protagonist parents give the time and energy necessary to provide it. While in their weaker moments they may succumb to more manipulative behavior, Protagonists mostly rely on their charm and idealism to make sure their children take these lessons to heart.

Owing to their aversion to conflict, Protagonist parents strive to ensure that their homes provide a safe and conflict free environment. While they can deliver criticism, it's not Protagonists' strong suit, and laying down the occasionally necessary discipline won't come naturally. But people with the Protagonist personality type have high standards for their children, encouraging them to be the best they can be, and when these confrontations do happen, they try to frame the lessons as archetypes, moral constants in life which they hope their children will embrace.

As their children enter adolescence, they begin to truly make their own decisions, sometimes contrary to what their parents want- while Protagonists will do their best to meet this with grace and humor, they can feel hurt, and even unloved, in the face of this rebellion. Protagonists are sensitive, and if their child goes so far as to launch into criticisms, they may become truly upset, digging in their heels and locking horns.

Career Paths

When it comes to finding a career, people with the Protagonist personality type cast their eyes towards anything that lets them do what they love most- helping other people! Lucky for them, people like being helped, and are even willing to pay for it, which means that Protagonists are rarely wanting for inspiration and opportunity in their search for meaningful work.

Don't Worry When You Are Not Recognized, but Strive to Be Worthy of Recognition

Protagonists take a genuine interest in other people, approaching them with warm sociability and a helpful earnestness that rarely goes unnoticed. Altruistic careers like social and religious work, teaching, counseling, and advising of all sorts are popular avenues, giving people with the Protagonist personality type a chance to help others learn, grow, and become more independent. This attitude, alongside their social skills, emotional intelligence and tendency to be "that person who knows everybody", can be adapted to quite a range of other careers as well, making Protagonists natural HR administrators, event coordinators, and politicians- anything that helps a community or organization to operate more smoothly.

To top it all off, Protagonists are able to express themselves both creatively and honestly, allowing them to approach positions as sales representatives and advertising consultants from a certain idealistic perspective, intuitively picking up on the needs and wants of their customers, and working to make them happier. However, Protagonists need to make sure they get to focus on people, not systems and spreadsheets, and they are unlikely to have the stomach for making the sort of decisions required in corporate governance positions- they will feel haunted, knowing that their decision cost someone their job, or that their product cost someone their life.

Having a preference for Intuitive (N) trait over its Observant (S) counterpart also means that careers demanding exceptional situational awareness, such as law enforcement, military service, and emergency response, will cause Protagonists to burn out quickly. While great at organizing willing parties and winning over skeptics, in dangerous situations Protagonists just won't be able to maintain the sort of focus on their immediate physical surroundings that they inevitably demand of themselves hour after hour, day after day. (This is the last thing, no I don't worry about what people have to say about me or how they treat me because I know everyone is different on that's what makes life more colorful, I wish all people have peace, joy, patience, self-control, faith and love. If we all show any or all of these, we have done a good thing toward all, and life can be better for everyone we meet but we cannot do it on our own.)

Always Bear In Mind That Your Own Resolution to Succeed Is More Important Than Any Other

It makes a great deal more sense for Protagonists to be the force keeping these vital services organized and running well, taking their long-term views, people skills and idealism, and using them to shape the situation on the ground, while more physical personality types manage the moment-to-moment crises. People with the Protagonist personality type are always up for a good challenge - and nothing thrills them quite like helping others. But while willing to train the necessary skills, Protagonists will always show an underlying preference for the sort of help that draws a positive long-term trend, that effects change that really sticks.

At the heart of it, Protagonists need to see how the story ends, to feel and experience the gratitude and appreciation of the people they've helped in order to be happy.

Careers operating behind enemy lines and arriving at the scene of the crime too late to help will simply weigh on Protagonists' sensitive hearts and minds, especially if criticized despite their efforts. On the other hand, Protagonists are a driven, versatile group, and that same vision that pulls them towards administration and politics can help them focus through the stress of the moment, knowing that each second of effort contributes to something bigger than themselves

Workplace Habits

People with the Protagonist personality type are intelligent, warm, idealistic, charismatic, creative, social... With this wind at their backs, Protagonists are able to thrive in many diverse roles, at any level of seniority. Moreover, they are simply likeable people, and this quality propels them to success wherever they have a chance to work with others.

Protagonist Subordinates

As subordinates, Protagonists will often underestimate themselves- nevertheless, they quickly make an Impression on their managers. Quick learners and excellent multitaskers, people with the Protagonist personality type are able to take on multiple responsibilities with competence and good cheer.

Protagonists are hardworking, reliable and eager to help- but this can all be a double-edged sword, as some managers will take advantage of Protagonists' excellent quality of character by making too many requests and overburdening their Protagonist subordinates with extra work. Protagonists are conflict averse and try to avoid unnecessary criticism, and in all likelihood will accept these extra tasks in an attempt to maintain a positive impression and frictionless environment.

Protagonist Colleagues

As colleagues, Protagonists' desire to assist and cooperate is even more evident as they draw their coworkers into teams where everyone can feel comfortable expressing their opinions and suggestions, working together to develop win-win situations that get the job done. Protagonists' tolerance, open mindedness and easy sociability make it easy for them to relate to their colleagues, but also make it perhaps a little too easy for their colleagues to shift their problems onto Protagonists' plates. People with the Protagonist personality type are sensitive to the needs of others, and their role as a social nexus means that problems inevitably find their way to Protagonists' doorsteps, where colleagues will find a willing, if overburdened, associate.

Protagonist Managers

While perfectly capable as subordinates and colleagues, Protagonists' true calling, where their capacity for insightful and inspiring communication and sensitivity to the needs of others really shows, is in managing teams. As managers, Protagonists combine their skill in recognizing individual motivations with their natural charisma to not only push their teams and projects forward, but to make their teams want to push forward. They may sometimes stoop to manipulation, the alternative often being a more direct confrontation, but Protagonists' end goal is always to get done what they set out to do in

a way that leaves everyone involved satisfied with their roles and the results they achieved together.
Conclusion

Few personality types are as inspiring and charismatic as Protagonists. Their idealism and vision allow Protagonists to overcome many challenging obstacles, more often than not brightening the lives of those around them. Protagonists' imagination is invaluable in many areas, including their own personal growth.

Yet Protagonists can be easily tripped up in areas where idealism and altruism are more of a liability than an asset. Whether it is finding (or keeping) a partner, staying calm under pressure, reaching dazzling heights on the career ladder or making difficult decisions, Protagonists need to put in a conscious effort to develop their weaker traits and additional skills. (I can see this happening; I am very careful.)

As a protagonist, I like to thank of myself as "a good person," I see my life moving toward the right decisions, I make in life. So, I do my best as not to make myself too powerful or too weak. Meaning I do my best not thinking I am better than one else or make myself weak, because I will not let anybody bully me or let them think they are better than me. No matter how much money they have or education they have because no matter where we live we live in the same world. One day everyone will see just where we are and supposed to be.

DNA

I did my DNA last year and who I have learned all I can say is I am Wow! My Ethnicity Melungeon which is a 'Free Person of Color'

I learned I am *Cameroon, -Congo, & Southern Bantu, -Benun & Togo, -Mali, -Ivory Coast/ Ghana, -Ireland & Scotland, -Germanic Europe, -Sweden, -Nigeria, -England, -Wales & Northwestern Europe, -Norway, -Senegal, -France, -and Native American.*

As I have said many times, I needed to know everything myself so I can help myself and save my life.

Therefore, I had it done, and I am glad I did.

I am who I am so be it, I belong to a lot of people. We all come from somewhere and it goes way, way back.

The reason why I did my DNA well was because I always felt like I was missing part of me. Like I was an adopted child and I needed to find out who and where I came from. Plus, with all my illnesses I needed to know what race carried what or why I have all these illnesses I have. And therefore, I did it and I am glad I did, it's a work in process.

There is something I live with just about every day. Many years I use to be a shame but through the years I *learned 'I rather be shame than to bust a gut and be lame.'* There are some days I 'cannot' leave the house this why...

TRIP TO THE STORE

I took my little cousin, to the store while we were there something happened. I was at the back wall with another customer about 6 feet. This were not one of my good days, anyway Tan was nearby and after I moved to another aisle, she came up to me and said,

Tan: "Cousin Janice, that man passed gas."

"No, he didn't!"

Tan: Yes, he did!"

"No, he didn't, it was me!"

As I was talking to her, she moved two aisles over.

"Where are you? Oh, you are acting like you don't know me. When you know came in the store with me."

Tan: "I don't know you!"

By this time, the man moved from where he was, suddenly, he stop.

Tan: "Cousin Janice, You, sent that man to 'Wonder Land' because when he walked into your stuff he couldn't move. His head and his eyes went rolling like where am I?"

"I know 'I can't help it; it just keeps coming out without my control."

It was time for me to check-out, and it was still coming up and out. The young man that checked me out he did it quickly, and he back-up to move out of its way. We both walked out of the store laughing so hard. We went to another store and this time I was walking in front of her.

Tan: "Oh, My Goodness, what was that? Why Didn't You Warn Me What I Was About to Walk Into?"

"I didn't know it came-out!"

By that time, a little boy and his dad came waking down the aisle and loudly said; "Dad somebody have Pooted!" We both looked at each other and smiled, but when we got outside, we both laughed so hard.

"I need to go in now before something else happened and I really will be shame."

So, this is why I wrote this poem you are about to read.

The Smell of Foul Gas That Has A Mind of Its Own

The very first thing we may notice is that we will start passing gas
that really do smell very foul it can be very, very foul.
We will pass it a lot, yes believe it or not, it will come out
without our control it can smell worse than the
movement of our bile.

It doesn't matter if we are sleep or awake, it doesn't matter if
we have a full stomach or if it's empty, if
we are setting or standing.
We do not have control, when it decides to take a trip,
when it shoots out like a cannon, I can't get a grip.
Just think about if we are dancing.
There are no way people can be understanding.

It doesn't matter when we are setting and talking,
or when we are standing or walking.

The smell of this very foul gas which has a
mind of its own,
It's comes out like it is one of the three top
selling colognes.

There are times I've notice this foul gas has a strong
odor of cognac,
it bubbles up and come through the front, yes, I have even notice
it bubbles up and ride up my back.

I can be out in public let's say when we are
out in a store, and I am walking down the
aisle a suddenly it's out.
Oh boy, the smell is so foul it will knock
you out, because it can smell like
brussels sprout!

Suddenly, someone would come down the aisle so I would rush
and leave that aisle so they wouldn't know it's me.
Who am I fooling I know they smell this very, very foul gas that
decided to go on a shopping spree?

What about when I am walking with a family member or a
friend, then suddenly it comes out silently.
They will walk right into it and suddenly I would hear oh my
goodness what a foul odor, what a pity, I would have to say I
can't help it, I have no control because it is as it has a mind
of its own, it like it's my rivalry.
I really do wish it would happen in privacy.

Do believe me this foul smell is no joke,
its smell will get in your nose
and throat.

Yes, this very, very foul smell has a
mind of its own.
When it happens, I really do wish I
could be at home.

So, I must ask do you think I am a
Survivor or what?
What would you do when something that
foul would come from your gut?
Would you feel like you are going crazy, or do you feel
like you are going nut?

Do I act like, or do I feel like I am a Survivor,
I know I am not Macgyve?

The Smell of Foul Gas That Has A
Mind of Its Own!
I do know this which it would smell
like cologne!

Wow I can't believe it my final word is Joy.

Dictionary's View: Joy is intense and especially ecstatic or exultant happiness, pleasure, or satisfaction. It is an instance of such feeling. It is expression of such feeling. Joy is a deep feeling or condition of happiness or contentment. It is something causing such a feeling, a source of happiness. It is an outward show of pleasure or delight, rejoicing.

Biblical View: Joy is a fruit of our Grand Creator's spirit after Love. It is not a mere personality trait that we are born with it is part of "the new personality," and we should "clothe ourselves with the new personality." Joy is a state of true happiness, even exultation.

This project has been a Joy for me, I will not confuse being joyful with simply being jovial or cheerful. will not be in a hilarious mood like when someone has had to many drinks or on drugs and when they sober up or comes down from a high, they will stop laughing and they will return to a life full of sorrow and troubles. Instead, I want my Joy to come from a deep-seated quality of my heart. Because I know I want to share my Joy to as many people as I can. This means when I see a person who's disturbed about something, I really do want to help them find the Joy in their heart. I want to help people develop Joy so they can be better able to cope with the stresses of life. Thanks for letting me share my life trials, illnesses, and more. Thank you for letting me share how I have survived the things I have shared with you and I am finding out there are even more things happening to me currently. But I will do all I can to survive if I can or as long as I can because.

"I AM A SURVIVOR" "I AM A SURVIVOR" "I AM A SURVIVOR!"

And so, can you, if you want to live, 'you can fight with all your might,' even when it is hard. Just remember it first starts with your mind because if you don't have the right mindset, you cannot help yourself because it will take will power. You will have to dig deep within yourself, you will need to see goodness in people and the things around you then you too can say.

"I AM A SURVIVOR" "I AM A SURVIVOR" "I AM A SURVIVOR!"

How Do I know If I Am A Survivor?

How can I endure when I am faced with trials? I know, I will look for the joy of better things ahead. I must have endurance, my faith, I must defend. I will fight with all my might and not give in, because my purpose I must defend.

Through the years I have seen much sorrow and pain, I do look beyond the tears, and I see the life I have gain. It makes me feel free, it keeps me determined to fight with assurance and it helps to keep me not wanting to give up.

If this is what makes a Survivor, I really hope this is in me. I see no need for doubt or fear because as long as I have Faith, Hope, Joy, Endurance and Love, I know I can endure to the end.

The End

POEMS TITLES

THE REPORT THEY HAD DONE

MoldREPORT

Date of Sampling: 10-20-2017
Date of Receipt: 10-20-2017
Date of Report: 10-23-2017

Table of Contents

Thank you for choosing MoldREPORT™ from EMLab P&K. Our mission is to provide industry leadership for the assessment of mold in the home indoor environment.

Your MoldREPORT™ is designed and intended for use by professional inspectors in office and residential home inspections to help in the assessment of mold growth in the living areas sampled by professional inspectors. Our laboratory analysis is based on the samples submitted to EMLab P&K. Please read the entire report to fully understand the complete MoldREPORT™ process. The following is a summary of the report sections:

1. Detailed Results of Sample Analysis - Laboratory results from the samples collected at the site.

2. Understanding Your Sample Analysis Results - Detailed summary of how to understand the analytical results from the air samples and/or surface samples including interpretive guidelines.

3. Important Information, Terms and Conditions - General information to help you understand and interpret your MoldREPORT™, including important terms, conditions and applicable legal provision relating to this report.

4. Scope and Limitations - Important information regarding the scope of the MoldREPORT™ system, and limitations
of mold inspection, air sampling, and surface sampling.

5. Glossary - Definitions and descriptions of frequently used terms and commonly found mold.

6. References and Resources - Literature, websites, and other materials that can provide more in-depth information about mold and indoor air quality.

MoldREPORT

Date of Sampling: 10-20-2017
Date of Receipt: 10-20-2017
Date of Report: 10-23-2017

Summary of Sample Analysis Results

Do not take any action based on the results of this report until you have read the entire report. .

Air Sample Summary:

The MoldSCORE™ was in the LOW range for the following area(s): 24181997, 24182032, 24182009, 24182017. A low MoldSCORE™ indicates the air sample did not detect, relative to the outside air, the presence of indoor mold growth in this room at the time of sampling.

Please see the sections titled "Detailed Results of the Air Sample Analysis" and "Understanding Your Air Sample Analysis Results" for important additional information.

Location	MoldSCORE™				Exposure Level					
24181997: Guest Bedroom * see p. 4 for details	Lower <110	200	Higher 300	Mold Score 124	Lower <200	1K	10K	Higher >70K	Location spores/m3 160	Outside spores/m3 3,000
24182032: Living Room * see p. 5 for details	Lower <110	200	Higher 300	Mold Score 111	Lower <200	1K	10K	Higher >70K	Location spores/m3 220	Outside spores/m3 3,000
24182009: Master Bedroom * see p. 6 for details	Lower <110	200	Higher 300	Mold Score 125	Lower <200	1K	10K	Higher >70K	Location spores/m3 140	Outside spores/m3 3,000
24182017: Dining/Kitchen * see p. 7 for details	Lower <110	200	Higher 300	Mold Score 131	Lower <200	1K	10K	Higher >70K	Location spores/m3 240	Outside spores/m3 3,000

(1) There is no outside for the Dining/Kitchen.

(2) As for the guest Bedroom this was done before they brought back my stuff that was in that room.

(3) As they say they only did an Air test.

(4) I had someone to come in that did Air test Also. They show me what the Air was and what it should/could be After using their Air machine ran for 10 mins.

(5) The test was done in the Living Room + Kitchen Counter.

(6) These Counts Are done for live spores. But there Are still dead spores Which is still As danger As live spores.

(7) Plus this test was done After A month running 1, 2+3 machines to dry out the Air.

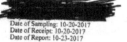

Date of Sampling: 10-20-2017
Date of Receipt: 10-20-2017
Date of Report: 10-23-2017

Detailed Results of the Air Sample Analysis

Location Lab ID-version:‡ 8508221-1 24181997: Guest Bedroom	Overall Mold Source Assessment* (Likelihood spores originated inside)			Overall Exposure Level (Shown on a log scale)				Outside 28514772-1 24182062	
	Lower <110	Higher 200 300	Mold Score 124	Lower <200 1K 10K >70K	Higher	Location spores m3 160	raw ct 6	Outside spores m3 3,000	raw ct 226

Indicators of Mold Growth Indoors

	Indicator Mold Source Assessment* (Likelihood spores originated inside)			Indicator Exposure Level (Shown on a log scale)					
	Lower <110	Higher 200 300	Mold Score	Lower <200 1K 10K >70K	Higher	Location spores m3	raw ct	Outside spores m3	raw ct
A) Penicillium/Aspergillus types**			124			160	6	210	8
B) Cladosporium species spores			100			<7	0	1,300	163
C) Basidiospores			100			<7	0	1,100	42
D) "Marker" spore types***			100			<7	0	<7	0
E) "Other" spore types***,****			100			<7	0	218	8

Other Sample Information

Sample clarity & visibility

	Good	Moderate	Poor
Location		X	
Outside		X	

"Good" = background debris is light enough to pose no difficulty in analyzing air samples.
"Poor" = background debris so heavy that it poses a significant difficulty in analyzing the air sample accurately. Results are most likely lower limits

what do maisnti mian?
Comments

Location | None

Outside | 152 of the raw count Cladosporium spores were present as several clumps. Data transferred from EMLab ID: 1817174 at client's request

Other "normal trapping" spores***

	Exposure Level (Highly unlikely to be from indoors)					
Lower <200 1K	10K >70K	Higher	Location spores m3	raw ct	Outside spores m3	raw ct
			<7	0	130	5

	Location	Outside
Sample volume (liters)	150	150

* Rated on a scale from low to high. A MoldSCORE™ rating of <150 is low and indicates a low probability of spores originating inside. A MoldSCORE™ rating of >250 is high and indicates a high probability that the spores originated from inside, presumably from indoor mold growth. A MoldSCORE™ between 150 and 250 indicates a moderate likelihood of indoor fungal growth. EMLab P&K's MoldSCORE™ analysis is NOT intended for wall cavity samples. It is intended for ambient air samples in residences. Using the MoldSCORE™ analysis on other samples (like wall cavity samples) will lead to misleading results.

** The spores of Penicillium and Aspergillus (and others such as Acremonium and Paecilomyces) are small and round with very few distinguishing characteristics. They cannot be differentiated by spore trap sampling methods. Also some species with very small spores are easily missed, and may be undercounted. The Penicillium Aspergillus indicator operates on the assumption that the majority of the spores in this category are, in fact, Penicillium or Aspergillus.

*** The spores reported in this category come from many different mold types. As a result, the mold types represented by the counts for the "Location" sample may be different than the mold types represented by the counts for the outside sample. The totals shown are the summation of the rounded values for the spores types in the category and may contain more than two significant figures

**** The spores of smuts, Periconia, and myxomycetes look similar and cannot generally be distinguished by spore trap analysis. Smuts are plant pathogens and are not likely to be on indoor surfaces. Periconia is rarely found growing indoors. However, myxomycetes, the spores of which look similar, can occasionally grow indoors. Because there is a small probability of indoor sources, these spore types are indicated in the "other" spore types category. False positives may result if the spores are smuts, not myxomycetes.

‡A "Version" indicated by "x" after the Lab ID# with a value greater than 1 indicates a sample with amended data. The revision number is reflected by the value of "x".
Total spores/m3 has been rounded to two significant figures to reflect analytical precision.
The analytical sensitivity is the spores/m³3 divided by the raw count, expressed in spores/m³3. The limit of detection is the analytical sensitivity (in spores/m³3) multiplied by the sample volume (in liters) divided by 1000 liters.
This report is generated by EMLab P&K, at the request, and for the exclusive use, of the EMLab P&K client named in this report. Important terms, conditions, and limitations apply. The EMLab P&K client and all readers of this report are advised to completely read the information, terms, conditions and limitations of this report.
© 2002 - 2010 EMLab P&K
EMLab P&K, LLC

MoldREPORT

Date of Sampling: 10-20-2017
Date of Receipt: 10-20-2017
Date of Report: 10-23-2017

Detailed Results of the Air Sample Analysis

Location	Overall Mold Source Assessment* (Likelihood spores originated inside)			Overall Exposure Level (Shown on a log scale)					Outside ‡8514072-1	
Lab ID-version:‡ 8508222-1	Lower	Higher	Mold	Lower		Higher	Location		24182062	
	<110	200	330	<200	1K	10K >70K	spores/m3	raw ct	spores/m3	raw ct
24182032: Living Room			Score 111				220	21	3,000	226

Indicators of Mold Growth Indoors

	Indicator Mold Source Assessment* (Likelihood spores originated inside)			Indicator Exposure Level (Shown on a log scale)						
	Lower	Higher	Mold	Lower		Higher	Location		Outside	
	<110	200	330	<200	1K	10K >70K	spores/m3	raw ct	spores/m3	raw ct
A) Penicillium/Aspergillus types**			Score 106				53	2	210	8
B) Cladosporium species spores			101				110	17	1,300	163
C) Basidiospores			100				27	1	1,100	42
D) "Marker" spore types***			100				<7	0	<7	0
E) "Other" spore types***,****			111				27	1	218	8
1) Bipolaris/Drechslera group										

Other Sample Information

Sample clarity & visibility

	Good	Moderate	Poor
Location		X	
Outside		X	

"Good" = background debris is light enough to pose no difficulty in analyzing air samples.
"Poor" = background debris so heavy that it poses a significant difficulty in analyzing the air sample accurately. Results are most likely lower limits.

Other "normal trapping" spores*

	Exposure Level (Highly unlikely to be from indoors)						
Lower		Higher	Location		Outside	
<200	1K	10K >70K	spores/m3	raw ct	spores/m3	raw ct
			<7	0	130	5

	Location	Outside
Sample volume (liters)	150	150

Comments

Location	17 of the raw count *Cladosporium* spores were present as a single clump.
Outside	152 of the raw count *Cladosporium* spores were present as several clumps. Data transferred from EMLab ID: 1817174 at client's request.

* Rated on a scale from low to high. A MoldSCORE™ rating of <150 is low and indicates a low probability of spores originating inside. A MoldSCORE™ rating of >250 is high and indicates a high probability that the spores originated from inside, presumably from indoor mold growth. A MoldSCORE™ between 150 and 250 indicates a moderate likelihood of indoor fungal growth. EMLab P&K's MoldSCORE™ analysis is NOT intended for wall cavity samples. It is intended for ambient air samples in residences. Using the MoldSCORE™ analysis on other samples (like wall cavity samples) will lead to misleading results.

** The spores of *Penicillium* and *Aspergillus* (and others such as *Acremonium* and *Paecilomyces*) are small and round with very few distinguishing characteristics. They cannot be differentiated by spore trap sampling methods. Also some species with very small spores are easily missed, and may be undercounted. The *Penicillium/Aspergillus* indicator operates on the assumption that the majority of the spores in this category are, in fact, *Penicillium* or *Aspergillus*.

*** The spores reported in this category, come from many different mold types. As a result, the mold types represented by the counts for the "Location" sample may be different than the mold types represented by the counts for the outside sample. The totals shown are the summation of the rounded values for the spores types in the category, and may contain more than two significant figures.

**** The spores of smuts, *Periconia*, and myxomycetes look similar and cannot generally be distinguished by spore trap analysis. Smuts are plant pathogens and are not likely to be on indoor surfaces. *Periconia* is rarely found growing indoors. However, myxomycetes, the spores of which look similar, can occasionally grow indoors. Because there is a small probability of indoor sources, these spore types are indicated in the "other" spore types category. False positives may result if the spores are smuts, not myxomycetes.

‡A "Version" indicated by -"x" after the Lab ID# with a value greater than 1 indicates a sample with amended data. The revision number is reflected by the value of "x".
Total spores/m3 has been rounded to two significant figures to reflect analytical precision.
The analytical sensitivity for the spores/m3 divided by the raw count, expressed in spores/m3. The limit of detection is the analytical sensitivity for spores/m3) multiplied by the sample volume (in liters) divided by 1000 liters.
This report is generated by EMLab P&K, at the request, and for the exclusive use, of the EMLab P&K client named in this report. Important terms, conditions, and limitations apply. The EMLab P&K client and all readers of this report are advised to completely read the information, terms, conditions and limitations of this report.
© 2002 - 2010 EMLab P&K
EMLab P&K, LLC

EMLab ID: 1817172. Page 5 of 18

MoldREPORT

Date of Sampling: 10-20-2017
Date of Receipt: 10-20-2017
Date of Report: 10-23-2017

Detailed Results of the Air Sample Analysis

Location Lab ID-version: SS0823-1	Overall Mold Source Assessment	Overall Exposure Level
24182009: Master Bedroom	125	140 · 6 · 3,000 · 270

Indicators of Mold Growth Indoors

	Indicator Mold Source Assessment	Indicator Exposure Level
A) Penicillium/Aspergillus types**	107	53 · 3 · 210 · 8
B) Cladosporium species spores	100	<7 · 0 · 1,300 · 56
C) Basidiospores	100	<7 · 0 · 1,100 · 42
D) "Marker" spore types***	111	7 · 1 · <7 · 0
1) Chaetomium		
E) "Other" spore types***,****	125	81 · 3 · 218 · 8
1) Curvularia 2) Nigrospora 3) Smuts, Periconia, Myxomycetes		

Other Sample Information

Sample clarity & visibility

Location	Good	Medium	Poor
Location		X	
Outside		X	

Other "normal trapping" spores***

	Exposure Level
	<7 · 0 · 130 · 5

	Location	Outside
Sample volume (liters)	150	150

Comments

Location	None
Outside	152 of the raw count Cladosporium spores were present as several clumps. Data transferred from EMLab ID: 1817174 at client's request.

* Rated on a scale from low to high. A MoldSCORE™ rating of <150 is low and indicates a low probability of spores originating inside. A MoldSCORE™ rating of >250 is high and indicates a high probability that the spores originated from inside, presumably from indoor mold growth. A MoldSCORE™ between 150 and 250 indicates a moderate likelihood of indoor fungal growth. EMLab P&K's MoldSCORE™ analysis is NOT intended for wall cavity samples. It is intended for ambient air samples in residences. Using the MoldSCORE™ analysis on other samples like wall cavity samples will lead to misleading results.

** The spores of Penicillium and Aspergillus (and others such as Acremonium and Paecilomyces) are small and round with very few distinguishing characteristics. They cannot be differentiated by spore trap sampling methods. Also some species with very small spores are easily missed, and may be underreported. The Penicillium/Aspergillus indicator spores are the assumption that the majority of the spores in this category are, in fact, Penicillium or Aspergillus.

*** The spores reported in this category come from many different mold types. As a result, the mold types represented in the counts for the "Location" sample may be different than the mold types represented by the spores for the outside sample. The totals shown are the summation of the rounded values for the spore types in the category, and may contain more than one significant figure.

**** The spores of smuts, Periconia and myxomycetes look similar and cannot generally be distinguished by spore trap analysis. Smuts are plant pathogens and are not likely to be on indoor surfaces. Periconia is rarely found growing indoors. However, in some cases, the spores of which look similar, can occasionally grow indoors. Because there is a small probability of indoor sources, these spore types are indicated in the "other" spore types category. False positives may result if the spores are smuts, but myxomycetes.

‡A "Version" indicated by "-x" after the Lab ID# with a value greater than 1 indicates a sample with unlimited data. The revision number is reflected by the value of "x".

Total spores/m3 has been rounded to two significant figures to reflect analytical precision.

The analytical sensitivity is the spores/m3 indicated by the raw count, expressed in spores/m3. The limit of detection is the analytical sensitivity (in spores/m3) multiplied by the sample volume (in liters) divided by the 1000 liters.

This report is generated by EMLab P&K at the request, and for the exclusive use, of the EMLab P&K client named in this report. Important terms, conditions, and limitations apply. The EMLab P&K client and all readers of this report are advised to completely read the information, terms, conditions and limitations of this report.

© 2002-2010 EMLab P&K
EMLab P&K, LLC

MoldREPORT

Date of Sampling: 10-20-2017
Date of Receipt: 10-20-2017
Date of Report: 10-23-2017

Detailed Results of the Air Sample Analysis

Location **Lab ID-version:‡ 8508224-1**	Overall Mold Source Assessment* (Likelihood spores originated inside)			Overall Exposure Level (Shown on a log scale)			Outside ‡8514072-1	
	Lower <110	Higher 500	Mold Score	Lower <200	Higher 10K	Location spores/m3	raw ct	Outside spores/m3	raw ct
24182017: Dining/Kitchen			131			240	9	3,000	226

Indicators of Mold Growth Indoors

	Indicator Mold Source Assessment* (Likelihood spores originated inside)			Indicator Exposure Level (Shown on a log scale)				
	Lower <110	Higher 300	Mold Score	Lower <200	Higher 10K	Location spores/m3	raw ct	Outside spores/m3	raw ct
A) Penicillium/Aspergillus types**			131			210	8	210	8
B) Cladosporium species spores			100			< 7	0	1,300	163
C) Basidiospores			100			< 7	0	1,100	42
D) "Marker" spore types***			100			< 7	0	< 7	0
E) "Other" spore types***,****			104			27	1	218	8
1) Smuts, Periconia, Myxomycetes									

Other Sample Information

Sample clarity & visibility

	Good	Moderate	Poor
Location		X	
Outside			X

"Good" = background debris is light enough to pose no difficulty in analyzing air samples
"Poor" = background debris so heavy that it poses a significant difficulty in analyzing the air
sample accurately. Results are most likely lower limits.

Other "normal trapping" spores***

	Exposure Level (Highly unlikely to be from indoors)				
	Lower <200	Higher 10K	Location spores/m3	raw ct	Outside spores/m3	raw ct
			< 7	0	130	5

	Location	Outside
Sample volume (liters)	150	150

Comments

Location	None
Outside	152 of the raw count Cladosporium spores were present as several clumps. Data transferred from EMLab ID: 1817174 at client's request.

* Rated on a scale from low to high. A MoldSCORE™ rating of <150 is low and indicates a low probability of spores originating inside. A MoldSCORE™ rating of >250 is high and indicates a high probability that the spores originated from inside, presumably from indoor mold growth. A MoldSCORE™ between 150 and 250 indicates a moderate likelihood of indoor fungal growth. EMLab P&K's MoldSCORE™ analysis is NOT intended for wall cavity samples. It is intended for ambient air samples in residences. Using the MoldSCORE™ analysis on other samples (like wall cavity samples) will lead to misleading results.

** The spores of Penicillium and Aspergillus (and others such as Acremonium and Paecilomyces) are small and round with very few distinguishing characteristics. They cannot be differentiated by spore trap sampling methods. Also some species with very small spores are easily missed, and may be undercounted. The Penicillium/Aspergillus indicator operates on the assumption that the majority of the spores in this category are, in fact, Penicillium or Aspergillus.

*** The spores reported in this category come from many different mold types. As a result, the mold types represented by the counts for the "Location" sample may be different than the mold types represented by the counts for the outside sample. The totals shown are the summation of the rounded values for the spores types in the category and may contain more than two significant figures.

**** The spores of smuts, Periconia, and myxomycetes look similar and cannot generally be distinguished by spore trap analysis. Smuts are plant pathogens and are not likely to be on indoor surfaces. Periconia is rarely found growing indoors. However, myxomycetes, the spores of which look similar, can occasionally grow indoors. Because there is a small probability of indoor sources, these spore types are indicated in the "other" spore types category. False positives may result if the spores are smuts, not myxomycetes.

‡A "Version" indicated by "v" after the Lab ID# with a value greater than 1 indicates a sample with amended data. The revision number is reflected by the value of "v".
Total spores/m3 has been rounded to two significant figures to reflect analytical precision.
The analytical sensitivity is the spores/m3 divided by the raw count, expressed in spores/m3. The limit of detection is the analytical sensitivity (in spores/m3) multiplied by the sample volume (in liters) divided by 1000 liters.
This report is generated by EMLab P&K at the request and for the exclusive use of the EMLab P&K client named in this report. Important terms, conditions, and limitations apply. The EMLab P&K client and all readers of this report are advised to completely read the information, terms, conditions and limitations of this report.
© 2002 - 2010 EMLab P&K
EMLab P&K, LLC

Date of Sampling: 10-20-2017
Date of Receipt: 10-20-2017
Date of Report: 10-23-2017

Understanding Your Air Sample Analysis Results

Description of the Air MoldREPORT™ Analysis
Mold spores are present in virtually all environments, both indoors and outdoors, with a few notable exceptions such as industrial clean rooms and hospital organ transplant rooms. Generally, in "normal" or "clean" indoor environments, indoor spore levels are lower, on average, than outdoor levels. However, even the most simple rules (such as "inside/outside" ratios) are not always appropriate for determining whether there is a source of mold growth indoors, and may provide false or misleading results. One reason these simple methods do not always work is because both outdoor and indoor spores levels vary widely due to factors such as weather conditions and activity levels within the room. For example, even in a "normal" home, spore levels can be higher than outdoors at certain times, such as after vacuuming (when airborne indoor levels could be unusually high) or after a heavy snow (when outdoor levels could be unusually low).

MoldREPORT™ is designed and intended to provide an easily understood report for residential home inspections to help in the assessment of mold growth in the living areas sampled. MoldREPORT™ relies on non-invasive and non-destructive tests, so it cannot guarantee that hidden mold problems will be detected and reported. MoldREPORT™ results apply only to the rooms or areas tested, at the time of sampling. Factors taken into consideration include, but are not limited to, the distribution of spore types, absolute levels inside and outside, relative levels inside and outside, the range and variation of spore levels that normally occur outside, and the types of spores present.

Providing you with a helpful, understandable and top quality interpretation requires special expertise. EMLab P&K recognizes this and has taken the following steps to provide the best possible interpretation of your air sampling results.

1. Your samples were analyzed by EMLab P&K.

2. We utilize the proprietary MoldREPORT™ analysis system, which was developed by a team including leading professionals in the indoor air quality (IAQ) industry.

MoldSCORE™
The MoldSCORE™ indicates the likelihood, based upon the air sample laboratory data, that there is unusual or excessive mold growth in the properly sampled indoor area(s). It is calculated using EMLab P&K's proprietary MoldREPORT™ system, based upon the indicator scores described in the following paragraphs. When the on-site inspection and sampling are done properly, MoldREPORT™ is less likely to give false results than other, simpler methods of interpretation often employed for routine home inspections, such as ratio analysis. It is important to bear in mind that any analytical method, findings, and interpretation should be used with a degree of caution and common sense. Any decisions related to health should be made in consultation with a medical doctor, and nothing in this report is intended to provide medical advice or indicate whether a medical or safety problem exists.

Descriptions of the indicators:

Quantity and concentration of *Penicillium/Aspergillus* spore types
This score indicates the likelihood that spores of *Penicillium* or *Aspergillus* present in the indoor sample originated from indoor sources. A high score suggests that there is a high probability that *Penicillium* or *Aspergillus* is originating indoors, such as from active mold growth. A low score indicates that the spores present are more likely to have originated from outdoor sources and come inside through doors and windows, carried in on people's clothing, or similar methods. *Penicillium* and *Aspergillus* are among the most common molds found growing indoors and are one of the more commonly found molds outside as well. Their spores are frequently present in both outdoor and indoor air, even in relatively clean, mold-growth-free, indoor environments. Additionally, their levels vary significantly based upon activity levels, dustiness, weather conditions, outside air exchange rates, and other factors.

Date of Sampling: 10-20-2017
Date of Receipt: 10-20-2017
Date of Report: 10-23-2017

Understanding Your Air Sample Analysis Results (continued)

Quantity and concentration of *Cladosporium* spores
This score indicates the likelihood that spores of *Cladosporium* present in the indoor sample originated from indoor sources. A high rating indicates that there is probably a source of *Cladosporium* spores in this location. *Cladosporium* is one of the most commonly found molds outdoors and is also frequently found growing indoors. Even more so than *Penicillium* and *Aspergillus*, spores from *Cladosporium* are generally present in outdoor and indoor air, even in relatively clean, mold-growth-free, indoor environments. Its levels also vary based upon activity levels, weather conditions, dustiness, outside air exchange rates, and other factors.

Quantity and concentration of basidiospores
This score indicates the likelihood that basidiospores present in the indoor sample originated from indoor sources. Basidiospores are extremely common outdoors and originate from fungi in gardens, forests, and woodlands. It is rare for the source of basidiospores to be indoors because basidiospores are produced by a group of fungi that includes mushrooms and other "macrofungi" (and are not technically molds). Their concentrations can be extremely high outdoors during wet conditions such as rain. Nevertheless, in certain conditions basidiospores can be produced indoors, and a high rating indicates that there is probably a source of basidiospores indoors. One reason basidiospores are important is that they can be an indicator of wood decay (e.g. "dry rot"), a condition that can dramatically reduce the structural integrity of a building.

Quantity and concentration of "marker" spore types
This score indicates the likelihood that certain distinctive types of mold present in the indoor sample originated from indoor sources. Certain types of mold are generally found in very low numbers outdoors. Consequently, their presence indoors, even in relatively low numbers compared to *Penicillium*, for example, is often an indication that these molds are originating from growth indoors. When present, these mold types are often the clearest indicator of a mold problem. Note, however, that the absence of marker spore types does not mean that a mold problem does not exist in a house; it just means that if a problem is present, it either involves types of mold that are more commonly found both indoors and outdoors, or that the spores from these molds were not airborne at the time of sampling.

Quantity and concentration of "other" spore types
This score indicates the likelihood that other types of mold present in the indoor sample originated from indoor sources. This score includes a heterogeneous group of genera that are not covered by any of the scores discussed above, and so it is difficult to make generalizations about this group. Molds in the "other" category are generally found outdoors in moderate numbers, and are therefore not considered markers of indoor growth. They are frequently found indoors but in lower numbers compared to *Cladosporium* and *Penicillium/Aspergillus* spores.

Other Sample Information:

Sample clarity and visibility
Air samples collect dirt and debris in addition to mold spores. Higher levels of debris make analysis more difficult, because they obscure the analyst's view of spores and can therefore lead to undercounting of the mold spores present. When sample clarity and visibility is rated "poor", the analytical results should be regarded as minimal and actual counts may be higher than reported.

Other "normal trapping" spores
Some molds do not grow on wet building materials and, consequently, are not usually indicative of building problems, or growth on building surfaces. Strict plant pathogens, for example, even if present in high numbers indoors, are not an indication of a building leak or mold growth on a wall or carpet. This section of the report focuses on the exposure level that may be due to these spore types.

February 9, 2018

Janice Holliman

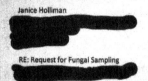

RE: Request for Fungal Sampling

Dear Mrs. Holliman,

On January 30, 2018 Healthy Air USA performed a limited environmental assessment of the apartment home located at the above address. The apartment was part of a larger building used for multifamily living. The purpose of this investigation was to determine if unusual or elevated levels of indoor mold and other air-borne contaminants were present. The scope of the investigation was limited to the accessible conditioned spaces of the home. Two fungal samples were taken for laboratory analysis. The assessment was restricted to fungal conditions and volume of air-borne particles only. No other environmental tests or assessments were conducted.

The type or method of construction is evaluated as the first step in assessing a building for conditions that support mold growth. Following that, a determination is made if conditions are present or can be present to sustain mold growth without an unusual water event. The assessment includes a thorough visual inspection, noting water marks and damage to ceiling including ceiling tiles, paint, cabinet, window frames/sills, wall, base trim, floor surfaces and swelling of wood trim and floor coverings. A visual inspection includes air registers, inside air-ducts, air-handler cabinet and cooling coil. Moisture measurements are taken in building materials located in areas moisture is likely to be elevated including concrete floors and walls. Although indoor humidity changes rapidly and frequently, it is also checked.

If evidence indicates building materials are holding or have held too much moisture in the past, one must assume that there is or was active mold growth. Additionally, if the building was constructed in a way that traps water in or around the foundation or floor slab that will allow moisture to migrate into the building, one must assume that there is or was active mold growth.

If conditions as described above are present, it should be assumed that there is mold growth, growth has occurred in the past or will most certainly occur in the future. Mold testing is merely a snapshot in time and should not be exclusively relied on to reflect the quality of the building's air. Contaminants that periodically become airborne and collect on surfaces due to various activities may not show up in fungal samples taken for laboratory test at a particular time. Therefore, mold testing should not be solely relied on to determine the health of a home or building.

OBSERVATIONS:

Interior:
The walls and ceilings of the home were finished with drywall. The flooring was covered with a mixture of vinyl and carpet.

The areas of stated concern were the exterior wall along the side of the home with the patio and the corner of the dining room adjacent to the mechanical room. The areas had been subject to water intrusion from either leaking plumbing or improper drainage of rainwater away from the building.

The relative humidity was not elevated throughout the apartment. The areas along the exterior wall with the patio had visible water staining. The staining was observed on the baseboards and the drywall. The carpet and padding were tested for trapped moisture with a moisture meter. Elevated moisture readings were obtained from the exterior wall to approximately 30 inches into the apartment. The door frame leading to the patio was stained from water exposure.

The corner of the dining room adjacent to the mechanical closet had staining on the baseboards. The carpet was slightly removed from the corner and the tack strip nails were rusted and the tack strips were dark brown and black, likely from water exposure. The carpet did not have elevated moisture content in the dining room.

The door leading to the mechanical room was locked at the time of our assessment. The interior of the mechanical room was observed by removing the return air register and photographing the interior of the room. The water heater was directly against the wall behind the return air register and was coated with dust and debris. The filter in the HVAC system did not appear to be properly seated, which can allow dust and debris to bypass the filter. The insulation visible on the air handler was coated with dust. The evaporator coils were not visible or accessible during our assessment.

Mold was observed on numerous surfaces around the apartment. Mold was observed on doors, window blinds, bags, around the HVAC system, and on drywall.

Particle Measurements:

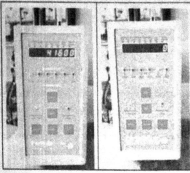

This group of pictures is provided to bring a frame of reference and comparison for volume of air-borne particles measured in your home and listed below. The laser particle scan displays the volume of particles in one cubic foot of air sizes 0.3 and 2.0 microns in size respectively. See explanation below.

The number of 0.3 and 2.0 micron air-borne particles were measured in one cubic foot of air using a laser particle scan. The particles can be atmospheric dust, smoke, pollen, fiberglass, bacteria, insect skeletal parts and mold spores. Point three micron particles are a measurement of air quality. Whenever measuring air-borne particulates where common household dust is present, high levels of 2.0 micron particles often indicate the presence of elevated mold spores. However fungal sampling for laboratory analysis must be done to confirm any assumption.

The table below shows the approximate levels of air-born particles Healthy Air finds in well maintained buildings and lists the actual numbers of particles found in the air. The temperature and relative humidity were measured and converted into grains of moisture per pound of air (actual amount of moisture present) and dew point. Dew point can determine the point at which materials will begin to absorb enough moisture from the air to create conditions for mold growth.

	0.3 microns	2.0 microns	Temp (°F)	Relative Humidity (%)	Grains of Moisture Per Pound of Air	Dew Point (°F)
Optimal	≤ 500,000	0	68° – 78°	35% - 45%	36 - 62	42° - 54°
Dining Room	172,875	11,695	65°	41%	37	41°
Living Room	128,672	7,249	65°	41%	37	41°
Master Bedroom	144,077	4,417	65°	41%	37	41°
Kitchen	190,319	14,555	65°	41%	37	41°
Guest Bedroom	136,771	2,803	65°	41%	37	41°

The particulate concentration was above Healthy Air's recommended optimal levels as bolded in the chart above. The HVAC system blower wheel was turned to "on" prior to taking measurements to assess potential particulate matter in the HVAC system.

Fungal Sampling:

Non-viable samples are taken in cassette slide impactors (also referred to as spore traps), tape lifts, or swabs. The sampling devises are designed for rapid collection and analysis of a wide range of airborne particles, including fungal spores. The cassettes are connected with a vacuum pump and up to 150 liters of air are drawn into the cassette and impacted onto a small slide between the two halves of the cylinder. Samples were sealed in a zip lock bag and delivered to Aerobiology Laboratory Associates, Inc. in Smyrna, GA for microscopic analysis. The technique detects fungal genus only and does not allow for differentiation between species.

There are currently no regulatory standards for acceptable or "safe" levels of indoor mold. Therefore, there are no numeric standards. Generally speaking, the overall concentration should be similar to or lower than outdoors. However, bio aerosol levels change throughout the day, week or season, and are also affected by the type and level of activity within the structure. (Air Quality Sciences, Technical Bulletins). We typically expect indoor counts to be 30% to 80% of the outdoor spore counts, with the same general distribution of spore types present. The presence or absence of a few genera in small numbers should not be considered abnormal (Environmental Microbiology Laboratory, Inc.).

Another method Healthy Air may use from time to time is to compare the results with EML (Environmental Monitoring Laboratories) regional averages. Over several years EMLab P&K has developed averages of fungal air samples in regions throughout the country. HealthyAir believes this is a better method since the indoor environment is a controlled climate/environment and outdoor fungal levels change with activity, season, temperature, wind, humidity, rain and other conditions.

Regardless of outdoor levels or other control sample comparisons, HealthyAir, LLC has zero tolerance for Stachybotrys sp, Chaetomium, Memnoniella, Trichoderma and/or Fusarium mold spores. Various types of fungal spores can cause health problems in immunocompromised individuals by being able to initiate infection only while they are alive. Others are capable of causing allergic disease, activation of asthma, or other health problems even when they are dead.

Results of lab analysis

Spore Identification	Sample Number / Location HA8105-1 / Living Room Spores per cubic meter of air	Sample Number / Location WR Outside / Breezeway Spores per cubic meter of air
ascospores	13	ND
basidiospores	13	187
Botrytis	13	ND
Chaetomium	40	ND
Cladosporium	167	327
Curvularia	7	ND
hyphal elements	73	40
Memnoniella	340	ND
Penicillium/Aspergillus group	1,973	80
Pithomyces	7	ND
Smuts, Periconia, Myxomycetes	7	27
Torula	7	ND

Spore Identification	Sample Number / Location	Sample Number / Location
	HA8105-1 / Living Room	WR Outside / Breezeway
	Spores per cubic meter of air	Spores per cubic meter of air

Air samples were collected in an Air-O-Cell spore trap.
Flow rate was 15 liters per minute and was field calibrated prior to sampling.
Sample time was 10 minutes per air sample.
ND: Not Detected / Not Observed

Based on the laboratory results, spores related to water damage in buildings were found in the samples. Chaetomium and Memnoniella spores can cause illness in even otherwise healthy individuals and are an indication of long term / severely water damaged building materials. Elevated concentrations of Penicillium / Aspergillus group spores can cause adverse reactions in sensitive individuals and are indicative of water intrusion. The detection of hyphal elements is indicative of active or recently active growth in the home. Determination of species was beyond the scope of this assessment. Based on these results, the home has been subjected to water intrusion, and water intrusion may be on-going in the home.

HEALTHYAIR

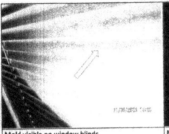

| Mold visible on window blinds. | Mold visible on the interior of the pantry door. |

CONCLUSIONS:

The water intrusion into the apartment has allowed fungal amplification to occur in the apartment. Based on the types of spores found in the air sample, the wetted materials were not dried within the recommended 48 to 72 hours to mitigate fungal amplification. The staining observed on the materials indicates that the wetted materials were not replaced, or the construction voids were not adequately dried prior to the replacement of the building materials.

It was unknown if the contractor who removed and replaced materials was properly licensed by the State of Georgia to conduct mold remediation.

RECOMMENDATIONS:

Gutter System / Exterior:
- Maintain the gutter system to divert water from rainfall events away from the foundation of the home.

Humidity Control:
- Keep the relative humidity in the conditioned spaces of the home between 35% and 45%.

HVAC Systems:
- Air-ducts
  - Cleaning / Sanitizing
    - The dust and debris should be cleaned from the HVAC system. After cleaning, the systems should be sanitized with an anti-microbial agent.
    - If fire dampers prevent the ductwork from being cleaned, the ductwork should be replaced.
- Internally Insulated Components
  - Components with exposed internal insulation should be removed and replaced. The replacement parts should be metal with insulation on the exterior. This should include plenums, housings, ductwork or other components with known or suspected fungal exposure.

HEALTHY**AIR**

leaking air ducts. Hard surfaces should be kept clean and dust free. According to the American Lung Association, carpets should be HEPA vacuumed regularly – three times each week. Carpet should be cleaned when soiled but no less than once each year. Since temperatures above 130 degrees will destroy mold spores carpets should be steam cleaned. HealthyAir recommends using a company that cleans under furniture. "Carpet with visible mold should be discarded".

Air Duct Cleaning
- Have the air ducts and the cooling coil (evaporator coil) cleaned and sanitized every three to five years. Use a company that follows **NADCA** guidelines for cleaning and sanitizing. Recommendations can be provided upon request.

CONDITIONS THAT SUSTAIN MOLD GROWTH

HVAC (HEATING VENTILATION AIR CONDITIONING) SYSTEM: As air moves through the ventilation system, particles collect on the cooling coil and air ducts. Water condenses on the cooling coil when air conditioner is operating and moisture migrates onto the dust particles which provide a food source for mold growth.

Some metal air ducts are internally insulated. As air is circulated through the ducts, problems with mold growth can result as the insulation collects cellulose particles over time. Moisture builds inside the air ducts and the particulate dust provides a food source to support mold growth. Supply air plenums are especially notorious for conditions that sustain mold growth. They are installed close to or attached to the cooling coil where water is condenses when the air conditioner is in operation. Supply air plenums (mixing box) are often made with fiberglass duct board. This porous coarse material collects dust and results in conditions that will sustain mold growth.

An oversized air conditioning system will create conditions to sustain mold growth within a home. The colder than normal air from the oversized air conditioner coming out of the supply vents cools surfaces to dew point levels, causing humidity to condense on the cold surfaces. Additionally, because it cools the home down so quickly, the air conditioner does not run long enough to remove enough humidity to prevent mold growth.

WHY MOISTURE CONDITIONS SHOULD BE CONTROLLED INSIDE YOUR HOME:

Molds can be allergenic, infectious or toxic. Authorities such as the CDC, US EPA, Canada's CHHC and the US Institute of Medicine all agree that fungus growth and associated dampness indoors are not acceptable. Fungi affects people differently, and health effects are determined by an individual's immune system, species or genus of the fungi, concentration, and amount of time exposed.

*Mycotoxins are biologically active metabolites produced by fungi that are known (or likely) to pose a health threat to humans and animals who come into contact with them. It is not a gas or VOC (Volatile Organic Compound). It is present in fungi particles (spores or mycelia) regardless of whether the fungi are viable or not. **Fungi can cause flu-like symptoms, runny nose, eye irritation, sore throat, cough, lethargy, congestion, skin rash, memory loss, joint pain, asthma and aggravation of asthma, cancer and even death.***

Since fungi is naturally present in outdoor environments, and we share the same air between indoors and the outdoors, it is impossible to eliminate all fungi and their spores from the indoor environment. Infants and elderly are more susceptible to health problems resulting from fungi because their immune system is likely to be underdeveloped or weakened.

It is just as important to eliminate the conditions that sustain mold growth as it is to clean mold. Mold growth can be controlled simply by dehydrating its food sources. Reduce moisture to 10% or less in drywall, wood and other materials that provide a food source and mold will become inactive or dormant. This can be accomplished by eliminating leaks and continuously keeping the relative humidity below 50% in crawl spaces, basements and living areas of the home.

Thank you for the opportunity to serve you.

Sincerely,

Healthy Air USA, LLC

Environmental Engineer
ABH/abh

CIH, CMR, IAQP

My Mom is still living. "Thank you for having me."

My Dad is part of me also. "Thanks!"

Emmeline Whitfield Jackson, my father's mother.

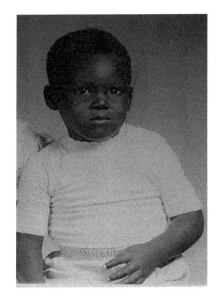

This is my brother at the age of two.

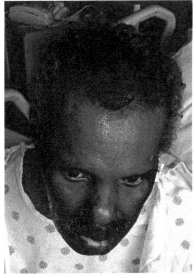

This is him, after his first stroke.

My mom at our 25 Wedding Anniversary!

This is a flower arrangement I made for my book interview.

This picture is two years old.

I am at our last International Jafra Cosmetic conference, in the year 2019 just before the pandemic and everything was shut down.

These are some of my passions:

This my first wedding cake I sold.

This is from one of my dinner party

These are of some of my dishes I came up with.

These are salads which I love to eat.

I made this stand for our 40th Anniversary.

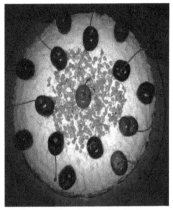

This is as a "Groom's Men Wedding Cake,
I call it the 'Cake of Life'." Because like life, you never know what you going to get.

This cake I made it two weeks ago. Cream Cheese/Raspberry Glaze Cake

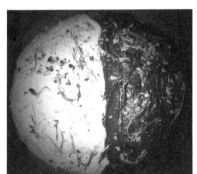

This one I made last week I just throw it together quickly; its taste is great!

I am a Jafra Cosmetic Consultant for over 20 years now!

These shows my work as an event planner.

These are some of my good day!

I wore this on the most important day of year, where I am incredibly happy to be.

I feel special today because I feel good.

I look like I am into what I am doing.

I am a woman mean business.

No, this is what I call sassy, not sexy!

I am posing for business.

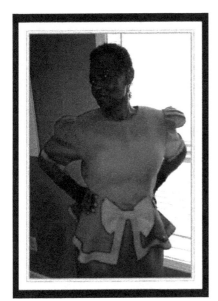

I am showing off my new haircut.

This one has me being thankful for being alive.

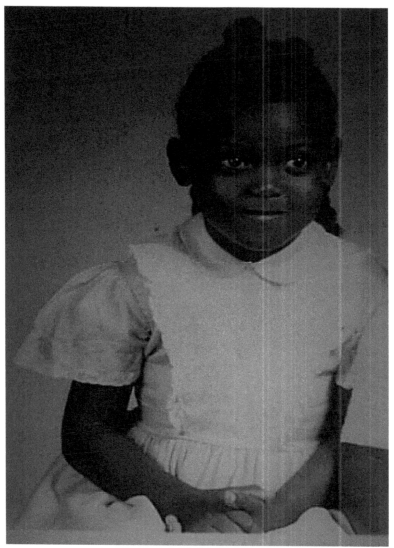

This picture is me at the age of 4.

This is from the beginning of year 2020, the start of another book or is it?

The Author has gone through so much in life like many different illnesses, accidents, trials and much more. She talks about how and why she keeps beating the odds. What she talks about most of all is what it takes for her to keep fighting all the things she has faced and still facing. She tells how her view of life helps her to be a survival. She tells how and why her learning about and getting to know herself and her body keep saving her, where she started the healing process first. She wrote this book because she felt that it would help so many by her encouragement. She talks about her Faith, her Hope, and her Endurance. She uses Poems, True Stories, Pictures, and Videos Links where you can see her personally. Where you can learn her personality, the why she is who she is. You will have wows, ohhs, what's, how's, and I can't believe it and many laughs.

NOTES

NOTES

NOTES

NOTES

NOTES

CPSIA information can be obtained
at www.ICGtesting.com
Printed in the USA
LVHW010416211121
704001LV00004B/18